THE ADULT SAFEGUARDING PRACTICE HANDBOOK

Kate Spreadbury and Rachel Hubbard

First published in Great Britain in 2020 by

Policy Press
University of Bristol
1-9 Old Park Hill
Bristol
BS2 8BB
UK
t: +44 (0)117 954 5940
pp-info@bristol.ac.uk
www.policypress.co.uk

North America office:
Policy Press
c/o The University of Chicago Press
1427 East 60th Street
Chicago, IL 60637, USA
t: +1 773 702 7700
f: +1 773-702-9756
sales@press.uchicago.edu
www.press.uchicago.edu

British Library Cataloguing in Publication Data
A catalogue record for this book is available from the British Library

Library of Congress Cataloging-in-Publication Data
A catalog record for this book has been requested

ISBN 978-1-4473-5167-2 paperback
ISBN 978-1-4473-5170-2 ePdf
ISBN 978-1-4473-5168-9 ePub

The right of Kate Spreadbury and Rachel Hubbard to be identified as authors of this work has been asserted by them in accordance with the Copyright, Designs and Patents Act 1988.

The statements and opinions contained within this publication are solely those of the authors and not of the University of Bristol or Policy Press. The University of Bristol and Policy Press disclaim responsibility for any injury to persons or property resulting from any material published in this publication.

Policy Press works to counter discrimination on grounds of gender, race, disability, age and sexuality.

Cover design by Andrew Corbett
Front cover image: Alamy
Printed and bound in Great Britain by CMP, Poole
Policy Press uses environmentally responsible print partners

Contents

List of figures and tables

Figures

Tables

About the authors

Kate Spreadbury is currently an independent social worker specialising in adult safeguarding; she works with Safeguarding Adults Boards and operational teams to review and develop policy and practice and is a lead reviewer for Safeguarding Adult Reviews. Kate qualified as a social worker in 1982. Working with adults who have experienced abuse has been a theme throughout her professional career in both mental health and adult safeguarding teams. Kate worked as an adult safeguarding manager in a local authority for 14 years, but now enjoys having time to immerse herself in all things adult safeguarding with no other work-related distractions.

Rachel Hubbard is Senior Lecturer in Social Work at UWE Bristol. She is a registered social worker and qualified Best Interests Assessor. She has practised adult safeguarding as a social worker in a variety of contexts and, as Safeguarding Adults, Mental Capacity Act and Deprivation of Liberty Safeguards training lead for North Somerset Council, was responsible for the learning of care workers, managers, social workers and health professionals about safeguarding practice. Rachel now teaches adult care and safeguarding, mental capacity and deprivation of liberty law and practice, as well as anti-oppressive practice, to undergraduate and postgraduate qualifying and continuing professional development social work students. She is co-author of the *Best Interests Assessor Practice Handbook* (Policy Press, 2018) and is a Professional Doctorate student at Cardiff University.

Acknowledgements

The authors would like to thank all the hardworking staff at Policy Press, especially Sarah Bird, Catherine Grey, Christie Smith and Shannon Kneis for their patience and guidance and Julia Mortimer for helping us to bring the idea for these books to Policy Press.

Kate would like to thank the past and present members of the South West ADASS adult safeguarding network who have been a source of wisdom and encouragement for the last 17 years. Thank you also to all members of the network who have shared their experiences, policies and procedures to inform the writing of this handbook, and to the West Midlands Editorial Group who inspire us all. Huge thanks to Lori, Anna, Rosa and Jen – so grateful you are on my team.

Rachel would like to thank Kevin Stone for his encouragement and enthusiasm about getting this book written. As ever, my contribution this book would not exist if it were not for the endless patience, tolerance, encouragement and good humour of Ali, Austin and Floyd Hubbard. You folks are the best.

Acronyms and commonly used abbreviations

ABH	actual bodily harm
ADASS	Association of Directors of Adult Social Services
AMCP	Approved Mental Capacity Professional (Liberty Protection Safeguards)
AMHP	Approved Mental Health Professional
BASW	British Association of Social Workers
BIA	Best Interest Assessor (Deprivation of Liberty Safeguards)
CHC	Continuing Health Care (NHS funded community healthcare)
COP	Court of Protection
COSHH	control of substances hazardous to health
CPS	Crown Prosecution Service
CQC	Care Quality Commission
CRPD	United Nations Convention on the Rights of Persons with Disabilities
DASH	domestic abuse, stalking and 'honour'-based violence
DH	Department of Health (to 2018)
DHSC	Department of Health and Social Care (since 2018)
DoLS	Deprivation of Liberty Safeguards
ECHR	European Convention on Human Rights
EHRC	Equality and Human Rights Commission
FGC	family group conference
FGM	female genital mutilation
GBH	grievous bodily harm
GP	general practitioner
HRA	Human Rights Act 1998
IDeA	Improvement and Development Agency
IDVA	Independent Domestic Abuse Advisor
IMCA	Independent Mental Capacity Advocate
IMHA	Independent Mental Health Advocate
ISVA	Independent Sexual Violence Advocate
LGA	Local Government Association
LGBTQ	Lesbian Gay Bisexual Transgender Queer/Questioning
LPS	Liberty Protection Safeguards
MAPPA	Multi-Agency Public Protection Arrangements
MARAC	Multi-Agency Risk Assessment Conference
MASH	multi-agency safeguarding hub
MCA	Mental Capacity Act 2005
MHA	Mental Health Act 1983 (2007)

MoJ	Ministry of Justice
MSP	Making Safeguarding Personal
NHS	National Health Service
NICE	National Institute for Health and Care Excellence
OPG	Office of the Public Guardian
PACE	Police and Criminal Evidence Act
PCSO	Police Community Safety Officer
PTSD	post-traumatic stress disorder
RIDDOR	reporting injuries, diseases and dangerous occurrences
RiPfA	Research in Practice for Adults
RJ	Restorative Justice
RPR	Relevant Person's Representative
RSPCA	Royal Society for the Prevention of Cruelty to Animals
SAB	Safeguarding Adults Board
SAR	Safeguarding Adults Review (post-Care Act 2014)
SCIE	Social Care Institute for Excellence
SCR	Serious Case Review (pre-Care Act 2014)
SSWWA	Social Services and Well-being (Wales) Act 2014
STIs	sexually transmitted infections
UDHR	Universal Declaration of Human Rights
UN	United Nations

1

Introduction

Chapter aim

In this chapter we will introduce the handbook, its purpose and structure. We will look at the importance of reflection in order to develop the practice wisdom needed to support good practice in adult safeguarding. We also describe the concept of 'well-being' and present a short summary of preventative approaches.

In this chapter we will explore:

- What is adult safeguarding?

- *The Adult Safeguarding Practice Handbook;*

- learning from experience as a practitioner;

- well-being;

- preventing abuse and harm.

What is adult safeguarding?

If you were to Google 'what is adult safeguarding in the UK?' you would collect a wide range of definitions. Is adult safeguarding a multi-agency procedure? A way of reducing risk? A means to promote well-being? We would argue that the central purpose of adult safeguarding is to promote and support the human and civil rights of adults who are unable to claim, and are sometimes prevented from claiming, their own rights. The practice of adult safeguarding is about working alongside adults to solve problems, to challenge discrimination, to give the same right of access to protection that all citizens can claim and to enjoy the same quality of life. You might argue that this is what all services should be promoting in their work with adults. This is true. However, if these rights were always respected and promoted there would be no need for adult safeguarding. Our role as practitioners is to promote these rights in every aspect of health and social care, indeed in our society, so there will be less need for adult safeguarding approaches.

This rights approach is what has motivated us through years of practice. We have been social workers, trainers and leaders in safeguarding roles. You will have your own perspectives and, as you gain more practice experience, your own wisdom. We hope that you enjoy dipping in and out of this handbook, you could read it chapter by chapter, but having had the comfort of handbooks or the advice of wise colleagues in moments of doubt and bewilderment during our practice we wanted to create one for you based on our learning, and hope that it is of help.

Adult safeguarding post-2014

> Safeguarding means protecting an adult's right to live in safety, free from abuse and neglect. It is about people and organisations working together to prevent and stop both the risks and experience of abuse or neglect, while at the same time making sure that the adult's wellbeing is promoted including, where appropriate, having regard to their views, wishes, feelings and beliefs in deciding on any action. This must recognise that adults sometimes have complex interpersonal relationships and may be ambivalent, unclear or unrealistic about their personal circumstances. (DHSC, 2018a, 14.7)

Adult safeguarding in Scotland, Wales and England is underpinned by legislation. Scotland passed legislation in 2007 (the Adult Support and Protection (Scotland) Act) while England (the Care Act) and Wales (Social Services and Well-being (Wales) Act) legislated in 2014. Northern Ireland works to the Adult Safeguarding: Prevention and Protection in Partnership (2015) policy, with legislation recommended for the future (Commissioner for Older People in Northern Ireland, 2014).

Adult safeguarding practice demands the use of excellent practice skills, many drawn from the social work knowledge base, together with the ability to reflect on and resolve ethical dilemmas. Practitioners must be able to use a range of approaches to make relationships with people and involve them in their own safeguarding enquiries and plans, working with people who may be in crisis, afraid and anxious or very unwell. They must be legally literate, understanding the application of legislation to real-life situations. Practitioners must be able to undertake risk assessments, form positive and creative working relationships with other agencies and make person-centred effective plans with adults to address risk and recover from the trauma of abuse. Adult safeguarding practice is at the core of all social work practice with adults.

Adult safeguarding work presents us with practice and ethical dilemmas, whether to respect the adult's wishes that we should not interfere, or continue in the knowledge that the harm the adult appears to be experiencing is having a serious impact on their well-being and could lead to serious injury or death, or that the influence of a controlling third party is preventing the adult from living a fuller, fulfilled life. The respect for the autonomy of an adult must be balanced with confidence in understanding the duty of care we have to the adults we work with. We can feel powerless or frustrated, anxious or despairing in the face of the misery of another human's experience and our own inability to support them towards a better quality of life. We can also feel the satisfaction of knowing that an adult is now free of abuse and developing their own life in the way they have long wished for. Adult safeguarding work can challenge us: we need to understand our own values and prejudices, be confident enough to work in risky situations without feeling we must be experts, but also know where and when to get the support to take action as needed.

The Adult Safeguarding Practice Handbook

The Adult Safeguarding Practice Handbook is designed as a practical guide to adult safeguarding for those new to practice, as well as those looking to develop their skills and knowledge. We hope to support students and practitioners with a range of professional and practice backgrounds to develop their skills, knowledge and value base to undertake the role of an adult safeguarding practitioner across the full range of adult safeguarding activities. Though much of adult safeguarding practice is conducted by social workers working within local authorities there are other roles and settings where adult safeguarding work is conducted. Whether you are a social worker or not this practice handbook can offer you insights and ideas for more person-centred and rights-based safeguarding practice. This practice handbook contains plenty of practice examples to illustrate legislative, policy and practice developments that you can use to reflect on in order to extend your competence in the complex area of adult safeguarding. The practice examples are based on real-life case studies, anonymised and changed to reflect common themes in practice. We suggest further reading at the end of each chapter so that you can take a deeper look at some of the topics we have introduced.

The focus of the legislation and statutory guidance in the handbook is on England. We are both English social workers with extensive experience of working in this part of the UK. However, we will compare legislation and policy across all four UK nations and use research undertaken across the UK to help us to explore different aspects of adult safeguarding.

The six government principles of adult safeguarding (DH, 2011) and the Making Safeguarding Personal approach are explored in detail in some chapters – these approaches also underpin everything within the handbook. Good safeguarding practice is about using the rights-based, person-centred, strengths-based approach of Making Safeguarding Personal and we will not explicitly reference MSP or the six principles as if they were separate from good practice.

Terminology

We will use the following within the handbook:

- *Adult* refers to a person with care and support needs who is alleged to be at risk of abuse or being harmed.

- The terms *harm* and *abuse* are used interchangeably. We generally use the convention that abuse is something that a third party or person does to an adult whereas harm is what is experienced by the adult.
- We will use the term *statutory guidance* to refer to the Care and Support Statutory Guidance which was originally published in 2014 and revised on a number of occasions since then and is used to support the implementation of the Care Act 2014 in England (see DHSC, 2018a).
- We refer to those undertaking adult safeguarding enquiries and other roles as *adult safeguarding practitioners*. Though we are aware that the majority of this work is undertaken by social workers in the UK there are others who undertake elements of these roles, such as care provider managers and safeguarding lead nurses working for hospitals and community organisations.

What is in the handbook?

We have used the English Care and Support Statutory Guidance (DHSC, 2018a) together with the English Care Act 2014 as a framework for considering the statutory adult safeguarding duties. This handbook attempts to clarify and illustrate the statutory guidance but is not a substitute for either this or the policies and procedures in use in your local area. You should always refer to your local policies and procedures and, if in any doubt, consult your manager.

The Care and Support Statutory Guidance (DHSC, 2018a) is interpreted differently across England, and is being updated at regular intervals, hence we recommend that you always access the guidance online and do not rely on a 2014 copy. Much has changed since then, including the deletion of the role of 'designated adult safeguarding manager' in the local authority and how self-neglect is considered in the context of a section 42 enquiry.

The book has been designed to consider some of the main practical elements of adult safeguarding, including the context for practice, the challenges of ethical decision making and the necessity for ongoing learning in the role. We have included case studies, summaries of key information and wider reading as well as reflective questions to help you consider important issues and support your development as a practitioner. Where available we have used research as a basis for evidencing good practice. However, there is little research on many of the different aspects of adult safeguarding practice and findings can be limited by the size of the research sample so there is still much research needed before we can establish a reliable evidence base for practice.

This introductory chapter sets out the structure of the book and introduces some of the key ideas and themes that will be considered. We will also think about the importance of being a reflective safeguarding practitioner and explore some of the ways we can prevent harm to adults. The handbook is divided into two parts: *the context of adult safeguarding* covering key contextual frameworks and themes and *good adult safeguarding practice*, which explores the skills and practical application of ideas and frameworks for positive adult safeguarding practice.

Part 1: The context of adult safeguarding

The first part of the book outlines the principles underpinning adult safeguarding, the legislation and statutory guidance within which contemporary practice is located and the definitions used in adult safeguarding work.

Chapter 2: Human rights: the principles that inform adult safeguarding

We describe how aspects of the European Convention of Human Rights and the United Nations Convention on Rights for Disabled People underpin adult safeguarding practice and give case studies of human rights in action. Human rights, as both a legal framework and a values-driven approach, are essential to person-centred adult safeguarding practice. Human rights are not referenced within the Care Act 2014 but are within another significant piece of legislation used in adult safeguarding, the Mental Capacity Act 2005. How can adult safeguarding practice address oppression and recognise the intersectional nature of discriminatory abuse? We detail each of the six principles of adult safeguarding (DH, 2011) and illustrate how good practice should adhere to each of the principles. The Care Act recommended a culture change in adult safeguarding practice, currently promoted by the sector led, person-centred MSP programme. We describe the principles of MSP and its relationship to human rights and anti-oppressive practice.

Chapter 3: Adult safeguarding legislation

This chapter examines adult safeguarding legislation and how it defines the parameters of practice in England, mostly focusing on the Care Act 2014. Differing legal frameworks for practice in Scotland, Northern Ireland and Wales are briefly considered in comparison to practice under the Care Act 2014 in England. Other significant legislation and legal frameworks will be explored including the High Court and its inherent jurisdiction, use of the provisions of domestic abuse legislation including the Serious Crime Act 2015 and responses to forced marriage and modern slavery. Finally, we detail how practitioners can develop legal literacy to keep their practice up to date and legally compliant.

Chapter 4: Mental capacity and adult safeguarding

This chapter explores the key role played by the Mental Capacity Act 2005 in adult safeguarding practice including its role in forming decision making and identifying the need for, and application of, advocacy and representation for adults within the safeguarding process. We also explore the use of the MCA to support autonomous decision making, especially in the context of risk, and what safeguards and duties remain where the adult at risk is assessed to have the capacity to make risky decisions that still require practitioners to be involved in safeguarding the adult from harm.

Chapter 5: Definitions in adult safeguarding

Adult safeguarding legislation applies to a small section of the population – adults in need of care and support. We begin this chapter with an analysis of who adults in need of care and support might be, and the challenges faced by different groups in protecting themselves and claiming the right to protection. We describe how abuse is defined and how harm may be identified if it is not disclosed. Key ideas about power, exploitation and coercive control inform our descriptions of abuse.

Part 2: Good adult safeguarding practice

The second part of the book focuses on adult safeguarding practice. Each chapter explores the knowledge, skills and values needed to undertake practice in adult safeguarding. The themes of anti-oppressive practice, adult safeguarding principles and the person-centred MSP approach appear throughout this section. Where available, the research evidence for practice approaches is introduced and illustrated in case studies in a range of adult safeguarding scenarios.

Chapter 6: Relationships, values and ethics

This chapter explores building working relationships with the adult and those who are close to them, including, when necessary, the person who has harmed them. We detail the essential precursors to forming a relationship that will support an adult through the process of identifying, acknowledging, addressing and recovering from harm including the ability to use the self in the creation of a relationship, and to understand oppression, the dynamics of power and how these change through the life course. Case studies are used to illustrate how practitioners can use relationship-building skills to engage with and empower people to change the dynamics of harm. We consider building relationships with colleagues from other agencies and reflect on the need to understand common organisational cultures and values, the impact of differences in these on adult safeguarding work, and how these can be resolved. Lastly, we reflect on the challenges to personal, professional and organisational identity, values and ethics, and how an understanding of one's own and others' value base provides a rich context for the development of good practice in adult safeguarding.

Chapter 7: Assessment of risk

We provide an overview of how risk assessment is used in adult safeguarding practice and explore how we understand and incorporate the adult's perception of their risk as well as what the evidence from research tell us about risk. We discuss the influence of organisations' attitudes towards risk and how multi–agency perspectives on risk contribute to assessment. Models of adult safeguarding risk assessment currently used in practice are presented in usable formats. Other useful risk assessments, for example those used in domestic abuse situations, or in organisational abuse, are introduced with guidance on where to get more information and training.

Chapter 8: Decision making in adult safeguarding

We describe the decisions that must be made in the course of adult safeguarding, and who makes them. In this chapter, we clarify decisions that must be made by a local authority as part of its statutory duty, and those that must be made by the adult at risk, or by using the best–interest decision-making process if the adult has been assessed as lacking the capacity to make those specific decisions. Adult safeguarding practitioners will encounter decision makers in other organisations, for example criminal justice, who make decisions that influence adult safeguarding enquiries and plans. We discuss how other agencies make decisions, the criteria and processes used.

Chapter 9: Adult safeguarding enquiries

We will describe the function of an enquiry and detail each component, from effective planning to quality assurance. The way in which the six principles of adult safeguarding are enacted throughout an enquiry is explored. We will look at examples of 'proportionate enquiry', observing the elements that must be part of any enquiry, no matter how brief or complex, or who is undertaking the enquiry. We will explore the involvement of adults at risk, how adults are involved in an enquiry, and how advocates support adults who have 'substantial difficulty' in being involved. We will explore the range of agencies that can be asked or 'caused' to undertake a specific enquiry on behalf of the local authority. We look at how such agencies should be supported, how caused enquiries are quality assured and actions that can be taken to promote partnership working, including the use of escalation pathways if necessary.

Chapter 10: Recovery and resolution

The Care Act requires that any enquiry should consider how the adult will recover from harm, and/or achieve a resolution of the experience. This element of adult safeguarding is often neglected, perhaps because harm has occurred within a family setting and practitioners are unsure how to support recovery and resolution between people, or because the long-term impact of harm on the well–being of adults is inadequately considered, or because agencies who might assist adults to recover are unknown. We use research studies, where available, to consider the long-term impact of harm on adults at risk through different stages of the life course and in different settings. We compare and illustrate approaches to recovery and resolution, including mediation, restorative justice and family group conferences together with access to counselling and other supportive interventions. Compensation and redress through the criminal courts are also considered.

Learning from experience as a practitioner

Developing practice wisdom

No one theory, no matter how well you can intellectually grasp it, will apply to all the situations you will encounter as a practitioner. Individuals are unique, as are the circumstances that they live in; their situations can be complex and may challenge everything you have previously understood. Safeguarding skills and knowledge are largely context-specific; you must adapt and extend what you know to address each situation. You must also be wise enough to understand how your personal value base may lead to bias in thinking and decision making, you must recognise your own ignorance, together with the expertise of the adults and others you are working with.

Thompson and West (2013) capture this element of practice wisdom:

> Wise professionals recognize not just their own knowledge and procedures in practice, they also recognize their own ignorance and the client's expertise. Thus, wisdom lies in intuitively recognizing when deficiencies present a need for further theoretical and procedural knowledge and when there is a need for deference to client or other knowledge. (p 125)

Dybicz (2004) emphasises how we use the power of our knowledge in helping relationships, and how awareness of our value base will provide a welcome compass as we descend into the unknown.

We are sometimes asked how long it will take to develop 'practice wisdom'. If you are wise enough to know that experience is not enough and have already engaged in reflection then you are already on the pathway to becoming wise. One of us was once told that 'the first ten years are the hardest' so perhaps it takes a while to really feel that you have a firm basis for your practice. Most of us can never sit back and feel truly 'wise' as every day can bring a different 'unknown'. Perhaps the real wisdom is knowing that you cannot know all the answers and indeed it is unhelpful to think that you should.

Reflecting on what you have learned from each piece of practice will help you to develop and extend practice wisdom. We may well be interpreting our experience unhelpfully and follow paths so influenced by our personal bias and values that we become jaded rather than wise practitioners. Practitioners need time to reflect, and to work in organisations that support learning from experience. Time to reflect also helps us to manage our everyday practice, how to prioritise and use time wisely, to focus our efforts and be as creative as possible in how we work with adults and with other agencies. You can develop 'practice wisdom' through reflecting on how you are using your skills and knowledge in individual circumstances, and how your values and professional ethics influence you in making judgements and decisions.

Reflecting on practice

> The practitioner allows himself to experience surprise, puzzlement, or confusion in a situation which he finds uncertain or unique. He reflects on the phenomenon before him, and on the prior understandings which have been implicit in his behaviour. He carries out an experiment which serves to generate both a new understanding of the phenomenon and a change in the situation. (Schön, 1983, p 68)

Reflecting on our emotions, our feelings of discomfort, shock or despair, is vital to keep us able to stay healthy when sometimes working in sad and at times seemingly hopeless situations. It is completely acceptable to feel a wide range of emotions in our practice, and important to observe and acknowledge how we feel and to take care of ourselves. Practitioners who believe they must behave as if they are not affected by the circumstances adults can experience are not perhaps allowing themselves to deeply reflect on their work and through reflection, and feeling emotions, begin to make authentic and genuine connections with the adults who they do have much commitment to working with. There are many ways of reflecting and several reflective models to use. The organisation you work for must support reflection via supervision arrangements and general support for group learning; it may also have an agreed framework for supporting reflective practice, or you may also find a model of reflection and framework that suits you best.

There are areas within this handbook that you can use as a reflective basis for the analysis of events. You could use one of the six principles of adult safeguarding, the five MCA principles, MSP approaches, research into what works when working with people who self-neglect or whatever you want to focus on at that time. For example, if you use the adult safeguarding principle of 'empowerment' you could evaluate how you used your professional power in an interaction, how you worked with the adult to make sure that their views were respected and that they were able to make a decision, and consider how effective this was. Where were the gaps in your understanding or conflicts with your value base?

Reflecting on mistakes or what could have gone better can be productive, and the wish to do better provides the motivation to reflect (Sicora, 2017). Reflecting on the errors of practice can create feelings of inadequacy without a reflection partner to provide context, you may find that reflecting with a colleague or manager is supportive. A 'critical friend' in your organisation can help you make sense of your reflections by contextualising your experience from an external perspective. While learning from our mistakes can generate the motivation to change, it is also important to reflect on what has gone well, and how this positive practice can be extended to other areas of work. Ghaye (2008, p 203) poses three questions to help think through and extend positive practice:

Think of a success that you achieved at work this week.
• What contributed to the success?
• What do you need to keep doing to create further success?
• What is the one behaviour you need to keep, and how will you keep doing it?

Learning events and opportunities

Reflecting on everyday practice provides a regular opportunity to develop. But sometimes we grow stale and need to be challenged and inspired; or we must understand a new way of practising that is consistent with new legislation or case law. Learning events, including training, are precious in providing opportunities to focus on a particular aspect of adult safeguarding practice, meet with other safeguarding practitioners and extend our own knowledge and understanding. We need to be active in making the most of these opportunities as it is often hard to get away from the 'day job' or travel long distances. SCIE (2019)'s Social Care TV or RiPfA (2019) offer webinars and videos on current topics for those of us who cannot get to distant or regular events and your learning will be maximised if you discuss and analyse these programmes with colleagues afterwards.

Safeguarding Adults Reviews (SARs) provide powerful learning opportunities. The purpose of a SAR is to identify lessons that can be learned from examining the case that will apply to similar cases in the future or will generally improve the systems and ways that agencies work together. That knowledge does not prevent practitioners and managers being initially fearful of a SAR in their area. It is sometimes only by experiencing a SAR process that treats practitioners respectfully and results in useful learning that we will stop being afraid. SCIE and RiPfA are producing 'quality markers' for SARs at the time of writing which urge SAR commissioners, managers and authors to enable practitioners and managers to have a constructive experience of taking part in the review. While learning from mistakes can be effective (Sicora, 2017) it can also be painful and if poorly managed creates stress in practitioners and teams. SARs can be commissioned to learn from good practice (statutory guidance 14.164) but at the time of writing no such SAR has been commissioned.

A SAR repository hosted by SCIE (2017) contains a wide range of published SARs and is a less stressful way of learning lessons from tragic circumstances. At the time of writing the repository is not indexed but is expected to be in the near future. It will be possible to input search terms, for example self-neglect, substance misuse, hospitals, and locate the SAR relevant to the topic you are interested in learning about.

Well-being

We will frequently refer to an adult's 'well-being' in the handbook. Local authorities have a duty under section 1 of the Care Act 2014 to promote an individual's well-being in all care and support functions. 'Well-being' encapsulates all aspects of an adult's life. Whenever we work with adults we must pay attention to the following areas:

- personal dignity (including treatment of the individual with respect)
- physical and mental health and emotional well-being
- protection from abuse and neglect
- control by the individual over day-to-day life
- participation in work, education, training or recreation
- social and economic well-being
- domestic, family and personal
- suitability of living accommodation
- the individual's contribution to society. (Statutory guidance 1.5)

The Care Act enshrines in legislation the approach we must take to the well-being of adults. As each individual is unique, some areas of well-being will be more important to one adult than others, but if we are mindful of an adult's well-being during every contact, assessment or review, we can make sure that we engage in conversations with a view to preventing harm. This may be about reducing isolation, making sure an adult is happy with their accommodation and in the community they live, that they have agency over their lives, that they have access to medical help as needed, or any other aspect of life that will contribute to a quality of life and desired level of safety. The observation of the well-being principle underpins both the prevention of harm and actions taken in response to harm.

▶ ESSENTIAL INFORMATION: LEGISLATION

Section 1(3) of the Care Act 2014 states that:

In exercising a function under this Part in the case of an individual, a local authority must have regard to the following matters in particular:

(a) the importance of beginning with the assumption that the individual is best-placed to judge the individual's well-being;

(b) the individual's views, wishes, feelings and beliefs;

(c) the importance of preventing or delaying the development of needs for care and support or needs for support and the importance of reducing needs of either kind that already exist;

(d) the need to ensure that decisions about the individual are made having regard to all the individual's circumstances (and are not based only on the individual's age or appearance or any condition of the individual's or aspect of the individual's behaviour which might lead others to make unjustified assumptions about the individual's well-being);

(e) the importance of the individual participating as fully as possible in decisions relating to the exercise of the function concerned and being provided with the information and support necessary to enable the individual to participate;

(f) the importance of achieving a balance between the individual's well-being and that of any friends or relatives who are involved in caring for the individual;

(g) the need to protect people from abuse and neglect;

(h) the need to ensure that any restriction on the individual's rights or freedom of action that is involved in the exercise of the function is kept to the minimum necessary for achieving the purpose for which the function is being exercised.

Preventing abuse and harm

The emphasis of this section is on how to prevent harm from happening. We do acknowledge that prevention also includes training staff to identify and respond to early signs of abuse and would suggest that the increasing number of referrals to adult safeguarding services in England across the last seven years (NHS Digital, 2018) evidences the impact of this training. Between 2011 and 2012 there were 136,000 adult safeguarding alerts in England, by 2017/18 this had risen to 394,655. But identifying harm is not the same as preventing harm occurring in the first place. How can we work in a way that reduces the possibility of harm to adults while respecting the elements of life which can serve as protective factors, especially the adult's self-determination about how they will live their life? Evidence on the effectiveness of preventative approaches is hard to obtain – how can we measure something which has not occurred? However, we can use the evidenced best practice available to reduce the likelihood of harm occurring wherever possible and to promote an adult's ability to self-protect.

How can individual practitioners prevent harm?

We have explored the well-being duty, section 1 of the Care Act 2014. Section 2 of the Care Act addresses the local authorities' prevention duty; the statutory guidance (Chapter 2) explicitly requires local authorities to work with partner agencies to actively promote people's independence and well-being (2.24), and not to only focus on responding to crises when they occur (2.1 and 2.7). 'Prevention' is one of the six principles of adult safeguarding; our aim in everything we do as practitioners must be to prevent abuse and neglect from occurring or recurring wherever possible.

How can we promote prevention as part of everyday practice? A starting point for practitioners is to ask adults with care and support needs how they want to live their lives, helping people to develop their resilience and retain their independence. The focus should be on all aspects of the person's well-being, not just their safety. Adults should be encouraged to think about their strengths, existing resources and any informal support networks they have around them. Such conversations can help adults to identify their particular needs, what complex situations may exist in their lives and whether they feel they face any risks to their well-being. Carers assessments and services are vital in supporting those caring for the adult, who may themselves be at risk of poor mental and physical health.

Isolation and loneliness have been identified as presenting a risk to the physical and mental health of older people (Age UK, 2011; Windle et al, 2011) and can also increase the vulnerability to abuse of all adults with care and support needs, whether through engaging with exploiters in order to experience 'friendship' or by being unable to discuss feelings of concern or dilemmas with their peers. Coercive control is about isolating the adult from any source of support so that the controller can impose their wishes and version of reality. If an individual has a connection to others this will maintain their physical and mental health and will also reduce the likelihood of harm.

Some adults do not feel comfortable in the company of others; we need to respect this but can discuss what level of connection they are engaged with or are interested in creating.

REFLECTIVE ACTIVITY

Case study: Roberta

Roberta lived on her own and did not willingly talk to other people. In order to calm her intrusive thoughts, she walked for miles each day, having a regular circuit which encompassed shops and cafes. The people who ran those businesses got to know her and looked out for her. Without intruding into her life, they provided her with sufficient companionship and connection, and when she later became ill, offered practical support to her through her daily perambulation.

Reflective question
–   How can you ensure that communities will support the people for whom they are a significant social support?

Our thoughts are that we need to promote the knowledge of shopkeepers, cafe owners and others about who to contact for advice should they have concerns. Your local authority and local Safeguarding Adults Board will have community engagement strategies, have a look on their websites or ask your principal social worker. You should see evidence of this in GP surgeries, hospitals, libraries, police stations and in the press. Get to know the community you work in, who frequents the local cafes, what the churches provide. Is there a community hub you can promote and engage with?

Some adults may prefer one-to-one regular contact rather than a group; a befriending volunteer may help. Others may be keen to extend or create a wider support network; practitioners may be able to identify opportunities in their community for the adult to connect with and may build the facilitation of these connections into the support plan. An adult who identifies with people in the LGBTQ community can be facilitated to find a social group, or an adult with a particular interest can be facilitated to join a group sharing their interests, whether that be birdwatching, trainspotting or fitness. You may be able to find creative ways of 'building bridges' between the isolated person and their community. Ideas from the 'circles of friends' work with people who have learning disabilities may also be valuable for people who have experienced long-term isolation from community and friendships for different reasons.

> ## ▶ ESSENTIAL INFORMATION: PRACTICE GUIDANCE
>
> *What is a circle of friends?*
>
> A 'circle of friends' is the intentional building of relationships around a person who may have become disempowered because of disability or difference. It is a group of people that care and come together at the request of the individual, the 'focus person', to help them think about their life. Circles were developed to support individuals to become connected in the community, and to make friendships and relationships and are a valuable tool for creating networks of friends and relationships and promoting empowerment and inclusion.
>
> The circle meeting is facilitated by another but chaired by the focus person who is respected as an individual with gifts and capacities, someone with their own views, beliefs and opinions; someone with the right to self-determination and a lot to offer to the community. It works with the focus person's vision of how they want to live their life and helps them to become connected with people who can support them to achieve that vision.
>
> The first step in creating the circle is to map existing relationships with the focus person. They will identify who should be invited to the circle and the meeting will be held at a venue where they feel most comfortable. Participants can be paid staff or advocates as these are sometimes the only people the adult has in their community. Family members and advocates may also be circle members as may neighbours, community volunteers or anyone the focus person wants to invite into their circle.
>
> The circle creates an action plan to fulfil the focus person's vision, however small or large that may be. The experiences of being part of the circle, which can continue to evolve through time, contribute to the development of confidence and self-esteem, the focus person experiences the ability to make changes in their lives, to be assertive and valued, and to be supported by a community of their choosing.
>
> Adapted from Burke, 2006

Adults and their families can be alarmed by the media attention to harm in provided services or from exploitative individuals, especially if the only knowledge the adult has of care services is a TV documentary depicting cruelty to people using services. The challenge to practitioners is on how to promote awareness of potential harm or poor quality without confirming an already bleak vision of care services. A positive approach can be taken by providing information about what a person can expect from services: what does good care look like, what should the adult expect? South Gloucestershire Safeguarding Adults Board (2019) have published a short guide 'What Makes a Good Care Home' emphasising the principle that everyone, practitioners, adults and their families, should ask themselves the question 'would I want to live here?' and if we would not, why not? What does good care mean to all of us? The standard should be one that anyone would be happy to live in. Encouragement and contact details are useful if the adult has any concern, however small, about their service. A person-centred, rights-based approach from the practitioner at all times puts the adult in control of what and who goes into their support plan.

Raising awareness about what abuse is also has a place; one of the challenging aspects of exploitation is the ease with which an exploiter can ready an adult to be coerced and harmed. It can be difficult for anyone to spot the initial signs of potential abuse. The skills of those perpetrating internet and postal scams and frauds evolve so quickly that it is hard to tell the difference between safe and unsafe approaches. You may wish to talk through these specific issues with adults who might be targeted via their everyday lives. There is a range of accessible information available to support such conversations via the British Institute for Learning Disabilities (BILD, 2019) or from your local Safeguarding Adults Board (SAB), Trading Standards or the police. Somerset County Council has produced a very simple sheet with telephone numbers for agencies who can help, if concerned about a range of keeping safe issues, which can be sent out to adults or given to them during a visit (Somerset County Council, 2016).

It is good practice to make sure that people are aware of the provisions of the Mental Capacity Act 2005 that are available to them. We can provide adults with information about the role of the Court of Protection and the Office of the Public Guardian as well as the mechanisms available (such as power of attorney, deputyship, Department of Work and Pensions appointeeship) to ensure their best interests are protected and to safeguard against financial exploitation, if they lose their capacity to make welfare and/or property and financial decisions in the future.

Recent SARs (Flynn, 2018; Spreadbury, 2018a) have highlighted the preventative role individual practitioners and commissioners can play in ensuring a care home or other setting is unlikely to cause harm to the adult living there:

- **Pre-placement** – visit the setting, with the adult if possible, and consider – is the building suitable for the adult? Can you observe person-centred care from a well-supported staff team? Will the adult be able to maintain existing networks of support if the placement is far from friends and family? How will connections be maintained?
- **Who else lives in the setting?** Are the needs of others who are living there compatible with those of the adult you are placing? How will adults be supported to live together? How will any tension or risk be managed?

- **After the adult begins to live in the setting** – do visit and review thoroughly and regularly. How does the adult feel about where they are living? How is their quality of life developing? What do they feel good about? Who do they get along with? What upsets them?

Do use the skills discussed in Chapter 6 to create a relationship with the adult to support them to tell you how life is for them. In the reflection, Mr Ralph shares his thoughts on the importance of having reliable contact with a social worker who was interested in your well-being.

REFLECTIVE ACTIVITY

Case study: Mr Ralph

Mr Ralph had lived in institutions for most of his adult life. He had social workers who were interested in how he was experiencing the care home he lived in; he also had social workers who he never saw. He lived in 'good places' where he felt at ease and useful and places where he was ill-treated, sometimes not having enough to eat or being cold in bed at night.

Mr Ralph said that in care homes other people have power over you; what you need is to have someone on your side who is also powerful, because you have no power in the situation at all. Mr Ralph thought that having a social worker who was interested in what happened to you and who could be relied on was vital in making the difference between having to tolerate poor care and abuse and being able to live in a comfortable place where you felt at home.

Reflective questions
- How do the adults you arrange placements for and review experience the care setting they live in?
- How can you make sure their experiences, thoughts and feelings are always understood, and that they have recourse to a 'powerful person' who is 'on their side' if needed?

Our thoughts are that all service users in institutional settings should be offered and supported to engage with outside advocacy, including development of their understanding of what is OK and what is not when being cared for. Advocacy and service user training on adult safeguarding should both be explored alongside working with organisations running institutions to develop positive, open and accountable working practices.

Some care settings are open to advocates having a presence in the service, or regular 'befrienders'. Openness to outside scrutiny is an essential trait to encourage in institutional settings to address the power imbalances that were identified in the case of Mr Ralph. An adult with no external connections in a care setting can be left in a vulnerable position regarding the need to confide concerns or in having no external person who cares about them to get alongside them.

FURTHER READING

- You can find the latest version of the Care Act Care and Support Statutory Guidance on this link. Always refer to the online version as it is often updated: www.gov.uk/government/publications/care-act-statutory-guidance/care-and-support-statutory-guidance.

- For a comprehensive and practical guide to reflection, and learning from our mistakes read Sicora, A. (2017) *Reflective Practice and Learning from Mistakes in Social Work*, Bristol: Policy Press.

- Maclean, S. (2010) *The Social Work Pocket Guide to Reflective Practice*, Lichfield: Kirwan Maclean Associates is also a simple and enjoyable guide to reflective practice.

- There is, as already mentioned, a growing body of research to support adult safeguarding practice. Much is still small scale, but to stay up to date it is worth subscribing or asking your organisation to subscribe to a regular e-journal such as *The Journal of Adult Protection*.

Part 1
The context of adult safeguarding

2

Human rights:
the principles that inform
adult safeguarding

Chapter aim

In this chapter we will explore the context for human rights informed adult safeguarding practice. We will consider how anti-oppressive practice plays a crucial part in ensuring that adult safeguarding practice is truly person-centred while acknowledging how diverse experiences and intersectionality may interact with vulnerability and risk.

This chapter includes:

- human rights and adult safeguarding in practice;

- oppression, anti-oppressive practice and identity;

- applying the six adult safeguarding principles of the Care Act 2014;

- Making Safeguarding Personal in practice.

Human rights and adult safeguarding in practice

All adult safeguarding practice must be informed by a human rights perspective and consider the legal framework that supports human rights. Fundamentally, adult safeguarding practice is about promoting and protecting the human rights of adults whose care and support needs make it difficult for them to exercise their autonomy and will. There are two main strands regarding human rights in adult safeguarding practice:

1. Human rights as a *legal framework* that provides structure, definitions of rights, duties and responsibilities and a template for action.
2. Human rights as a *perspective* that informs our values and actions in practice.

To use a human rights perspective, we must understand what human rights are as set out in law, where we might see abuses of the human rights of adults with care and support needs and how our decisions must be informed by values based on the principles of human rights.

The first legal framework for addressing the abuse of vulnerable adults in England, 'No Secrets' (Home Office and Department of Health, 2000) described 'abuse [as] a violation of an individual's human and civil rights by any other person or persons' (para. 2.5), placing human and civil rights at the centre of adult protection practice. The Care Act 2014 does not reference the Human Rights Act 1998 or UN Rights Conventions, for example the United Nations Principles for Older Persons (1991). The Equality Act 2010 is referenced only with regard to accessible information and in one chapter (16.78) with reference to discrimination in schools for disabled people. The statutory guidance chapter on adult safeguarding does include the statement 'safeguarding means protecting an adult's right to live in safety, free from abuse and neglect' (Chapter 14.7) but gives no further context for these rights. The lack of reference to the human and civil rights of adults with care and support needs, unable to protect themselves, is troubling, and indicates a different perspective, one of principles rather than rights – a subtle but important distinction. Collingbourne (2014) finds that, while many of the provisions of the Care Act correspond with the UN Convention on the Rights of Persons with Disabilities 2006 and are an improvement on previous legislation, the Care Act legislates for welfare not rights:

> successive governments have chosen to view international socio-economic rights not as 'rights' but as principles and objectives to guide politicians in the allocation of scarce resources. They argue that these 'principles and objectives' are implemented through the policies, laws and practices of the British welfare state – such as, for example, the Care Act 2014. Under this argument, rather than being identified as constitutional rights of equal importance to and indivisible from the civil and political rights they enable, support services become 'welfare entitlements' subject to the gift (or denial) of the State. (p 5)

The role of an adult safeguarding practitioner has always been to support people to claim their human and civil rights because, by reason of their care and support needs, they have been unable to do so by themselves. Human rights law remains an essential underpinning to the rights and freedoms violated when adults are abused by others.

Human rights law in the UK

Human rights law has evolved over centuries round the world, with key developments, like Magna Carta, being created in the UK. Most of the legal structures were fixed in the 20th century and have been formed by at least six fundamental ideas.

> ### ▶ ESSENTIAL INFORMATION: LEGISLATION
>
> *Six fundamental ideas of human rights law*
>
> 1. That the power of a ruler (monarch or the state) is not unlimited.
> 2. That the subjects have a sphere of autonomy that no power can invade and some rights and freedoms that need to be respected by a ruler.
> 3. That there exist procedural mechanisms to limit the arbitrariness of a ruler and protect the rights and freedoms of the ruled (points 1 and 2 above have already transformed subjects into the ruled) who can make valid claims on the state for such protection.
> 4. That the ruled have rights that enable them to participate in decision-making (with this, the ruled have changed into the citizens).
> 5. That the authority has not only powers but also some obligations, which may be claimed by the citizens.
> 6. That all these rights and freedoms are granted equally to all persons (this transforms individual rights/privileges into human rights).
>
> Osiatyński, 2013, p 9

Essentially, this means that those who can be identified as citizens of a country where human rights laws apply (for example, nations who are signatories to human rights conventions such as the Universal Declaration of Human Rights (UDHR), European Convention on Human Rights (ECHR) and the Convention on the Rights of Persons with Disabilities (CRPD)) may theoretically use these laws to challenge the decisions made by those acting as rulers, such as representatives of the state. These protections, in the context of adult safeguarding, are available to all those in the care of public bodies, for example local authorities, the NHS (including hospitals, GPs and other community health and ambulance services), the police and criminal justice system, and those acting on behalf of the state, for example care and support providers commissioned by local authorities or the NHS to provide care and support in the adult's home, community or in institutions like care homes, for instance, and those commissioned using public funds, such as Direct Payments and Continuing Health Care (CHC).

This leaves an obvious gap in the human rights legal protections available to adults at risk: those who buy their care from private providers with no state involvement in either making decisions about what that care involves or assistance with paying for care (known as 'self-funders'). Self-funders have limited ability to use human rights law unless there is state involvement to question. Case law in both European and UK courts about what is imputable to the state – for example, what decisions the state should be considered to be responsible for, and as a result have recourse to human rights – has a very low bar. In the case of *Staffordshire CC v SRK and Ors* (2016), care provision that was organised for an adult without support, funding or the knowledge of the local authority or the NHS was considered to be imputable to the state because the care was paid for with money awarded by a court as compensation for personal injury resulting from an accident. This resulted in the local authority being required to take authorisation of the care, which met the threshold for deprivation of liberty, to the Court of Protection for legal authorisation despite having had no involvement in planning the care provision. It was planned, when the Care Act 2014 was being drafted, to directly address this issue; however, nothing appeared in the final legislation related to explicitly offering protection to self-funders in order to ensure that they were included in protections available to others receiving care via the state.

The necessity of state involvement in some form to attract the protections of human rights law creates issues regarding the protections available to self-funders setting up their own private contracts with care providers. For example, care homes and home care agencies where there is no involvement of the state in either decision making or funding. Consumer rights established under legislation, such as the Consumer Rights Act 2015, or regulatory frameworks, such as the Care Quality Commission (CQC) in England (or Care Inspectorate Wales in Wales), apply to the contract between the individual and the care provider so these are available to self-funders, though these offer different rights from the framework of safeguards offered by human rights law where the state is involved. It is also important to note that these kinds of arrangements do not mean that adult safeguarding processes are not available. Local authorities still have statutory duties to undertake enquiries under section 42 of the Care Act 2014, however care arrangements have been made.

Section 6 of the HRA gives public bodies the duty to ensure that their actions do not infringe a citizen's human rights unlawfully, known as their *negative obligation*. Public bodies also have a *positive obligation* to act to prevent human rights abuses, for example where care is provided by public and non-public bodies. In addition, public bodies must also ensure that there are systems in place to protect human rights – known as the *procedural obligation* (BIHR, 2013, p 7). This range of obligations means that the actions of those responsible for the care, support and treatment of those who might be subject to safeguarding arrangements must fundamentally act to protect from, address and prevent human rights abuses as part of adult safeguarding arrangements.

Which rights relevant to adult safeguarding are protected under human rights law?

Key human rights for adults at risk of harm and abuse set out within the European Convention on Human Rights (ECHR) and the Human Rights Act 1998 (HRA) include:

Article 2: right to life

This right is absolute as, except in states where lawful execution may be legally sanctioned, this right cannot be removed. This right also gives states the positive obligation to protect life, though this obligation is not absolute, as the state may make decisions that may lead to the person's death, for instance by choosing not to provide certain life-sustaining medical treatments. This also means that care decision making made by state bodies should act to protect life such as by taking efforts to prevent suicide (Johns, 2014, p 31) or providing care to an acceptable standard (SCIE, 2013) so that a person's life is maintained.

REFLECTIVE ACTIVITY

Case study: Sylvia and Ted Jones

Sylvia Jones is a 73-year-old woman with a Parkinson's diagnosis who lives in a housing association tenancy flat with her husband, **Ted Jones**. Sylvia was assessed by the local authority under the Care Act 2014 as needing help with personal care, assistance to mobilise as she cannot bear weight, assistance with eating, drinking and taking medication and assistance to leave her home to shop and visit family and friends. Ted declined the carer's assessment from the local authority. Their GP had made the referral as they were concerned about the amount of stress that caring for Sylvia was putting on Ted. The GP noticed that Sylvia did not speak when they met and appeared scared of Ted.

Ted told the social worker that he was able to meet all of Sylvia's care needs and refused an assessment. The social worker joined a routine GP appointment with Sylvia so they could meet without Ted present. Sylvia explained that Ted often does not wash or dress her and leaves her in a soiled bed for hours at a time. He limits her food and drink intake so she does not need the toilet as often and does not give her medication as he believes it makes her worse. She refused to let the GP examine her physically, though the GP noticed that she appeared to have lost weight. Sylvia did not want to talk about Ted as she feels she makes his mood worse because of all the help she asks for. The social worker asked what Sylvia wanted to do about her care – she explained that she would like Ted to have more help so he wouldn't be so stressed but she knows he would refuse as he does not like people coming into their home. Sylvia does not want to live apart from Ted and is adamant that she wants him to care for her.

The social worker considered assessing Sylvia's capacity but decided that this was not appropriate as she has no mental disorder that could affect her ability to make decisions. The social worker offered Ted another carer's assessment but he refused this and any offers of care again. With Sylvia's capacitated refusal to receive care or to live apart from Ted there were limited options for reducing or managing the risks to her. The social worker asked the GP to monitor Sylvia and Ted during routine appointments and to contact adult safeguarding should there be further concerns.

Three months later, Sylvia was admitted to hospital severely malnourished and dehydrated and with significant pressure sores. She was delirious as a result of the infected sores and staff used the Mental Capacity Act 2005 and Deprivation of Liberty Safeguards to keep her on the ward to treat her as she was frequently asking to go home. Ted had been rude to staff on the ward and asked that Sylvia should return home; this was refused until her health improved. After three weeks' treatment with antibiotics and improved nutrition and hydration, Sylvia regained mental capacity and chose to discharge herself to Ted's care. The social worker offered Sylvia alternative accommodation or assistance with care at home as they were concerned that without additional support Sylvia's health was likely to deteriorate again and there was a significant risk to her life, considering her state of health when she was admitted to hospital. Sylvia refused any care or support and Ted arrived to take her home again.

Reflective questions

- What responsibility does the local authority have regarding Sylvia's right to life?
- How does the local authority's obligation regarding her right to life interact with Sylvia's capacity and autonomy to make decisions that may put her at risk?
- What challenges would this pose for you as a safeguarding practitioner?

Our thoughts are that the following areas should be considered during safeguarding:

- The local authority's duty to protect the right to life must be considered when weighing risks against the adult's right to autonomy and self-determination. Sylvia's capacitated views should be recognised and her autonomy promoted while considering supporting protective factors to monitor her health and well-being, such as regular contact with the GP, as Sylvia accepts this contact, and housing-related support as well as continuing to attempt engagement with home care and/or carer support.

– Offering options to promote Sylvia's voice and begin engagement with domestic abuse services should be pursued, for example the involvement of an Independent Domestic Violence Advisor (IDVA).

Article 3: freedom from torture and inhuman and degrading treatment

Article 3 is also an absolute right.

The United Nations Torture Convention (United Nations Human Rights, 1984) (Article 1) definition of torture is complex but has been summarised as:

- the intentional infliction of severe mental or physical suffering
- by a public official, who is directly or indirectly involved
- for a specific purpose. (Association for the Prevention of Torture, 2017)

The implication here is that torture is sanctioned by the state and is carried out for a purpose, either to gain information or to punish so is very likely not to be relevant to adult safeguarding. The second part of this human right, 'freedom from inhuman and degrading treatment' is a more common theme seen in adult safeguarding concerns. The British Institute of Human Rights (BIHR, 2008) have produced a useful range of real-life examples of breaches of Article 3 together with other human rights breaches, relevant to people with care and support needs in various situations. For example:

> a young man with mental health problems was placed in residential care on a short-term basis. During a visit one day, his parents noticed unexplained bruising on his body. They raised the issue with managers at the home but their concerns were dismissed (*breach of his Article 3 rights*). They were also told that they were no longer permitted to visit their son (*breach of his Article 8 rights*). After participating in a BIHR training session the parents approached the care home once again and invoked their son's right not to be treated in an inhuman and degrading way and their right to respect for family life. As a result, the ban on their visits was revoked and an investigation was conducted into the bruising on their son's body. (BIHR, 2008)

Other examples of potential breaches of Article 3 in care settings include:

- people who do not have incontinence being forced to wear incontinence pads because staff say they do not have time to take them to the toilet;
- people left in soiled beds or clothes;
- people shouted at or called names.

Article 5: right to liberty and security of person

This right protects citizens from unnecessary detention. It is not absolute so the article sets out the circumstances that lawful action can be taken to infringe this right. Of particular interest in adult safeguarding are the provisions for detention under a legal framework for those of unsound mind, meaning where a person has a medically diagnosed mental disorder. This right underpins the necessity for legal frameworks such as the Mental Health Act 1983 (as amended in 2007) (MHA) in England, Wales and Northern Ireland and Mental Health (Care and Treatment) (Scotland) 2003, as amended by the Mental Health (Scotland) Act 2015, in Scotland. In addition, Article 5 also underpins the current Deprivation of Liberty Safeguards (DoLS) amendment to the Mental Capacity Act 2005 (MCA) and the planned revision of DoLS set out in the Mental Capacity (Amendment) Act 2019, resulting in the Liberty Protection Safeguards (LPS) in England and Wales.

People who have been assessed as lacking mental capacity to make these decisions are considered to be deprived of this right when their care and treatment meet the three criteria for deprivation of the Article 5 right to liberty. The three elements are:

1. *Objective*: detention in a specific place for a not-negligible period of time. The 'acid test' defined the threshold as 'under continuous supervision and control and not free to leave' the establishment where they are residing for care and treatment in the *P v Cheshire West and Chester Council* and *P and Q v Surrey County Council* (2014) Supreme Court cases (known as the 'Cheshire West' judgment).
2. *Subjective*: consent to reside in the location for care and treatment amounting to a deprivation of liberty, including deciding that the person lacks mental capacity to make this decision.
3. *Imputable to the state*: responsibility for deciding on the care and treatment in the location can be attributed to the state in some way, for example through planning, providing, funding, monitoring or supervising the care or treatment.

This article requires legal frameworks for the lawful deprivation of a person's right to liberty to include speedy access to appeal, for example via tribunal or managers hearing (MHA) or application to the Court of Protection (MCA DoLS/LPS), and support for individuals to exercise these rights, via advocacy and representation, for instance.

DoLS/LPS can be used in three ways in the context of adults safeguarding, to:

- **Prevent** violation of the adult's Article 5 rights, for example by identifying where restrictions are unnecessary and prompting changes in care practice to promote autonomy.
- **Alert** to adult safeguarding concerns through the scrutiny offered currently by the Best Interests Assessor and Mental Health Assessor roles in DoLS assessments

or the assessing professional, review scrutiny and, in some cases, Approved Mental Capacity Professional in LPS assessments, as well as the representative and advocacy roles.

• **Protect** adults at risk from abuse in institutional settings by imposing conditions of changes in care practice through conditions attached to DoLS authorisations, regular monitoring by representatives and advocates and during reassessment and promoting the right to appeal against authorisations.

DoLS/LPS cannot be used to protect other rights – there have been cases where DoLS was used by local authorities to restrict Article 8 rights. For example by limiting contact with family and placing in residential care in order to safeguard from alleged harm (reported cases include *MK v Somerset County Council*, 2014, *Milton Keynes Council v RR and Ors*, 2014, *Essex County Council v RF and Ors*, 2015). The judgment in each of these cases clearly show that using DoLS to infringe Article 8 rights offers no legal protection to practitioners as DoLS was designed solely as a legal framework for lawful deprivation of the right to liberty.

In our experience, practice within DoLS has intersected with adult safeguarding to a great extent, especially where Best Interests Assessors (BIAs) scrutinise care practice for individuals. The BIA can identify and draw attention to decision making that does not respect the adult's right to autonomy or organisational abuse during their assessment, facilitate safeguarding reporting and develop monitoring, for example with conditions attached to DoLS authorisations (McNichol, 2016). For example, a BIA assessment noted that an older man with a dementia diagnosis was being kept in bed for the majority of the day in a care home because the care staff were concerned about him repeatedly lying on the floor whenever he was moving around the home independently. In order to stop him doing this the home had chosen to restrict him to bed, which had the result of increasing the risks of pressure sores, muscle wastage, frustration and boredom. An occupational therapy assessment identified little risk to him from lying on the floor when he chose to but greater risks to him in preventing him from leaving his bed – the BIA assessment noted the restriction to his bed as unnecessary and recommended a DoLS authorisation with the condition that he be supported to move freely within the home and to choose how he spent his time. The involvement of the local authority safeguarding team encouraged the home to reconsider their approach to risk management in this case and to see the importance of noting the severity of risks inherent in the range of potential options for managing his care in the context of his right to live a life as free from restrictions as possible.

Article 5 does not just offer a right to protection to those subject to restrictions amounting to deprivation of liberty in institutional settings like care homes and hospitals (for example, where DoLS applies at the time of writing). People without decision-making capacity regarding their care and treatment can be considered to be deprived of their liberty where there is any state involvement in decision making about, or funding of, their care and treatment in supported living, residential schools or Shared Lives arrangements or when receiving care in their own home. These circumstances can be relevant to adult safeguarding as unnecessary restrictions that interfere with the person's right to liberty can also be seen as abusive (physically or psychologically).

Where unnecessary restrictions are applied in settings without the oversight and scrutiny that institutions are subject to, via inspection regimes like the CQC, these may continue unchecked without scrutiny. For example, a care home agency was asked to lock an older woman with dementia into her home when they left as the family who had organised them to provide care visits were concerned that she would leave the property and be at risk of wandering at night and getting lost or being injured on the road because of poor road safety awareness. The care agency raised a concern about the family's request, the social worker identified that the family were acting proportionately and in her best interests but without legal authority. The social worker educated the care agency about community deprivation of liberty applications under section 16 of the MCA (at the time of writing or LPS, once implemented), organised the involvement of an Independent Mental Capacity Advocate as a litigation friend and made the application to the Court of Protection for authorisation of the care arrangements.

▶ **ESSENTIAL INFORMATION: LEGISLATION**

Protections for Article 5: Mental Health Act, Deprivation of Liberty Safeguards, the Court of Protection and Liberty Protection Safeguards

The legal **safeguards** available for people with mental disorders in England and Wales with regard to their Article 5 rights at the time of writing include:

- A range of procedures prescribed by law including the Mental Health Act 1983 (2007) (MHA), the Deprivation of Liberty Safeguards (2007) amendment to the Mental Capacity Act 2005 (DoLS) and application to the Court of Protection for what may be called 'community', 'domestic' or 'judicial' deprivation of liberty under section 16 of the Mental Capacity Act 2005. DoLS and community deprivation of liberty frameworks will be replaced by the Liberty Protection Safeguards (LPS) through the implementation of the Mental Capacity (Amendment) Act 2019 which, at the time of writing, is planned for October 2020.
- These legal frameworks each include the **right to appeal** (to meet ECHR Article 5(4)) via the managers of the hospital where the person is detained or the two-tier tribunal system under the MHA, via the Court of Protection for DoLS authorisations and via the Court of Appeal where the Court of Protection has made the decision to deprive the adult of their liberty.

- Each legal framework includes support to the right to appeal through *advocacy* whether via the rights of access to an Independent Mental Health Advocate (IMHA) and free representation by a solicitor for appeals to those detained under the MHA, to a Relevant Person's Representative (RPR) and Independent Mental Capacity Advocate (IMCA) (Department for Constitutional Affairs, 2007) under DoLS or appropriate person or advocate under LPS to a litigation friend for Court of Protection applications and appeals. Appeals under each of these legal frameworks attract Legal Aid and the applications for Legal Aid funds can be signed off by IMCAs.
- The MHA offers *specific safeguards* to those in institutional care. For example, it stipulates that 'the local safeguarding team should be made aware of any patient being supported in longer term segregation' (Code of Practice, Chapter 26.153) as an extra layer of scrutiny when a patient is confined to one area on a ward and prevented from mixing with other patients on a long-term basis.

Each of these legal frameworks has been criticised regarding their safeguards to people deprived of their Article 5 human rights including:

- *Complexity*: DoLS and the Court of Protection (COP) have been criticised for the complexity of assessment, language used and ability to be understood by lay people. Guidance for professionals, families and people subject to these legal frameworks are available from user organisations such as Age UK or government run/funded organisations such as the Social Care Institute for Excellence (SCIE) or the Office of the Public Guardian (OPG) but this does not solve the inherent complexity of the decisions being made and the language used in law to describe them.
- *Inability to meet demand for assessment and authorisations following the Cheshire West decisions*: the effective lowering of the threshold for deprivation of liberty has meant the number of applications for DoLS and community deprivation of liberty have risen hugely (data on DoLS applications available from NHS Digital and on COP applications in Family Court Reports). This has led to long waiting lists for assessments under DoLS, even with local authorities prioritising and managing waiting lists, and local authorities not actively pursuing community deprivation applications in the COP. Following the Cheshire West decision, a streamlined version of the community deprivation of liberty application to the COP process (known as 'Re. X') was proposed in anticipation of increased numbers of applications and was widely criticised for missing out access of the detained person to representation in the court process, so the role of the litigation friend was promoted in the knowledge that applicants will be unlikely to have the mental capacity to act on their own appeal. There is no indication that the overall number of deprivation of liberty applications will reduce under LPS since the safeguards will bring together

DoLS and COP applications and additionally include 16- and 17-year-olds. However, assessments will be conducted by frontline health and social care staff rather than specialists, which should make assessments more accessible.

- *Limitations on appeal processes*: DoLS and community deprivation of liberty applications to the COP have been criticised regarding access to appeal. The demand for appeals against DoLS decisions has grown since the Cheshire West decisions in line with increased numbers subject to these detentions. The ability of the COP to respond in a speedy manner to applications for appeal is limited. It is our experience from practice that the appeals of people subject to DoLS authorisations are not always followed through to a hearing in court for reasons including inexperience of RPRs, belief that an appeal would not succeed or be in the person's interests or the person's objections to their care not being interpreted as a desire to appeal against their deprivation of liberty.
- *Availability of advocacy*: the increase in numbers of DoLS and community deprivation of liberty applications to the COP since the Cheshire West judgment and the judgment in the *Re. AJ* (2015) case, which promoted the importance of RPRs to aid access to appeals, have both led to increased pressure on local authority funded advocacy services who are commissioned to provide IMCAs and where needed are often also acting as paid RPRs. In the context of local authority budget cuts, many advocacy services have not had the capacity to meet this increased demand and are not always able to respond as needed.

As a result of these critiques, all mental health rights legislation in England and Wales has recently been reviewed.

Mental Health Act 1983 (2007)

- MHA was reviewed and a final report laying out the plans for reform was published in December 2018. It particularly sets out the need for the MHA to be compliant with the United Nations Convention on the Rights of Persons with Disabilities (CRPD) (2006). The report specifically sets out why the recommendation from the UN's Committee on the Rights of Persons with Disabilities in October 2017, that the UK abolish all substitute decision making and repeal legislation for involuntary and compulsory treatment and detention, is not supported by the review (DHSC, 2018b, p 61).
- The report states the need to improve how human rights are embedded in this crucial piece of mental health law for England and Wales. Suggestions for reform of the MHA include a range of 'rebalancing the system to be more responsive to the wishes and preferences of the patient' (DHSC, 2018b, pp 11–12) through greater respect for individual decision making through 'proposals on advance directives, nearest relatives, access to advocacy, better safeguards and a new right of appeal against compulsory treatment' (p 12). The introduction of advance care planning by the person regarding future

compulsory treatment, giving detained people the right to choose their own representative and the ability of tribunals to hear appeals against treatment as well as detention may all act to expand the control of the person over their own mental health treatment. What action the government will take on these recommendations is not clear at the time of writing.

Deprivation of Liberty Safeguards (DoLS)

The House of Lords (2014) report on the implementation of the MCA, recommending that DoLS be scrapped and replaced by a simpler and more rights-based version, and the Cheshire West (2014) Supreme Court judgment causing a massive increase in the number of DoLS and COP applications prompted the UK government into making the replacement of DoLS a priority. As a result the Mental Capacity (Amendment) Act 2019 was given Royal Assent in May 2019.

The passage of the Mental Capacity (Amendment) Bill 2018 through Parliament was remarkable considering it took place in the context of highly charged Brexit negotiations and the stalling of much of the rest of the government's legislative agenda. The amendments changed considerably from the original Law Commission proposals to the final Act. The main safeguards offered by the LPS which, at the time of writing, were due to be implemented from October 2020, are set out in the box.

▶ ESSENTIAL INFORMATION: LEGISLATION

Liberty Protection Safeguards

Who?
Adults from *16* years of age, with a *mental disorder* that means they *lack capacity* to make decisions about their care and whose care plan amounts to a *deprivation of liberty* (defined via case law, as defined in the Cheshire West (2014) judgment regarding the 'acid test'). The assessment must note whether the arrangements are *necessary and proportionate* (without defining what the arrangements are proportionate to), whether detention would be more appropriate under the *MHA*, that those interested in their care have been *consulted*, how *representation* is available to the person and whether additional scrutiny from a specialist *Approved Mental Capacity Professional* (AMCP) assessor is required.

Where?
Applies in England and Wales to people living in their own home, sheltered or supported housing, residential schools, extra care housing, care homes and hospitals. Scotland and Northern Ireland have their own legal frameworks.

How long?
Up to one year, renewal for up to one year then up to three years.

How organised?
Responsible bodies manage the LPS processes with relevant NHS bodies responsible for people in hospital or with CHC funding and local authorities responsible for everyone else, including inpatients in private psychiatric hospitals.

What is the process?
1. *Assessments* – those conducting health and social care assessments identify those whose care is likely to amount to a deprivation of liberty and complete an LPS necessary and proportionate assessment. LPS assessments can be conducted by anyone with relevant experience and knowledge though the mental capacity and mental health elements of the assessment are likely to need a professional.
2. *Pre-authorisation check* – the responsible body identifies a person not involved in the assessed person's care to scrutinise the written assessments. If the assessed person is objecting, they reside in a private psychiatric hospital or for another reason at the responsible body's discretion, the reviewer can ask an AMCP to review the assessments including visiting the person and consulting those involved in their care.
3. *Authorisation* – the responsible body authorises the LPS detention.

What safeguards does LPS offer?
As with the MHA and DoLS, the LPS offers access to *appeal* (via the COP), *representation* by an appropriate person or advocate and right to *review*.

Summarised from Edge Training, 2019

Article 8: respect for private and family life, home and correspondence

When considering intervention to safeguard an adult from the risk of harm and abuse, you must consider the adult's right to respect for their private and family life, home and correspondence which is designed to protect the individual from unnecessary intervention in their right to live their life as they choose. It is not an absolute right – as suggested by the use of the phrase 'respect for' – but something that all those representing the state in their work must consider and balance with risks to the adult's well-being before intervening in their life.

When making decisions about the nature of harm an adult is experiencing and how to address this, you will be balancing a range of rights and responsibilities towards the individual in a proportionate manner, such as using the legal principle of proportionality. At times, it can feel like protection of the adult can only be best achieved through the use of legal measures to remove the adult from the risky situation and place them in an apparently 'safer' institutional setting. However, it is essential to ensure that the correct legal safeguards are used to interfere with the person's right to privacy. A range of judgments in the COP show that legal measures regarding deprivation of liberty, such as DoLS, should not be used to restrict contact with family. Depriving an adult of their liberty to safeguard them from harm where safeguarding concerns are unproven or uninvestigated has been criticised in the courts (*Milton Keynes Council v RR* (2014), *Somerset Council v MK* (2014), *Essex County Council v RF* (2014)) as has using DoLS to deprive a person of contact with a family member where no evidence of harm has been presented in justification (*London Borough of Hillingdon v Steven Neary* (2011)). If the circumstances of an adult safeguarding concern mean that legal measures are required to remove the adult from their home or deprive them of contact with their family or friends, only the COP can make this decision and issue a lawful order to restrict this right. In the vast majority of cases this will not be either necessary or desirable.

REFLECTIVE ACTIVITY

Case study: Jay and Daisy

Jay Jones and Daisy Smith have been engaged to be married for ten years. Their parents have opposed their marriage for all of this time, saying that as they both have learning disabilities and live in supported living, they have no idea what marriage is and have no right to marry. Jay and Daisy's support workers are convinced that both do understand marriage and what this entails but are worried about the parents' reactions would be if they were to bring this up with them.

The support workers became concerned about the breach of the couple's Article 8 rights in not supporting their rights to choose to marry and contacted the local adult safeguarding team who arrange a number of interventions. These included conversations with Jay and Daisy about the nature of marriage, where they show their understanding and desire for this legally binding arrangement, and meetings, with the couple's permission, with their families. Jay's family remain adamantly against him marrying. Jay and Daisy marry and move into a double flat in the supported living complex.

Reflective questions

- How has recognition of Jay and Daisy's rights under Article 8 affected their choices about their family life?
- How can you use these insights into practice with adults at risk?

> *Our thoughts* are that the following areas should be considered in similar circumstances:
>
> –   Jay and Daisy's understanding of marriage and relationships should be explored in a manner that recognises their rights to form relationships and their mental capacity.
> –   Care planning should include consideration of education regarding sexuality, positive relationships and sexual health.

The British Institute for Human Rights (Hosali, 2015) identified that care providers are not always clear in their understanding of their responsibilities to protect their service users' human rights. In this example, Admiral Court Care Home in Hartlepool did not recognise their responsibility to protect a resident's Article 8 rights by respecting the need to have the adult's consent to a Do Not Attempt Resuscitation (DNAR) order. Rights to refuse or accept medical treatment should be considered as Article 8 issues as they are concerned with who chooses what happens to the person's body. This right should be balanced with the Article 2 right to life and the adult's views and wishes should be considered when concluding whether a DNAR order is appropriate.

Article 14: protection from discrimination in the exercise of these rights

This article is what the BIHR call a 'piggy-back right' (Rebours, no date), meaning that it gives citizens the right to not be discriminated against in accessing the other rights offered within the ECHR and HRA. This ensures equality of access to rights by all – echoing the universality of access to rights that Baroness Hale referred to in the Cheshire West (2014) judgment when considering the rights of disabled people to have the same expectations of what amounts to a deprivation of liberty as other people.

The adult's disability, age, sex, gender identity, sexual orientation, race and ethnicity or religion or belief may be a factor in discrimination though this right also offers protection for discrimination for other reasons, for example advertising specifying gender when employing a personal carer for an individual.

Oppression, anti-oppressive practice and identity

Discrimination and oppression are prevalent throughout the lives of adults at risk of harm and abuse. Social work has long acknowledged the impact of oppression and its responsibility to work to counter this and to provide lead professionals in safeguarding these ideas should be influential on all adult safeguarding practice. Burke and Harrison (2016) note that 'working with people who experience discrimination and oppression, who are excluded and at the margins of society, places a moral duty on the social work profession and those who work within it to move from a position of noticing and witnessing to one of engaging in political and social action' (p 41). This should not be ignored as a factor in the experiences and situations of those subject to adult safeguarding processes, though the low numbers of enquiries considering discrimination as a factor suggest that the vast majority of safeguarding work does not explicitly acknowledge the impact of discrimination and oppression.

Discriminatory abuse only accounted for 0.6 per cent of all concluded adult safeguarding enquiries in England in the year 2017/2018 (NHS Digital, 2018). The significance of discrimination in the lives of adults at risk is not sufficiently understood. Beliefs about older or disabled people, or about the impact of sex and gender, the experiences of transgender people, ethnicity, sexual orientation or religion/belief should be considered in the context of all abuse of adults at risk.

If people are marginalised and considered somehow less valuable in society, the risk of harm increases and may not be recognised in how adult safeguarding concerns are raised, enquiries made and plans devised. For example, cuts to local authority and NHS budgets in the context of the UK government's austerity policies since 2010 have had an impact on the availability and quality of care, which are an often unconsidered factor in adult safeguarding – especially concerning organisational abuse where understaffing, lack of training and poor leadership can have a significant impact on the nature of care received. The challenge for individual safeguarding practitioners is how to introduce effective measures to reduce and prevent risk of abuse and harm to adults in organisations where socio-economic conditions are a factor in increasing risks. Close work with local authority contracting services and regulatory bodies, such as the CQC, can be valuable in these circumstances.

Discriminatory abuse is a powerful factor in the lives of disabled people. Mortimer (2015) on the increasing rates of disability hate crime reported to the police (up by 41 per cent in 2014/15 compared to 2013/14) and how campaigners consider this to be the 'tip of the iceberg' in the context of low confidence among disabled people that their concerns will be taken seriously by the police. Discriminatory abuse is perpetrated by both individuals and organisations, meaning that all categories of abuse can be intensified by a discriminatory element. For example, in terms of abuse based in discrimination against people with learning disabilities, campaigns such as 'Death by *Indifference*' (Mencap, 2012) and research by the University of Bristol in the Learning Disabilities Mortality Review (*LeDeR*) programme (2018) have shown that people who have learning disabilities have life spans of 15 to 20 years less than the general population, and that early mortality can be associated with the attitudes and beliefs of medical staff caring for them.

► **ESSENTIAL INFORMATION: LEGISLATION**

The Care and Support Guidance provides a direct link to information on the nine Equality Act 2010 protected characteristics that apply to England, Wales and Scotland. Northern Ireland did not implement the Equality Act so previous laws on discrimination apply.

Types of discrimination: protected characteristics
It is against the law to discriminate against anyone because of:

- Age
- Gender reassignment [e.g. the person's gender identity]
- Being married or in a civil partnership
- Being pregnant or on maternity leave
- Disability
- Race including colour, nationality, ethnic or national origin
- Religion or belief
- Sex
- Sexual orientation

You are protected from discrimination:

- At work
- In education
- As a consumer
- When using public services
- When buying or renting property
- As a member or guest of a private club or association

You are also protected from discrimination if:

- You are associated with someone who has a protected characteristic, for example a family member or friend
- You have complained about discrimination or supported someone else's claim

HM Government, 2018

In practice, it is essential to have a sense when discrimination is affecting the experience of care and support and to be aware that the presenting concern might not place discrimination in the foreground.

REFLECTIVE ACTIVITY

Case study: Benjamin/Barbara Broad

Benjamin Broad lived in a hospital for people with learning disabilities for much of his childhood and now, in his early sixties, he lives in a supported living flat. A support worker has reported a safeguarding concern about another worker who has refused to take Benjamin to an LGBTQ support group arranged by his social worker. The reporting support worker overheard the other worker say, "You shouldn't be mixing with people like that".

The social worker making enquiries talked to Benjamin who said that he had met younger people who feel as he does, that they have a different gender identity from the one they were labelled with at birth. Benjamin has told his support workers that he wishes to be known as **Barbara** and wants them to support her to go shopping for women's clothing. The support worker refused to support Barbara with buying clothes or attending the group as they believe that she does not understand what she is saying.

Reflective question

- What would your response to this situation be, considering both the legal and values-driven approach to human rights-based safeguarding?

Our thoughts are that the following areas should be considered:

- Barbara's expression of her gender identity should be respected and supported and ongoing contact with the LGBTQ support group should be facilitated. She has legal rights to protection from discrimination from the Equality Act 2010 in accessing the support service commissioned for her who should be acting in a person-centred manner towards her. She is also able to call on her Article 8 rights to privacy and a family life to express her identity without discrimination and to ensure only those with a need to know are aware of her transition.
- Staff training regarding LGBTQ identity and care needs should be provided for those working in the organisation.

There has been increasing recognition of the experiences and rights of transgender people to be recognised for who they are, and the inadequacy of health and social care services to acknowledge this (Bachman and Gooch, 2018a, 2018b). The interaction of discrimination on the grounds of gender identity can intensify the experiences of discrimination on the grounds of disability and multiply the intensity and severity of abuse and its psychological impact on the adult's mental health and well-being. Recognition of multiple forms of abuse can be informed by the concept of *intersectionality* (Crenshaw, 1991), which started by exploring the difference in experiences of oppression of black women where oppression on the grounds of gender and race intersect. Since then this concept has been used to acknowledge the differences that those subject to multiple oppressions experience that the usual discourse ignores as it tends to focus on single issues as affecting individuals homogeneously. In Barbara's case, her access to a supportive community that validates her identity is controlled because of her disability and the values of those paid to care for her as a result. A safeguarding approach that does not acknowledge this as having a detrimental effect is likely to compound the neglect and psychological impact of this experience.

Well-being under the Care Act 2014 and human rights

The Care Act 2014 is legislation based on principles including the overarching principle of well-being and the six principles of adult safeguarding. In Table 2.1, we map the well-being principle against the relevant ECHR and CRPD human rights.

Applying the six adult safeguarding principles of the Care Act 2014

The six adult safeguarding principles (DH, 2011) were issued as a statement of government policy prior to the creation of the Care Act 2014 to form a statement of intent about adult safeguarding practice. The principles should inform all aspects of adult safeguarding work, from operational practice by individual practitioners through to strategic and policy decisions made by organisations and SABs. Here we explore the meaning of each principle and present an account of how these principles can be used in practice through Freda Johnson's story.

Empowerment

Empowerment means people being supported and encouraged to make their own decisions and give informed consent: *"I am asked what I want as the outcomes from the safeguarding process and this directly informs what happens."*
    The empowerment principle in practice is typified by the Making Safeguarding Personal approach described here and illustrated throughout this book. We can support adults who have been marginalised and/or harmed, and are unable to protect themselves, by:

* exploring with them what will improve their quality of life;
* using this understanding to support them to make decisions; and
* making sure the adult's decisions, views and wishes inform what we do.

Table 2.1: Care Act 2014 well-being principle mapped to the European Convention on Human Rights and Convention on the Rights of Persons with Disabilities

Well-being principle *Care Act 2014*	Human right *ECHR or CRPD as stated*
Personal dignity (including treatment of the individual with respect)	**Article 3 ECHR** The right not to be tortured or treated in an inhuman or degrading way **Article 8 ECHR** Right to respect for family and private life
Physical and mental health and emotional well-being	**Article 2 ECHR** Right to life The right to life also includes the positive duty of state organisations to support health.
Protection from abuse and neglect	**Article 2 ECHR** Right to life is an **absolute** right. Absolute rights are rights that can never be interfered with by the state. The state has a positive duty to protect Article 2 rights by taking action to protect people at risk of abuse and neglect. **Article 3 ECHR** Right not to be subjected to torture or inhuman or degrading treatment – also an **absolute** right. **Article 16 CRPD** Freedom from exploitation, violence and abuse; also includes the right to 'appropriate measures to promote the physical, cognitive and psychological recovery, rehabilitation and social reintegration of persons with disabilities who become victims of any form of exploitation, violence or abuse, including through the provision of protection services. Such recovery and reintegration shall take place in an environment that fosters the health, welfare, self-respect, dignity and autonomy of the person and takes into account gender- and age-specific needs.'
Control by the individual over their day-to-day life (including over care and support provided and the way they are provided)	**Article 19 CRPD** Living independently and being included in the community **Article 20 CRPD** Personal mobility
Participation in work, education, training or recreation	**Protocol 1 Article 2 ECHR**
Social and economic well-being	**Article 14 ECHR** Rights under the **Equality Act 2010** regarding employment **Article 20 CRPD** Personal mobility
Domestic, family and personal domains	**Article 8 ECHR** Right to respect for family and private life **Article 12 ECHR** Right to marry and found a family **Article 23 CRPD** Respect for home and the family Rights under the **Equality Act 2010** regarding the protected characteristics of pregnancy and maternity and marriage and civil partnership
Suitability of the individual's living accommodation	**Protocol 1 Article 1 ECHR** Protection of property **Article 19 CRPD** Living independently and being included in the community
The individual's contribution to society	**Article 19 CRPD** Living independently and being included in the community **Article 21 CRPD** Freedom of expression and opinion, and access to information in accessible formats

This practice can have a huge impact in a variety of areas, from increased self-esteem to a reduction in the chances of the adult being harmed again.

FREDA'S STORY I

Freda Johnson lives in a care home with five other people who have physical and learning disabilities. Josh, one of the other people living there, is beginning to show the symptoms of dementia. He shouts at Freda and hit her yesterday. Freda initially appears resigned to tolerating his behaviour; they lived together in a large hospital for people with learning difficulties some years ago and she is fond of him. Yesterday she said that the care home was "getting like the old hospital" – she isn't happy with the situation. Freda meets with her key care worker and social worker; she talks about how she feels and is asked what she wants to happen regarding Josh's behaviour towards her and what thoughts she has about how her current life could be improved.

Prevention

Prevention means it is better to take action before harm occurs: *"I receive clear and simple information about what abuse is. I know how to recognise the signs, and I know what I can do to seek help."*

Prevention begins with good commissioning of services and good healthcare and social work; if the adult is using services which are of good quality and meet their assessed needs, a large amount of harm will be prevented. However, life is not risk- or harm-free and so building prevention into everything that we do, including giving clear information and promoting awareness, will enable us to support the adult's human rights and well-being.

FREDA'S STORY II

The staff involved make sure that Freda understands that although Josh does not always have control over his behaviour at the moment, they know that she is being harmed by the situation and she should not have to tolerate this. They take the opportunity to talk about any other experiences of harm that Freda has encountered in her life, emphasising that she should not have had to experience any of this. The first thing that Freda asks for is a plan about how to reduce the risk that Josh will shout at her again, or hit her, and to know when, how and who to ask for help if she is concerned about Josh or anyone else who might harm her. After some discussion with Freda the staff also start thinking about how to promote general 'staying safe' awareness throughout the home.

Proportionality

Proportionality means the least intrusive response appropriate to the risk presented: *"I am sure that the professionals will work in my interest and they will only get involved as much as is necessary."*

Proportional responses are essential to maintaining the adult's autonomy and promoting their human right to minimal intervention and can be clearly informed through dialogue with the adult. Practitioners should establish what is important to the adult and what the key changes are that the adult wants to achieve. Prescribed procedural approaches can get in the way of proportionate approaches; for example, practitioners believe that an enquiry must be complex and time-consuming when a flexible response may be less intrusive and more appropriate.

FREDA'S STORY III

Freda's social worker is in contact with Josh's social worker who is reviewing how Josh's needs may have changed and the level of support he requires. Part of this work will involve a compatibility risk assessment to understand how changes in Josh's behaviour affect others in the home. Freda only needs to know that Josh will get help with his behaviour; her focus must be on how she can be supported to be and feel safer. Freda's social worker has written up her outcomes and the safeguarding plan made with her and has agreed to return the following week to review whether Freda feels and is safe from harm.

Protection

Protection means support and representation for those in greatest need: *"I get help and support to report abuse and neglect. I get help so that I am able to take part in the safeguarding process to the extent to which I want."*

Protection from abuse and neglect is a fundamental aspect of the 'well-being' principle (Chapter 1:1.1–1.26 of the statutory guidance) and of the human rights enjoyed by all. There is no interpretation of 'those in greatest need' in either government policy or statutory guidance; however, the definitions given within the guidance would suggest that these are people with care and support needs.

FREDA'S STORY IV

Freda doesn't expect Josh to be moved away from the home – she is fond of him and concerned about how he is coping. But she does want to know that her experience is taken seriously and that she will be protected. After a full discussion with Freda and her key care worker, the social worker agrees an interim safeguarding plan with both. Freda has been supported to devise a slightly different daily routine she is more comfortable with and is now aware that her well-being is valued by all staff who will support her throughout the day.

Partnership

Partnership means local solutions through services working with their communities, as communities have a part to play in preventing, detecting and reporting neglect and abuse: *"I know that staff treat any personal and sensitive information in confidence, only sharing what is helpful and necessary. I am confident that professionals will work together and with me to get the best result for me."*

The reference to communities in the government adult safeguarding policy (DH, 2011) reflects both that governmental aspiration of wider community involvement in society, a 'Big Society' that trusts in the people for ideas and innovations (Conservative Party, 2010) and the localist approach to the implementation of adult safeguarding policies and legislation. However, the follow-up statement references professionals working together. Both approaches are key factors in adult safeguarding work; the mechanisms of adult safeguarding bring together the agencies who can help the adult. The community the adult lives in is also of relevance: what strengths and what resource exist in what the adult considers as 'community'?

FREDA'S STORY V

Freda understands that information about Josh will not be shared with her, or information about her shared with Josh. The professionals working with Josh will get anonymised information needed for a compatibility risk assessment. Freda agrees to this as she understands the explanation that some work needs to be done to understand how the people in the care home, with all their different strengths and challenges, can live together with the best quality of life for all.

Accountability

Accountability means accountability and transparency in safeguarding practice: *"I understand the role of everyone involved in my life and so do they."*

Safeguarding plans and discussions are key to ensuring that the people involved in a piece of safeguarding work are clear about their role and are held to account by the local authority to complete the actions they have agreed to undertake within the agreed timescale. The adult at the heart of this work must also be informed and supported if necessary, to understand the roles of all and the way in which they are being held to account on their behalf.

FREDA'S STORY VI

Freda understands the role of her social worker and the staff at the home, including the role of the manager. She has a copy of the safeguarding plan which has been written simply, in clear language, and includes how staff are supporting her and what she can do to ask for further help if needed before her social worker returns to review the plan next week.

Making Safeguarding Personal in practice

The Making Safeguarding Personal (MSP) development project was initiated in 2009 in response to feedback from people using safeguarding services and from multi-agency partners and practitioners that the focus of safeguarding work was on process and procedure, not on the experience and outcomes of the adults at the heart of adult safeguarding practice. People using safeguarding services wanted to be part of their own safeguarding but reported that safeguarding was something that was 'done to them'. One of us was carrying out large-scale audits of adult safeguarding work in 2010 and found that older people in particular would sometimes not be informed that a concern had been received about them, in case this 'upset them'. Practitioners and SAB members wanted to know what difference they were making to the lives of the people they worked with, but local and national indicators and data only measured the processes used, for example how many alerts (concerns) had been received and how many of the defined timescales had been met.

In 2009 the Improvement and Development Agency (IDeA), now the Local Government Association (LGA), the Social Care Institute of Excellence (SCIE), the British Association of Social Workers (BASW) and Women's Aid worked together to form a body of knowledge that would assist in promoting empowerment and support for people making difficult decisions. The progress of this work can be found within annual reports held on the Association of

Directors of Adult Social Services website (ADASS, 2017). The statutory guidance (Chapter 14.207) references the importance of practitioners having confidence in using an MSP approach to adult safeguarding.

MSP seeks to achieve:

- A personalised approach that enables safeguarding to be done with, not to, people.
- Practice that focuses on achieving meaningful improvement to people's circumstances rather than just on 'investigation' and 'conclusion'.
- An approach that utilises social work skills rather than just 'putting people through a process'.
- An approach that enables practitioners, families, teams and SABs to know what difference has been made. (ADASS, 2017)

MSP in practice is a relationship-based and anti-oppressive practice approach to adult safeguarding, the rights of adults, including the right to take risks and to have choice and control over your own life, run through all aspects of practice.

Practitioners report that using the MSP-based approach is refreshing and satisfying: you are using the full range of social work skills and working with individuals and their families face to face, supporting them to engage in problem solving and to achieve the outcomes they hope for whenever possible. Instead of a decision that harm is 'substantiated' or not at the end of the adult safeguarding process, the focus is on whether the adult's outcomes were achieved, whether their 'well-being', or quality of life, is any better as well as whether their safety has increased and the possibility of further harm been understood and where possible reduced. People who do not have the capacity to make decisions about their own well-being or safety are also included within the MSP approach by involving the adult as much as possible using observation, conversations and the perceptions of those around them, together with known current and previous wishes, and crucially by using 'best interests' (MCA 2005) processes.

Practitioner's enthusiasm for MSP approaches can be frustrated if there is no organisational sign-up to the approach as it is challenging to use when workloads are predicated on a defined workflow system. Once used, the MSP approach can change practitioner's approaches to other social work activities, which may have been previously bound by procedural imperatives, for example care and support assessment or reviews.

What does an MSP approach to practice involve?

Fundamental to the MSP approach is the focus on what the adult hopes will be achieved by the adult safeguarding process and what will be a meaningful improvement in their lives (the 'outcomes'). This is an important part of any initial or subsequent discussion with the adult. Lawson (2017, p 22) describes this as '(having conversations) to understand what supports wellbeing in their lives; seeking to support wellbeing alongside safety'. Once the adult becomes more aware of the facts or what support may be available, they may change the outcome that they want, and for this reason it is important to revisit outcomes during the process of enquiry. Whether and how the adult's outcomes are being met should be discussed when safeguarding plans are reviewed or ended. It may not be possible to achieve the adult's initial outcome request as it may be unreasonable or impractical; in these situations explaining what is possible and renegotiating from a position of respect and honesty is important.

REFLECTIVE ACTIVITY

Case examples: Harriet George and Arthur Evans

Harriet George is upset and angry about the behaviour of the care worker who shouted at her during her last stay at the respite centre. She would like the care home closed down.

Reflective question
–   How would you respond to Harriet's initial thoughts on her preferred outcome?

Our thoughts are that we must be clear with Harriet what is and isn't possible, and she may need time to discuss what happened to her in more depth. Are there more concerns about the care home that Harriet hasn't talked about yet? What other outcome would feel satisfactory to her? What restorative approaches might feel comfortable to her – possibly an apology in person or via letter from the care home manager?

*   *   *

Arthur Evans was shouted at by a domiciliary care worker and badly frightened. He has asked that "no one mentions this again and no action should be taken". Arthur does not like to be a bother and wonders if he did something that upset the worker.

Reflective question
–   How would you respond to Arthur's initial thoughts on his preferred outcome?

Our thoughts are that you will need to discuss your obligation to take the matter further as the care worker works with others whom they may also shout at. You need to be honest and open. Arthur may feel that he does want to be involved as this will help others, or he may want assurances that he does not have to see that worker again. Arthur may want to know more about what to expect from a care worker or anyone employed to provide a service to him, his rights and who to talk to in the future if he is ever concerned again.

In order to make sure people have enough information and understanding about what is involved and what their rights and options are, we must provide the right support for each individual. For some this may be accessible written information and good verbal explanations; others, who may have no one else to support them and have 'substantial difficulty' (Care Act 2014 S68(3)) in understanding and being involved, must have an independent advocate.

Information and advice must be tailored to the adult and their situation, so that they can understand their situation and the risks involved and weigh up the options they find acceptable and think workable to manage risk. This may involve continuing to live in a situation of risk or engage in relationships that are risky, but this decision will be understood by both adult and practitioner and other agencies involved, with the adult having an opportunity to think through acceptable strategies to minimise risk. ECHR Article 8 rights (the right to respect for private and family life) are upheld while the impact of family relationships is considered with the adult involved. Practitioners must develop skills and confidence in a range of responses to enable people to achieve safety, resolution, recovery and access to justice.

We will revisit MSP practice again when exploring adult safeguarding practice. MSP practice is good adult safeguarding practice; the empowering principles of this person–centred approach will feature in case studies and commentary as we explore how practitioners can develop their knowledge, skills and confidence in working with adults at risk of harm.

▶ KEY MESSAGES

- Human rights, as both a legal framework and a values-driven approach, are essential to person-centred adult safeguarding practice.

- Your practice as a professional and as a representative of an organisation with duties and responsibilities as a public body can have a significant influence on how the adult's rights are respected within adult safeguarding.

- You should be aware of the potential for discrimination to affect the quality and nature of support that an adult receives and act to address oppression in how care and support is provided on an individual and organisational basis to adults at risk of abuse and harm.

- Using the Making Safeguarding Personal approach is an essential tool in anti-oppressive safeguarding practice as it will ensure that the views of the adult are central to safeguarding enquiry and planning.

KNOWLEDGE REVIEW

- WHAT are the two ways that human rights can influence adult safeguarding practice?

- WHICH articles of the ECHR and HRA are relevant to adult safeguarding practice and why?

- HOW can adult safeguarding practice address oppression and recognise the intersectional nature of discriminatory abuse?

- HOW do the six principles of adult safeguarding run through all practice?

FURTHER READING

- The British Institute for Human Rights (BIHR) have developed a range of excellent resources for practitioners on using a human rights-based practice in health and social care, which can be accessed at: www.bihr.org.uk.

- For more information on applying the MCA and, at the time of writing, DoLS read Hubbard, R. and Stone, K. (2018) *The Best Interests Assessor Practice Handbook*, Bristol: Policy Press.

- For training events, regular updates and summaries of the Liberty Protection Safeguards, sign up to the email alerts from Edge Training at: www.edgetraining.org.uk.

- A wealth of resources on Making Safeguarding Personal for practitioners and Safeguarding Adults Boards can be found on:

  - The Local Government Association *Making Safeguarding Personal* website at: www.local.gov.uk/our-support/our-improvement-offer/care-and-health-improvement/making-safeguarding-personal.
  - And the Association of Directors of Adult Social Services website at: www.adass.org.uk/making-safeguarding-personal-publications.

- Putting the six principles into practice is explored and well illustrated in Lawson, J. (2017) 'The "Making Safeguarding Personal Approach" to Practice' (pp 26–9) together with 'Top Tips for Making Safeguarding Personal' (pp 30–1), both in Cooper, A. and White, E. (eds) *Safeguarding Adults Under the Care Act 2014: Understanding Good Practice*, London: Jessica Kingsley.

3

Adult safeguarding legislation

Chapter aim

In this chapter we will explore the legal context for adult safeguarding practice, including the central role played in England by the Care Act 2014 in providing a framework for adult safeguarding practice. Other key legal frameworks will also be considered that are not always acknowledged as having a role to play in addressing safeguarding concerns. Finally, we will explore how practitioners can develop 'legal literacy'.

- The framework for adult safeguarding within the Care Act 2014;

- other legislative frameworks for adult safeguarding practice;

- developing legal literacy.

We will cover the crucial interaction between the Mental Capacity Act 2005 and adult safeguarding in Chapter 4.

The framework for adult safeguarding within the Care Act 2014

The Care Act 2014 was implemented in 2015 accompanied by statutory guidance. It is worth looking at what the actual legislation says about each of the sections relating to adult safeguarding before looking in more depth at the accompanying statutory guidance so that we can be clear about our own, and others', legal duties.

While all children under the age of 18 can be protected via children's legislation, only specific groups of adults are protected under the Care Act 2014 in England, and in similar legislation in Wales and Scotland and policy in Northern Ireland. Who the duty to enquire applies to is often subject to misunderstanding and controversy. The guidance issued with the Care Act 2014 is statutory; therefore, it must be acted on by a local authority unless a legally sound reason for not doing so can be demonstrated. The Care Act statutory guidance is not detailed, and can be subject to wide interpretation, particularly regarding who the duty to enquire applies to, and what an enquiry is. We will focus on the legal definition of an enquiry in Chapter 9 but in this chapter we will look at who the duty to enquire applies to and the other sections of the Care Act which apply to adult safeguarding.

▶ **ESSENTIAL INFORMATION: LEGISLATION**

Section 42 of the Care Act 2014 stipulates to whom the duty to enquire applies:

Enquiry by local authority

(1) This section applies where a local authority has reasonable cause to suspect that an adult in its area (whether or not ordinarily resident there)—
   (a) has needs for care and support (whether or not the authority is meeting any of those needs),
   (b) is experiencing, or is at risk of, abuse or neglect, and
   (c) as a result of those needs is unable to protect himself or herself against the abuse or neglect or the risk of it.

(2) The local authority must make (or cause to be made) whatever enquiries it thinks necessary to enable it to decide whether any action should be taken in the adult's case (whether under this Part or otherwise) and, if so, what and by whom.

(3) 'Abuse' includes financial abuse; and for that purpose, 'financial abuse' includes—
   (a) having money or other property stolen,
   (b) being defrauded,
   (c) being put under pressure in relation to money or other property, and
   (d) having money or other property misused.

There is a detailed account of the term 'financial abuse'. This may be because there was concern that financial abuse was not being taken seriously as a safeguarding matter (see Chapter 5).

► **ESSENTIAL INFORMATION: LEGISLATION**

The nature of a statutory duty

The Care Act 2014 introduced a number of new safeguarding adults statutory duties relating to practice for local authorities. These specific duties are:

Section 1: The local authority has an overriding duty to promote individual well-being which also covers the protection from abuse or neglect.

Section 11: The local authority is under a specific duty to undertake a section 9 assessment (when an adult is refusing) if there is reasonable belief that the adult is under coercion, or the adult is experiencing, or is at risk of, abuse or neglect.

Section 42: If the criteria for the section 42 duty are met, the local authority must make, or cause others to make, whatever enquiries it deems necessary to determine what actions (if any) are necessary to safeguard the adult. The local authority cannot delegate its duty under section 42 and when it causes an enquiry to be made by an external partner, it must satisfy itself that the enquiry has been concluded effectively and determine if it needs to undertake any further enquiries under section 42.

Section 68: Places a duty on the local authority to provide an advocate to support an adult who would experience significant difficulties participating in a section 42 enquiry, or a Safeguarding Adults Review under section 44. The local authority is not under a duty to provide an advocate if they believe there is an appropriate independent person to support the adult.

A duty must be undertaken: For example, while adults should be asked to consent to an enquiry the local authority can progress the enquiry without their consent. The statutory guidance (DHSC, 2018a, 14.95) gives examples of where the local authority may choose to progress without consent, but the vital point to remember is that the adult's consent is not necessary for the enquiry to progress. The adult should contribute to the enquiry and even if they do not wish to do this must be kept as fully informed as they wish, but an enquiry cannot be ended simply because the adult has not consented.

To whom the duty to enquire applies

The three elements are set out in part 1 of section 42. This section applies where a local authority has reasonable cause to suspect that an adult in its area (whether or not they are ordinarily resident there).

(a) 'has needs for care and support (whether or not the local authority is meeting any of those needs)'

The Care Act statutory guidance is not always clear in providing definitions. The statutory guidance does not consistently use the term 'adults at risk' although the phrase has entered common usage as a way of defining this specific population. The statutory guidance does specify that the local authority duty only applies to those 'in need of care and support' but does not define 'care and support', only saying that whether the local authority is meeting these care and support needs is not relevant. Government updates on the Care Act have included this definition – '"Care and support" is the term used to describe the help some adults need to live as well as possible with any illness or disability they may have' (DH, 2015, para 1). A useful position is to take 'care and support' at face value. In order to be an 'adult at risk', a disabled adult or adult with a long-term health condition must have a need for care to be provided, either by a service, a relative or a friend, in order to be able to live their life. 'Care' must be present as well as 'support'. Some English local authorities have added the Skills for Care (2014) glossary definition of 'care and support' to their policies to clarify to which adults the section 42 duty applies.

> ▶ **ESSENTIAL INFORMATION**
>
> *Skills for Care, care and support definition*
>
> Care and support is:
>
> the mixture of practical, financial and emotional support for adults who need extra help to manage their lives and be independent – including older people, people with a disability or long-term illness, people with mental health problems, and carers. Care and support includes assessment of people's needs, provision of services and the allocation of funds to enable a person to purchase their own care and support. It could include care home, home care, personal assistants, day services, or the provision of aids and adaptations. (Skills for Care, 2014)

Reflective question
- Who do you encounter in the course of your practice who will meet this definition?
- Who might not? What actions outside the section 42 duty may be needed where the person does not meet this criteria?

Our thoughts are that the kinds of wider universal support services that those not eligible for care and support under the Care Act can access (including voluntary sector agencies, GPs and so on) can also offer points of contact for safeguarding information, monitoring and concern raising when the person is at high risk and further advice or problem solving is needed.

(b) 'is experiencing, or is at risk of, abuse or neglect'

It is vital to remember that harm may not yet have occurred, but that there are indicators that there is a strong risk of harm in the future. This risk must be explored and preventative measures taken. Indicators of the risk of harm need to be explored thoroughly as, after all, merely living a life involves a degree of risk of harm and the impact on the adult's well-being, and their perspective on risk, are important considerations to explore.

Examples may include that a person with physical and learning disabilities is cared for by a sibling who drinks heavily to the point of unconsciousness. No harm has come to her while her carer has been affected by alcohol but an enquiry as to what her views are about any risks and how these might be planned for should be considered.

(c) 'as a result of those care and support needs is unable to protect himself or herself from either the risk of, or the experience of abuse or neglect'

This guides us to think about what the barriers are to the person being able to protect themselves. That the adult 'is unable to protect himself or herself' suggests they do not have the skills, the means nor the opportunity to do so. The adult may live in a group setting and have no control over the way that they are treated or of the environment they live in, simply because as a resident or patient they have less power than those working in or running the establishment. The adult may lack life experience because their care and support needs have resulted in them living a secluded life and they may not understand an intention to harm them. Because of their care and support needs, the adult may be trapped in a domestic situation that they cannot physically leave. They may have disabilities that impair their capacity to make decisions about protecting themselves, although it is important to note that many people who are unable to protect themselves do have the mental capacity to do so, but need support, including advocacy, to enact their decision. It is also important to be aware that the services that others use to support them in protecting themselves may not be accessible to the adult. For example, it can be harder for a disabled woman to access a refuge (BBC News, 2018) and domestic abuse services report rarely receiving referrals for people who have learning disabilities (SafeLives, 2016b).

What if a person has no care needs, but does need support? Someone giving informal care to a person with care and support needs may also have 'support needs' and may well be unable to protect themselves from harm because they are caring for a person with care and support needs. The statutory guidance does allow a local authority to choose to undertake a safeguarding enquiry for people where there is no section 42 duty to enquire, if the local authority believes it is proportionate to do so and will improve the person's well-being and support prevention of further harm. This is called a 'non-statutory' enquiry, and sometimes an 'other' enquiry.

REFLECTIVE ACTIVITY

Case study: Mrs Kaur

Mrs Kaur hopes that she and her husband can stay together at home for the rest of their lives. He has lately been quick to anger over small frustrations. These are many as he was visually impaired after a stroke and now finds it hard to navigate life after a second stroke damaged his cognition. Mrs Kaur has to continually watch and prompt him now, and, at times, also takes care of his personal needs. Mr Singh hit his wife yesterday, something that has never happened before in their relationship, which has always been one of mutual respect and affection. Mrs Kaur is distraught: how can she continue to care for her husband when she feels afraid of him? She wants to leave the house but worries about what would happen to her husband with no one to care for him. She confides in her GP who asks for her consent to contact adult safeguarding services.

Reflective questions
– What harm are both Mrs Kaur and Mr Singh at risk of?
– Is the GP's response the most helpful one in this situation? What alternatives may offer a more person-centred approach?

Our thoughts are that Mrs Kaur may experience further physical assaults from her husband. She may have to leave the house in an emergency situation; Mr Singh will then be unsupported. The GP could explore with Mrs Kaur during her appointment what support she has in her networks that may help, and what options are available, explaining a referral to adult safeguarding, an assessment of Mr Singh's care and support needs,

> and a carer's assessment for Mrs Kaur herself. Mrs Kaur may want an opportunity to think through a plan to protect herself immediately and, should the situation escalate, have ready contacts for the emergency duty team and police.

Local authorities in England are using non-statutory enquiries in a variety of ways, most usually for people who have no care needs but require support to manage issues such as substance misuse, or mental health issues which impact on their well-being.

It is useful to compare legislation in England with the legislation and policies in the three other UK nations.

▶ ESSENTIAL INFORMATION: LEGISLATION

Law and policy in adult safeguarding in Scotland, Wales and Northern Ireland

The earliest piece of legislation in the UK designed to protect adults is the **Adult Support and Protection (Scotland) Act 2007**. Section 4 of the Act specifies that councils have a duty to

> make inquiries about a person's well-being, property or financial affairs if it knows or believes—
> (a) that the person is an adult at risk, and
> (b) that it might need to intervene (by performing functions under this Part or otherwise) in order to protect the person's well-being, property or financial affairs.

There are powers within the Act to support intervention in situations where access to an adult at risk is prevented or to use in the protection of an adult at risk. These are generally referred to as 'protection orders' and are authorised by the local sheriff.

- Assessment orders: allow professionals to enter premises and either interview an adult at risk on site or take him or her to another place for the purpose of conducting a private interview.
- Removal orders: enable professionals to take the adult at risk to a place of safety for up to seven days (the duration is set in the order).
- Banning orders: exclude a third party from a specified place (usually the home of the adult at risk), for up to six months.

- Temporary banning orders: can be granted, pending the determination of an application for a banning order.

The Act enshrines the adult's right to participate as fully as possible (S2) and for advocacy to be considered (S6) to support participation.

The **Social Services and Well-being (Wales) Act 2014** (SSWWA) was implemented in April 2016. This adult social care legal framework for Wales has much in common with the Care Act 2014 in England. SSWWA has a similar definition to the Care Act 2014 as to whom the duty to enquire applies, however the legislation does specify that this group of individuals are 'adults at risk' (S126). This legislation stipulates that regulations made must ensure that the conclusions of any enquiry must be recorded. In Wales, practitioners authorised by the local authority are able to apply to magistrates for an 'adult protection and support order'. This order enables a practitioner to enter premises where there is reasonable belief that there is an adult at risk; a 'constable' must accompany the worker. The purpose of the order is to gain access to the person in order to assess whether the person is an adult at risk and to make a decision as to whether an enquiry, or some other action, if any, should be taken. The magistrate authorising the order must be assured that exercising the power of entry conferred by the order will not result in the person being at greater risk of abuse or neglect.

In Northern Ireland, the **Adult Safeguarding: Prevention and Protection in Partnership** (2015) policy gives a detailed description of situations when an adult may be at increased risk of exposure to harm, and differentiates between 'adults at risk' and 'adults in need of protection':

An 'Adult at risk of harm' is a person aged 18 or over, whose exposure to harm through abuse, exploitation or neglect *may* be increased by their:

(a) personal characteristics

AND/OR

(b) life circumstances

Personal characteristics may include, but are not limited to, age, disability, special educational needs, illness, mental or physical frailty or impairment of, or disturbance in, the functioning of the mind or brain. Life circumstances may include, but are not limited to, isolation, socio-economic factors and environmental living conditions.

An 'Adult in need of protection' is a person aged 18 or over, whose exposure to harm through abuse, exploitation or neglect *may* be increased by their:

(a) personal characteristics

AND/OR

(b) life circumstances

AND

(c) who is unable to protect their own well-being, property, assets, rights or other interests;

AND

(d) where the action or inaction of another person or persons is causing, or is likely to cause, him/her to be harmed.

In order to meet the definition of an 'adult in need of protection' *either* (a) or (b) must be present, *in addition to both* elements (c) *and* (d) (Northern Ireland Department of Health, 2015, pp 10–11).

In summary, each piece of legislation or policy in the UK defines a specific group of adults in need of protection, usually associated with the adult being unable to protect themselves because of illness or disability, and practitioners should be familiar with the adult safeguarding legal framework for the nation where they practice.

Scotland, England and Wales all have legislation that requires a duty to be enacted. Northern Ireland at the time of writing has a policy approach. Scotland and Wales have attached provisions for a practitioner to apply for an order to give power of entry and in the case of Scotland, removal of the adult at risk or banning of the source of harm form the premises. The Commissioner for Older People in Northern Ireland (2014) has called for adult safeguarding legislation to include powers of access, removal and banning the source of harm.

While the Care Act 2014 gave local authorities the duty to enquire, English legislation has no powers to intervene in support of that duty to enquire such as through powers to access the person in order to assess. Stevens et al (2017) explore some of the reasons for this, noting that professional submissions to the Department of Health (2012) in the pre-Care Act consultation were in favour of introducing such powers. However, in its response to the consultation results, the Department of Health (DH) (2013) emphasised that only 18 per cent of members of the public were in favour, compared with 72 per cent of social care and 90 per cent of health professionals. Manthorpe et al (2016) have succinctly analysed the debates within both Houses of Parliament concerning the three attempted amendments to introduce powers, identifying themes regarding concerns about the overuse of state intervention in private life and a belief that powers of entry via the police already existed. Ultimately the Care Act was passed with no statutory powers of access for practitioners.

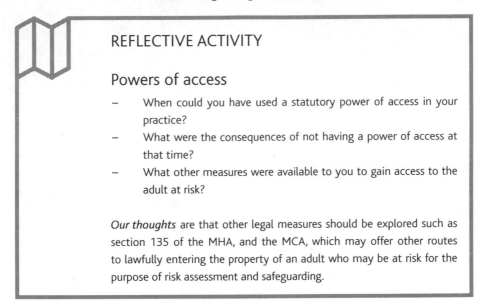

REFLECTIVE ACTIVITY

Powers of access

- When could you have used a statutory power of access in your practice?
- What were the consequences of not having a power of access at that time?
- What other measures were available to you to gain access to the adult at risk?

Our thoughts are that other legal measures should be explored such as section 135 of the MHA, and the MCA, which may offer other routes to lawfully entering the property of an adult who may be at risk for the purpose of risk assessment and safeguarding.

Other adult safeguarding sections of the Care Act 2014

The duty to cooperate

Section 6 of the Care Act 2014 sets out the duties that local authorities have to cooperate 'with each of its relevant partners' and that 'each relevant partner must co-operate with the authority' (6.1) regarding adults with needs for care and support and their carers. These relevant partners include providers of care and support, medical services, hospitals and providers of social housing. These are essential underpinning relationships for safeguarding prevention work and for organisational safeguarding enquiries. Cooperation at an organisational level with providers of care, support and housing, health services including the NHS, and the police, for example at SAB level, are also essential for prevention, addressing organisational issues and SARs, for example to publicise and apply lessons learned.

Advocacy

Under **section 68** a local authority must arrange for a person who is independent of the local authority (an 'Independent Advocate') to represent and support the adult who is subject to a section 42 enquiry or a SAR. This provision is crucial in ensuring that an adult is involved in any adult safeguarding process, and that that process is built around their wishes and well-being.

Safeguarding Adults Board

Section 43 stipulates that each local authority must establish a SAB for its area and that the objective of a SAB is to 'help and protect adults in its area in cases of the kind described in section 42(1)' (Care Act 2014 S43.2). A clear understanding of who the section 42 duty applies to is important in enabling the SAB to focus on the parameters of its role and responsibility. The role of the SAB is to coordinate and ensure the effectiveness of what each of its members does. Some agencies must be members of the SAB. These 'statutory partners' are:

- the local authority which set the SAB up;
- the clinical commissioning groups in the local authority's area;
- the chief officer of police in the local authority's area.

Other agencies *may* be invited to be SAB members, according to local need, and include the agencies listed here together with any agency the SAB deems necessary to carry out its duties. You can find the full list in the statutory guidance (14.146–7); these can include representatives of providers of health and social care services, housing and housing support providers, local Healthwatch and members of user, advocacy and carer groups. SABs must be linked with other partnerships to maximise their impact and minimise duplication of work, other partnerships include community safety partnerships, local children safeguarding boards, health and well-being boards, and quality surveillance groups.

A 'SAB may do anything which appears to it to be necessary or desirable for the purpose of achieving its objective' (S43.4). This section demonstrates an important principle behind the Care Act, the idea that the legislation serves as a framework that should be adapted to meet the needs of the local population. In the Statement of Government Policy on Adult Safeguarding, this position is clearly set out:

> The State's role in safeguarding is to provide the vision and direction and ensure that the legal framework, including powers and duties, is clear, and proportionate, whilst maximising local flexibility. This framework should be sufficient to enable professionals and others to take appropriate and timely safeguarding action locally while not prescribing how local agencies and partnerships undertake their safeguarding duties. (DH, 2011, 2.3)

REFLECTIVE ACTIVITY

Safeguarding Adults Board (SAB) activity

Go to your local authority web page devoted to the local Safeguarding Adults Board. You should find the strategic adult safeguarding plan for your area and the Annual Report there. The SAB is legally obliged to publish these documents. You may also find:

> – published SARs or learning briefings relating to the SARs the SAB has commissioned;
> – policies, procedures and protocols agreed by the SAB for local use.
>
> By publishing these documents, all SABs aim to meet the adult safeguarding principle of 'accountability and transparency'.
>
> ## Reflection
> Consider the strategic adult safeguarding plan for your area
>
> – What impact does or should the plan have on your adult safeguarding practice?

Safeguarding Adults Reviews

Section 44 covers the duty of the SAB to 'arrange for there to be a review of a case involving an adult in its area with needs for care and support (whether or not the local authority has been meeting any of those needs)' (S44.1) if the following conditions are met:

• there is reasonable cause for concern about how the SAB, members of it or other persons with relevant functions worked together to safeguard the adult, and the adult has died, and the SAB knows or suspects that the death resulted from abuse or neglect (whether or not it knew about or suspected abuse or neglect before the adult died), or
• the adult is still alive, and the SAB knows or suspects that the adult has experienced serious abuse or neglect.

The law emphasises that the purpose of a SAR is learning, and that each member of the SAB must cooperate in and contribute to carrying out the SAR and applying the lessons learned to future cases.

The law also says that the SAB can arrange a review of any other case involving an adult in its area with needs for care and support. The statutory guidance suggests that SARs 'may also be used to explore examples of good practice where this is likely to identify lessons that can be applied to future cases' (DHSC, 2018a, para 14.164). At the time of writing a SAR has not been arranged to derive lessons from good practice; we hope that this happens as not only would this be a powerful vehicle to disseminate good practice, but a focus on good practice would help to emphasise the true nature of a SAR, which is to learn, not to blame.

Supply of information

Lastly, **section 45** covers the supply of information to the SAB. Agencies and individuals must comply with requests for information made by the SAB for the purpose of the SAB exercising its functions. This section is particularly important in ensuring that all agencies supply information to SARs and to enable the SAB to carry out its duties to ensure the effectiveness of adult safeguarding arrangements in the local area.

Legislation that underpins adult safeguarding practice is still relatively new in England and interpretation of the provisions of the Care Act is evolving, particularly regarding the duty to enquire and to whom the duty applies.

Other legislative frameworks for adult safeguarding practice

In this section we will provide a brief overview of some of the other pieces of legislation which support adult safeguarding including:

- powers of entry
- domestic abuse offences, including coercive control, forced marriage and female genital mutilation
- hate crime
- organisational abuse
- offences relating to physical, sexual, psychological and financial abuse and neglect
- modern slavery

We will include enough detail for you to connect the harm identified with the possibility of a criminal offence, which will prompt you to discuss the matter with police colleagues.

Powers of entry

There are a few legal means of gaining access to people's homes that are relevant to safeguarding. To breach an adult's human right to a private life under Article 8 of the ECHR, there must be significant grounds on the basis of their health and welfare. The following legal measures may be available depending on the circumstances.

Police

The police only have powers of entry in very specific circumstances and you should not automatically assume that police colleagues can enter a private property when there are concerns. The police may enter a property without a warrant only in the following circumstances under section 17 of the Police and Criminal Evidence Act (PACE) 1984:

- arresting a person for an indictable offence, for example where it is believed that a serious crime has been committed;
- arresting a person for an offence under section 4 of the Public Order Act 1986, for example where it is considered that someone may be causing threatening behaviour, cause fear or provoke violence; and/or
- saving life or limb or preventing serious damage to property.

Officers may use reasonable force in the exercise of these powers, if necessary (PACE S117). 'Saving life or limb' means that there is a concern that a person is at imminent risk of death or serious bodily injury, not just a concern about a person's welfare. Officers can also enter without warrant if there is a real and imminent risk of a breach of the peace, for example when there is imminent violence or threat of violence. This is a measure that exists in common law (that is, not in legislation) and can only be used in an emergency.

Approved Mental Health Professional (AMHP)

AMHPs have powers of entry and inspection under section 115 of the Mental Health Act 1983 (2007). Under section 115, an AMHP may 'enter and inspect any premises (other than a hospital) in which a mentally disordered patient is living, if he has reasonable cause to believe that the patient is not under proper care' (MHA 1983 S115(1)). The AMHP cannot force entry to a premises under this section or remove the person, and they cannot override the property owner's refusal to give permission to enter, although a co-owner can give permission to prevent a trespass occurring.

Under sections 135(1) and (2) of the MHA 1983, AMHPs have the power to apply to a justice of the peace at a magistrates' court for a warrant to enter a person's property for the purpose of conducting, or removing them to a place of safety to conduct, a Mental Health Act assessment. The AMHP will need to evidence that the appropriate criteria are evident, which are usually associated with high levels of risk to the person as a result of their mental health and that all other options for conducting the assessment have been unsuccessful, before the justice of the peace can grant the warrant. This may be relevant to accessing an adult at risk to safeguard them from harm but the criteria for sections 135(1) or (2) MHA must be met in order for this to be a legal option, not just that there is concern about the person's welfare in a safeguarding sense. It is worth noting that for a section 135(2) warrant, a non-AMHP (as long as they are authorised to do so) can apply for a warrant to retake a person who is liable to be detained or absconded from hospital. For more information see Stone et al (2020).

SCIE (2014a) have produced a useful guide on using the law to gain access to an adult at risk, including consideration of the Mental Capacity Act 2005 and the

Mental Health Act 1983 (2007), as well as the Police and Criminal Evidence Act 1984, the inherent jurisdiction of the High Court and the common law powers of the police to prevent or deal with a breach of the peace. There is a link to the SCIE guide in the further reading section at the end of this chapter.

Domestic abuse offences, including coercive control, forced marriage and female genital mutilation

There is no specific offence of 'domestic violence or domestic abuse' in statute. The term can be applied to a number of offences committed in the person's domestic environment. The Crown Prosecution Service's view (CPS, 2018c) of the domestic nature of the offending behaviour is an aggravating factor because of the abuse of trust involved. Domestic abuse could be considered as offences under:

- Offences Against the Person Act 1861 – physical assaults such as grievous bodily harm (GBH) and actual bodily harm (ABH);
- Malicious Communications Act 1998 – use of phone, text, internet and so on, to abuse;
- Sexual Offences Act 2003 – sexual assaults, rape and so forth.

Coercive control

Section 76 of the Serious Crime Act 2015 created a new offence of controlling or coercive behaviour in an intimate or family relationship. The new offence only applies to offences committed from December 2015. An offence of coercive control could have been committed if person with a personal connection to another (for example as a family member or through an intimate personal relationship) repeatedly or continuously engages in controlling or coercive behaviour that the person is aware will have a serious effect on the other person.

- 'Serious effect' can include fear of violence (on at least two occasions) or causing alarm or distress that has a substantial adverse effect on the other person's day-to-day activities.
- 'Substantial adverse effect' could include:
  - stopping or changing the way the affected person socialises;
  - physical or mental health deterioration;
  - change in routine at home including mealtimes or household chores;
  - attendance record at school;
  - putting measures in place at home to safeguard themselves or their children;
  - changes to work patterns, employment status or routes to work.

Evidencing this offence can be complex. The Statutory Guidance Framework on controlling or coercive behaviour in intimate and family relationships (Home Office, 2015a) suggests the following types of evidence may be needed:

- Copies of emails, phone records or text messages or records from the internet, digital technology and social media platforms.
- Evidence of assault, such as photographs of injuries including defensive injuries to forearms, latent upper arm grabs, scalp bruising or clumps of hair missing.
- Tapes and/or transcripts of 999 calls, CCTV recordings, body-worn video footage or at scene photographic evidence.
- Records of interaction with services such as support services or medical records.
- Evidence of isolation such as lack of contact between family and friends, withdrawal from activities such as clubs or the perpetrator accompanying the victim to medical appointments.
- Bank records showing financial control, previous threats made to children or other family members or diaries kept by the victim.

Make sure that your records are detailed regarding instances of coercive control of an adult at risk, as these will form useful evidence if an offence is prosecuted in the future.

Forced marriage

Forcing someone to marry against their will is a criminal offence under the Anti-social Behaviour, Crime and Policing Act 2014 (ASBCP). This offence applies to an individual who intentionally forces another person to enter into marriage, believing the person does not consent, or an individual who deceives someone into going abroad for the specific purpose of forcing them to marry, an offence is committed whether or not the forced marriage goes ahead. A person is considered to have committed an offence under section 121 of the ASBCP 2014 if they:

- use violence, threats or any other form of coercion for the purpose of causing another person to enter into a marriage; and
- believe, or ought reasonably to believe, that the conduct may cause the other person to enter into marriage without free and full consent.

People subject to forced marriage who lack capacity to consent to marriage within the definition used within the MCA 2005 are referred to under section 121(2) of ASBCP 2014, and section 121(3) refers to where a person deceives another person to leave the UK and intends them to be subject to forced marriage. For example, in the case of *XCC v AA* (2012) the Court of Protection (England and Wales) ruled under inherent jurisdiction that an arranged marriage in Bangladesh between a British citizen with severe learning difficulties (DD) and her cousin was a forced marriage because DD lacked capacity to consent to the marriage, which was compounded by DD having been taken from the country to conduct the marriage. The judgment also clarified that any sexual relationship within that marriage would be a criminal offence because DD lacked capacity to consent and that social services should be informed in these circumstances.

Female genital mutilation

The Female Genital Mutilation (FGM) Act came into force on 3 March 2004 and was amended by sections 70–5 of the Serious Crime Act 2015. These provisions introduced FGM protection orders and a mandatory duty for front-line professionals to report FGM in under-18s. Criminal offences under the Act include offences of FGM as well as assisting a female to mutilate her own genitalia and assisting a non-UK person to mutilate a female's genitalia overseas. Failing to protect a female aged under 16 from the risk of FGM is also an offence.

Hate crime

Hate crime encompasses a wide range of criminal offences, including offences against the person, theft, fraud, sexual assault and so on. Hate crime relates to the sentencing tariff used in court; for example, if the offence can be shown to be motivated by hostility or prejudice based on the victim's disability or other characteristics, then sections 145 and 146 of the Criminal Justice Act 2003 may be used to impose a general duty on criminal courts to treat any offence more seriously (an aggravating factor) when sentencing. The court must consider if hostility during the offence from the perpetrator towards the victim related to their (or presumptions about their):

- religious belief and ethnicity
- sexual orientation
- disability
- transgender identity

Hate crime can be considered as a form of discriminatory abuse.

Organisational abuse

Key pieces of criminal legislation related to the abuse of adults at risk within organisational contexts, such as care homes, care and support agencies, and hospitals include:

- Ill treatment or wilful neglect of adults who lack capacity (section 44 of the MCA): this offence could have been committed if a person has the care of (is paid to care for the person, for instance) a person who lacks, or can be reasonably believed to lack mental capacity, or if they have a lasting or enduring power of attorney for the person or are a court-appointed deputy for the person and they ill-treat or wilfully neglect the person.
  - 'Ill treatment' is considered as a deliberate act, where the perpetrator recognises that they are ill-treating a person or behaved recklessly.
  - The 'wilful' element of the neglect offence requires that the perpetrator acted deliberately or recklessly.

- Ill treatment or wilful neglect of adults who are receiving treatment for mental disorder (section 127 of the MHA): this offence could have been committed where a person employed by a mental health organisation (such as a hospital or care home) ill-treats or wilfully neglects a person in their care whether as an inpatient, outpatient, under guardianship or another caring role.

These MCA and MHA offences apply to individuals being cared for by people employed by organisations. Organisations with responsibilities to care for adults at risk can be considered to have committed offences under the Criminal Justice and Courts Act 2015. Offences under sections 20–5 comprise two criminal offences of ill treatment or wilful neglect which apply both to individual care workers and care provider organisations who are working with adults, whether those adults have mental capacity or not. The creation of these offences was a part of the government's response to the public inquiry into the events at Mid-Staffordshire NHS Foundation Trust which identified routine neglect of patients between 2005 and 2009 (Francis, 2013).

- Section 20(1) concerns 'an individual who has the care of another individual by virtue of being a care worker to ill-treat or wilfully to neglect that individual'. The individual concerned must be in paid employment as a care or health worker or in receipt of a benefit such as a carer's allowance to support their caring role.
- Section 21(1) concerns an organisation where:
  - an individual who has the care of another individual by virtue of being part of the care provider's arrangements ill-treats or wilfully neglects that individual;
  - the care provider's activities are managed or organised in a way which amounts to a gross breach of a relevant duty of care owed by the care provider to the individual who is ill-treated or neglected; and
  - in the absence of the breach, the ill treatment or wilful neglect would not have occurred or would have been less likely to occur.
- Care provider in this context includes both health and social care providers, for example hospitals, care homes, domiciliary care agencies and so on.

Corporate manslaughter charges may be relevant under the Corporate Manslaughter and Corporate Homicide Act 2007, which can apply when the way in which an organisation's activities are managed or organised cause or are a significant element in the breach of a relevant duty of care which has caused death. There may also be relevant offences under the Health and Safety at Work Act 1974 and subsequent regulations which cover topics such as manual handling, use of bed rails, control of substances hazardous to health (COSHH), reporting injuries, diseases and dangerous occurrences (RIDDOR) and falls. The CQC has the lead role in the investigation of breaches of health and safety legislation in health and care settings and is part of the Key Line of Enquiry of Safety in health and social care services.

Offences relating to physical, sexual, psychological and financial abuse, and neglect

Physical abuse

Common assault is considered under section 39 of the Criminal Justice Act 1988, while assault occasioning ABH or unlawful wounding/inflicting GBH are covered by the Offences Against the Person Act 1861. False imprisonment may be charged under section 44 of the MCA, section 127 of the MHA or under sections 20–5 of the Criminal Justice and Courts Act 2015 as described earlier.

Sexual abuse

Sexual abuse can be considered offences under the Sexual Offences Act 2003 which includes:

- **Rape** – section 1(1) defines rape as when a person (A) 'intentionally penetrates the vagina, anus or mouth of another person (B) with his penis'.
- **Assault by penetration** – section 2(1) defines this offence as when: (a) a person (A) 'intentionally penetrates the vagina or anus of another person (B) with a part of his body or anything else, and (b) the penetration is sexual, and (c) B does not consent to the penetration, and (d) A does not reasonably believe that B consents'.
- **Sexual assault** – section 3(1) defines this offence as when a person (A) commits an offence if: '(a) he intentionally touches another person (B), (b) the touching is sexual, (c) B does not consent to the touching, and (d) A does not reasonably believe that B consents'.
- **Causing a person to engage in sexual activity without consent** – section 4 defines this offence as when a person (A): '(a) he intentionally causes another person (B) to engage in an activity, (b) the activity is sexual, (c) B does not consent to engaging in the activity, and (d) A does not reasonably believe that B consents', based on what efforts that A has made to establish consent.

Mental disorder and sexual offences

The Sexual Offences Act 2003 (sections 30–3, 34–7 and 38–44) considers the situations of people defined as having a mental disorder. The legislation draws a distinction between:

- persons who have a mental disorder impeding choice, persons whose mental functioning is so impaired at the time of the sexual activity that they are unable to make any decision about their involvement in that activity, that is, that they are 'unable to refuse'; and

- those who have the capacity to consent to sexual activity but who have a mental disorder that makes them vulnerable to inducement, threat or deception; and
- those who have the capacity to consent to sexual activity but who have a mental disorder and are in a position of dependency on the carer.

In all these offences, mental disorder is defined as set out in section 1 of the MHA, as 'any disorder or disability of the mind'. As well as including serious mental illness, this definition ensures the protection of those with a lifelong learning disability and persons who develop dementia in later life. Medical evidence will usually be required to prove that a person has a mental disorder.

Psychological abuse

Offences which relate to psychological abuse may include those covered by the section 76 of the Serious Crime Act 2015 offence of controlling or coercive behaviour in an intimate or family relationship; section 44 of the MCA; section 127 of the MHA; or sections 20–5 of the Criminal Justice and Courts Act 2015 all referred to earlier. The Malicious Communications Act 1988 created the offence of sending or delivering letters or other articles for the purpose of causing distress or anxiety. It was updated in 2001 to include electronic communications.

Financial abuse

Criminal legislation regarding finances can generally be divided between two offences: theft and fraud.

The Theft Act 1968 covers the offence of dishonestly appropriating property belonging to another with the intention of permanently depriving the other of it (S1). It is important to note that 'it is immaterial whether the appropriation is made with a view to gain, or is made for the thief's own benefit' (S1(2)) but that the act may not be dishonest if the perpetrator has the belief that they would have the owner's consent if they knew of the 'appropriation and the circumstances of it' (S2(1)(b)).

The Fraud Act 2006 covers three ways of committing a fraud: fraud by false representation (S2), fraud by failing to disclose information (S3) and fraud by abuse of position (S4). Section 4 (fraud by abuse of position) offences can be pertinent to the behaviour of trustees, attorneys and carers. The offence is committed when a person occupies a position in which he or she was expected to safeguard, or not to act against, the financial interests of another person and he or she has abused that position 'dishonestly' intending by that abuse to make a gain/cause a loss. Crown Prosecution Service guidance (CPS, 2018b) on prosecuting offences of fraud underlines the difficulty of deciding between a theft or fraud charge. This is a matter for the police and the CPS; it is enough for practitioners to be aware of the criminal offences relating to financial abuse to the extent of knowing when the police are likely to be interested in a crime possibly having been committed.

Neglect

Criminal offences relating to neglect will include section 44 of the MCA, section 127 of the MHA or sections 20–5 of the Criminal Justice and Courts Act 2015 as referred to earlier. There may also be relevant offences under the Health and Safety at Work Act 1974 and subsequent regulations which cover topics such as manual handling, bed rails, COSHH, RIDDOR and falls as well as, in tragic cases, the Corporate Manslaughter and Corporate Homicide Act 2007.

Discriminatory abuse offences have been covered under 'Hate crime', earlier in this chapter.

Offences relating to modern slavery or human trafficking

These offences can be addressed under various pieces of legislation, including offences against the person laws and the Sexual Offences Act 2003. The Modern Slavery Act 2015 consolidated and updated criminal legislation on human trafficking, slavery, forced labour, cannabis farming, organ harvesting, forced begging and domestic servitude. The two key offences under the Act relate to 'slavery, servitude and forced or compulsory labour' and 'human trafficking'.

In determining whether a person is being held in slavery or servitude or required to perform forced or compulsory labour, regard may be had to all the circumstances including the person's personal circumstances (such as the person being a child, the person's family relationships, and any mental or physical illness) which may make the person more vulnerable than other persons. The Act makes provision for the police or immigration services to apply to a magistrates' court for prevention orders (S15) and for protection for people compelled to commit crimes while in slavery (S45).

Developing legal literacy

Adult safeguarding practitioners need to be well acquainted with the law and policy that sets out their duties, responsibilities and powers (and lack of them) in order to offer effective protections to adults at risk of harm and abuse. The term commonly used for this is 'legal literacy'.

Defining legal literacy

Legal literacy means that you understand how the law guides your practice, you can apply the law consistently in a range of circumstances and you can demonstrate how the law influences the decisions you make.

Legal literacy in adult safeguarding includes being able to:

- understand your legal duties in order to undertake these as part of everyday practice;

- recognise when a legal solution is needed;
- know how to practise using the law so that the adult's rights are upheld;
- know how to find information about the law;
- know when to get legal advice;
- recognise when colleagues or agencies are acting outside the law and challenge or remedy this.

Practitioners in agencies involved in adult safeguarding have been noted to struggle to develop legal literacy. It can be argued that the implementation of the MCA and the Care Act 2014 came as a cultural shock to health and social care organisations working with adults. Practitioners had focused on procedures and organisational priorities, including budgetary constraints, when making decisions rather than the ethical structures and values needed for rights-informed and person-centred decision making. The confusing patchwork of law used in adult safeguarding has added to anxiety about using the law correctly. At the same time, practitioners felt that the absence of a legal framework left them powerless when attempting to intervene in the lives of adults (Jones and Spreadbury, 2008).

Legal literacy and the implementation of the MCA

The MCA gives clarity about how decisions are made, who can make them, and how the rights of people who do not have the capacity to make specific decisions can be protected. The government hoped that the legislation would 'over time bring about a quiet revolution in public attitudes and practice' (Lammy, 2004). In 2014 the House of Lords Select Committee on the Mental Capacity Act reported that no such quiet revolution had taken place, the empowering ethos of the Act had not been widely implemented and practice was poor across all professional groups.

Williams et al (2012) researched the best-interest decision-making practice of 400 practitioners from the health, social care and legal professions following implementation of the MCA and identified that good practice correlated with 'strong leadership' in the organisation and ready access to sources of advice about specific cases. Bishop (2012) observed the difficulties practitioners had in taking cases to the Court of Protection when the local authorities involved were concerned that enacting this legal duty was too costly. We observe that senior managers in both health and social care organisations often have a poor understanding of how to use the MCA in practice, and do not always provide the daily leadership necessary to ensure that the MCA's principles are evident in all policies and procedures. The development of a culture of legal literacy in an organisation needs to be promoted by the informed actions of its leaders.

Practitioners can think through implementing the principles of the MCA in specific cases if they have ready access to advice. In many local authorities, access to legal advice is tightly managed and direct advice from a solicitor is hard to arrange. Dedicated Deprivation of Liberty Safeguards (DoLS) teams are an excellent source of advice and guidance, but these teams have been overwhelmed with the volume of work following the Cheshire West judgment of 2014. Some (Braye and Preston-Shoot, 2017; Preston-Shoot, 2017) have argued that the MCA is complex and hard to enact. We believe that attention must be paid to an organisational culture that promotes legal literacy in order to effectively implement the MCA and that in many ways it is not that the legislation is too complex but that practitioners often misunderstand how to use it.

How is legal literacy developing in use of the Care Act 2014?

The Care Act 2014 is the legal framework that local SABs must use to inform their local policies and procedures. The statutory guidance sets the expectation that policy and procedures should be regularly updated to incorporate learning from case law so that all practitioners are able to identify and apply changes in legislation in their practice (DHSC, 2018a, para 14.53). The statutory guidance for the Care Act 2014 is regularly updated online so reference must always be made to the most up-to-date version. See the further reading section at the end of this chapter for the link to the statutory guidance.

There are significant challenges in ensuring that adult safeguarding practice is grounded in legislation. Human rights legislation is enshrined within the MCA but not within the Care Act; in addition, new criminal legislation has been implemented since the Care Act but is not always widely understood or used. Case law can be complex to understand and apply to practice. How can the individual practitioner continue to attend to the development of their legal literacy?

REFLECTIVE ACTIVITY

Developing your legal literacy: top tips

Do:

- Ask expert practitioners about case law, and if you do not understand the explanation ask them to simplify it. It can help to think about a case together: how would the law apply to the case?
- Keep your knowledge updated. Go to training and seminars. Subscribe to an update service – see the further reading section for recommendations. Read short articles in trade journals and discuss with your colleagues. Use your learning as soon as you can in practice and reflect on how this worked with others or via your reflective journal.
- Practise applying legal knowledge to practice – have a regular discussion slot with colleagues, work through case studies or

presentations of practice, ask an experienced colleague to tell you what they did in a particular case from a legal perspective.

– Find out where you can get legal advice. Specialist in-house teams can be a great source. How can you access a solicitor for more expert advice? How do you find out more about criminal law? Find out where to get advice now rather than in a crisis so you are clear about arrangements.

Don't:

– Assume that using the law will not help and will make you more anxious. If you are struggling, do raise this with your manager; make a plan together to build your knowledge and confidence.

– Get overwhelmed. Break down what the law requires you to do and identify one or two changes you will make to your practice now. You will feel more in control of your practice.

Understanding how to use the law

How to use legal duties and powers is an important element of legal literacy. We have described here and in Chapter 2 how the misapplication of legislation can result in breaches of the adult's human rights, resulting in them coming to further harm. An overly legalistic approach can be unhelpful without careful planning, relationship building and a consideration of the dynamics of the networks around the adult. Without careful planning and consideration, at best the practitioner's efforts will be ineffective and at worst the situation for the adult will deteriorate.

REFLECTIVE ACTIVITY

Case study: The Malins

For the last month, social worker George has been concerned that **Mrs Malin** is unable to cope with caring for her husband any longer. The district nurse has referred **Mr Malin** for an assessment of his care and support needs. Mrs Malin is frail and tired, but she will not accept any care in the house. Mr Malin has dementia and is spending most of the day in bed, he is incontinent and although he can stand and walk, he isn't responding to Mrs Malin's prompts any more. The Malins' son and daughter-in-law live around the corner. Mrs Malin says that they help to care for her and her husband but George is not convinced of this – it may be wishful thinking on her part or she may be finding it hard to face what is happening in her life.

Mrs Malin telephones George and is very upset. Mr Malin has hit her and she cannot cope any longer; she wants him to go into a home. George goes straight round to the house. He talks to Mrs Malin about the options, he explains that as Mr Malin has dementia he will need to assess his capacity to make a decision about where to live, and if he does not have capacity then George can arrange for him to be admitted to a care home 'in his best interests'. Mrs Malin looks bewildered by this and says she will get her son to come round. Mr Malin junior arrives, Mrs Malin explains that Mr Malin has hit her and that George has come to take him into a home. Mr Malin junior looks very shocked. He orders George to leave the house and raises his arm in a way that George feels threatened by. George leaves, but is very worried about the couple. He calls the police and asks for their assistance in getting back into the house. The police arrive and are invited into the house. After 30 minutes the officers emerge, telling George that the family do not to wish to see him but that there does not seem to be any imminent risk to either Mrs Malin or her husband.

Reflective question

– Using your knowledge of the law and creating relationships, how could you manage this situation differently?

Our thoughts are that we think that George is reacting to the crisis that Mrs Malin now finds herself in. George has powers under legislation, such as the MCA and DoLS, but they must be used to support Mr Malin's well-being and if needed, in his best interests, and not to facilitate a reactive intervention.

* * *

A cup of tea with Mrs Malin while George carries out a calm assessment of the situation is needed. Mr Malin is usually in bed – has this changed? When did he hit Mrs Malin? Is Mr Malin all right, physically and emotionally? Is there a reason to assume he does not have mental capacity today regarding this situation? He may be ill or have a urinary infection. He may be upset about hitting his wife. Talking over what happened may help Mr and Mrs Malin think about options now and later. Do the couple want their son and daughter-in-law to come over to contribute to thinking about what to do next or would they prefer to wait for a family meeting when feelings are calmer?

* * *

You can add to these ideas that may help George calm the situation and keep himself safe while engaging all in thinking about how to resolve the current crisis together. Diffusing the situation without police intervention would have been ideal but in these circumstances social work skills in reducing tension and building relationships are crucial to rebuild the relationships needed to safeguard both Mr and Mrs Malin.

▶ KEY MESSAGES

- While an organisational culture of legal literacy can be supported by strong leadership, individual practitioners must also pay attention to the development of their own legal literacy.

- Knowledge of your legal powers and duties is essential to positive adult safeguarding practice but you must balance this with attention to careful planning around risks, relationship building with the adult, their family and other key elements of their network and a consideration of the dynamics of the networks around the adult.

- You need to know how the criminal law applies to different types of harm, but you do not need to be an expert in criminal law; you must work with the police and other agencies who can bring prosecutions under legislation.

KNOWLEDGE REVIEW

- WHAT is meant by the term 'legal literacy' and what can you do to develop and maintain yours?

- WHAT are the key legal frameworks for adult safeguarding in your part of the UK?

- HOW confident are you that you can use them effectively and in the spirit of the law?

FURTHER READING

- The most up-to-date version of the Care Act 2014's Care and Support Statutory Guidance, including Chapter 14 on adult safeguarding, is to be found at: www.gov.uk/government/publications/care-act-statutory-guidance/care-and-support-statutory-guidance.

- Social Care Institute for Excellence (SCIE, 2014a) 'Gaining Access to an Adult Suspected to Be at Risk of Neglect or Abuse: A Guide for Social Workers and Their Managers in England'. Available from: www.scie.org.uk/care-act-2014/ safeguarding-adults/adult-suspected-at-risk-of-neglect-abuse/files/adult-suspected-at-risk-of-neglect-abuse.pdf.

  This gives a useful overview of what legal powers may be considered in situations when a social worker in England cannot get access to speak with or see an adult who is at risk of harm.

- Home Office (2015a) 'Controlling or Coercive Behaviour in an Intimate or Family Relationship: Statutory Guidance Framework' is a useful guide to this offence and can be accessed at: https://assets.publishing.service.gov. uk/government/uploads/system/uploads/attachment_data/file/482528/ Controlling_or_coercive_behaviour_-_statutory_guidance.pdf.

4

Mental capacity
and adult safeguarding

Chapter aim

In this chapter we will explore the crucial interaction between decision making and adult safeguarding in the context of practice using the Mental Capacity Act 2005. We will consider the crucial and often complex role played by the Act in supporting decision making or making substitute decisions in the person's best interests.

- What is the Mental Capacity Act 2005 and how does it apply to adult safeguarding practice?

- Advocacy, representation and autonomy in adult safeguarding;

- risk and mental capacity in adult safeguarding decision making.

What is the Mental Capacity Act 2005 and how does it apply to adult safeguarding practice?

Fundamental to practice with adults at risk is the law that supports their rights to make decisions as adults. The MCA offers a framework that asks professionals and others supporting the decision making of adults, where there may be conditions that affect their abilities to make decisions, for example as a result of mental ill health or learning disability, to promote their rights to decide for themselves or to have decisions made on their behalf in accordance with their best interests. The MCA sets out principles, tests and checklists to enable practitioners to ensure that they practise in a manner that is compliant with the values and purpose of the Act.

▶ **ESSENTIAL INFORMATION: LEGISLATION**

Mental Capacity Act 2005

Five principles of the Act
1. A person must be assumed to have capacity unless it is established that they lack capacity.
2. A person is not to be treated as unable to make a decision unless all practicable steps to help them to do so have been taken without success.
3. A person is not to be treated as unable to make a decision merely because they make an unwise decision.
4. An act done, or decision made, under this Act for or on behalf of a person who lacks capacity must be done, or made, in their best interests.
5. Before the act is done, or the decision is made, regard must be had to whether the purpose for which it is needed can be as effectively achieved in a way that is less restrictive of the person's rights and freedom of action.

Two-stage test of mental capacity
1. **Diagnostic test**: does the person have an impairment of the mind or brain, or is there some sort of disturbance affecting the way their mind or brain works? (It doesn't matter whether the impairment or disturbance is temporary or permanent.)
2. **Functional test**: if so, does that impairment or disturbance mean that the person is unable to make the decision in question at the time it needs to be made?

Evidence must be available that the diagnosed impairment has caused the inability to decide (not another factor, such as coercion) – known as the 'causative nexus'.

Four capacity assessment questions
A person is unable to make a decision if they cannot:

1. understand relevant information about the decision to be made;
2. retain that information in their mind long enough to decide;
3. use or weigh that information as part of the decision-making process; or
4. communicate their decision (by talking, using sign language or any other means).

Best interests checklist
If the person has been assessed to lack capacity to make the decision at the time the following must be considered when making the decision on the person's behalf:

- Encourage the person's participation in making the decision.
- Identify all relevant circumstances.
- Find out the person's views, past and present wishes and feelings, beliefs and values and any other factors the person themselves would have taken into account.
- Avoid discrimination on the basis of the person's age, appearance, condition or behaviour.
- Assess whether the person might regain capacity.
- If the decision concerns life-sustaining treatment, to not be motivated in any way by a desire to bring about the person's death.
- If it is practical and appropriate to do so, consult other people for their views about the person's best interests and to see if they have any information about the person's wishes and feelings, beliefs and values.
- Avoid restricting the person's rights by considering less restrictive options.
- Take all of this into account when deciding by weighing up all of these factors.

Summarised from the MCA Code of Practice (2007)
in Hubbard and Stone, 2018, pp 7, 41, 45, 65

For adult safeguarding practitioners, questions of the person's mental capacity most often arise when there is concern that the person does not understand or acknowledge the risks that they are facing and may choose to remain in an environment or situation with high levels of risk to themselves. However, all health and social care practice should be informed by human rights and consideration of the person's ability to make meaningful choices about their lives. The key point when adult safeguarding and mental capacity intersect is when considering whether the adult has the capacity to be involved in their own safeguarding, particularly when considering whether the adult understands and weighs key points regarding the risks to themselves in the situation. Baker (2017, p 128) notes three questions that often arise when exploring the adult at risk's views of the safeguarding concern:

- Can and should this individual make their own decisions in this situation or be protected from harm?
- Do they understand the concerns? Do they understand the likely and foreseeable consequences?
- Who would be blamed if the individual came to harm? Whose risk is it to take?

Though we would question whether the attribution of blame is a valuable driver for mental capacity decision making, these questions aid our focus on key considerations for considering the involvement of adults in decision making about safeguarding.

Advocacy, representation and autonomy in adult safeguarding

Mental capacity should also be considered when exploring the arrangements needed for advocacy and representation within the safeguarding process. Often these are not considered in a timely fashion, either leaving the person at increased risk because of their inability to recognise and deal with the risks in their situation or leading the adult to disengage with the safeguarding process because decisions have been made that have not sufficiently involved them. For example, a social worker involved with an adult with a learning disability, where allegations had been made about the brother stealing his money, assessed his mental capacity regarding his finances. They decided that the adult's desire to remain in contact with his brother overrode their assessment that the adult did not understand the risk that his savings would decline and he would no longer be able to live independently. The social worker observed the ongoing reduction in funds available to the adult and stood by their capacity assessment even in the face of allegations that the brother was verbally abusive to the adult. Without independent advocacy and safeguarding arrangements because the adult was judged to have the mental capacity to make decisions about how he spent his money, the adult remained at further and escalating risk of abuse.

The MCA is designed to offer guidance and prompt professionals to recognise and promote the rights to autonomy that adults at risk have, provide safeguards that ensure their views are heard and addressed and to act and intervene when required. Rogers et al (2015) recognise that:

> while there remain too many instances of professionals making decisions on behalf of others without properly consulting or assessing capacity, we have certainly moved on from the times when the apparently omnipotent and omniscient professional would regularly make life-changing decisions for people without consulting or informing them or their families in advance. (p 25)

It is probably naive to suggest that health and social care professionals have altogether stopped seeing themselves as omnipotent in terms of their application of the MCA. The MCA has been in force for 11 years at the time of writing and it is disheartening to see that criticism of the implementation of the Act has been consistent since 2007 (Williams et al, 2012; House of Lords, 2014; Braye and Preston-Shoot, 2017; Preston-Shoot, 2017), much of which focuses on the poor understanding of how the Act directs practitioners to support the rights of people to make autonomous decisions and to respect the rights of the individual to make their own decisions rather than acting in an overprotective and paternalistic manner. It is important to note that Preston-Shoot is critical of practitioners often privileging autonomy and self-determination for adults in their decisions to the extent that they abandon their duty of care (Preston-Shoot, 2017, section 6.3.1). It is vital to note that autonomy and self-determination sit on one side of a set of scales with the practitioner's duty of care and responsibilities such as the ECHR Article 2 right to life on the other. It is essential that practitioners look overall at the balance between individual autonomy and their duty of care when weighing decision making under the MCA so that these legal provisions are used accurately and are not merely used to justify and support inaction, especially where engagement with an individual or their family is difficult or complex.

As practitioners who work within adult safeguarding processes, you will be very aware that you tread a line at all times between the impetus to protect adults from harm, often under pressure from families and other professionals to intervene to reduce risks, and the need to support adults to make decisions about their own lives free from interference. The MCA can be a useful tool to prompt scrutiny of choices that you have made to ensure that the person's views and wishes have not been lost in decision making and also to ensure that you have fully considered the person's right to autonomy within the protective safeguarding framework.

Take a common example from social work practice with older adults: a frail older adult, with memory issues, who is living alone and is being financially exploited, either by a friend or family member. Often the adult has people involved (such as other family, friends, neighbours or a care agency) who are expressing concern about the risk to the adult and who contact the local authority to consider the situation as a safeguarding concern. The social worker visits and, as part of the enquiry, conducts a mental capacity assessment to consider whether the adult understands the risks in the situation and whether to intervene to prevent further risk. Two possible outcomes can be considered.

Mental capacity assessment decision and intervention

1. The social worker forms the impression that the adult knows that the situation is not ideal but can see that they gain benefit from contact with the alleged abuser and decides that the adult *has capacity* to make the decision not to change the situation. *Consequently*, the social worker offers the adult ways to reduce the identified risks by suggesting ways to minimise the alleged abuser's access to the adult's finances and encouraging them to share any further concerns with others involved (for example, the care agency). The adult is free to choose whether they take up the offered assistance.

2. The social worker decides that, despite the adult's view that they need the alleged abuser involved, the adult is not able to understand the risks involved or to weigh up the risk that the abuse poses to their independence. They may decide that the adult *lacks capacity* to make the decision. *Consequently*, the social worker needs to make a best-interests decision on the adult's behalf. They decide after consulting with the adult and others interested in their welfare to apply to the Court of Protection for a deputyship for property and affairs, as they assess that the adult lacks the mental capacity to appoint a lasting power of attorney, and could suggest that the local authority would be better placed to manage the adult's finances than the alleged abuser or other individuals.

Risk and mental capacity in adult safeguarding decision making

The process of mental capacity assessment and, where relevant, making a best-interests decision should be a rights-driven and, when needed, collaborative effort that allows for a detailed exploration of the individual's rights, views and the likely impact of risks on their abilities to remain as independent as possible. Williams et al noted that 'risk was a very common trigger for a best interests process' (2012, p 5) and that safeguarding concerns often drove the need for a mental capacity assessment of the person's understanding of their risks. Interestingly, the researchers found that often the MCA was not used where concerns were raised about one-off risks but was more likely to be a feature of safeguarding when there were repeated incidents causing concern, leading to more formal systems coming into effect to reduce risk (p 44). It may be that practitioners see one-off incidents as less likely to indicate more severe harm or more likely to be accidental. Without a history of incidents it can give less confidence that abuse has occurred or that an ongoing safeguarding plan, including the use of powers under the MCA, might be necessary. This can obscure the possibility of the one-off high-risk incidence of abuse that could reoccur being identified and addressed.

Where situations involve risks to people who are seen as vulnerable it can be difficult to resist the urge to protect the person from further harm. Often those around an adult perceived as vulnerable want action taken, even where intervention may breach the person's rights to make decisions for themselves. However, the challenge with adult safeguarding is that adults have the right to make decisions that we do not just think are unwise but may actually be actively harmful to them. Assessment under the MCA will enable you to decide whether the person can make the decision or not on the basis of whether their mental health or learning disability is affecting their decision-making abilities about the risks. Understanding the person's mental capacity will also form part of the adult safeguarding enquiry and should inform your discussion with the adult about their preferred way forward. However, if the person has capacity to make the decision the routes to intervention to protect can become limited.

The case study shows the challenges for practitioners who can perceive risk when the adult does not.

REFLECTIVE ACTIVITY

Case study: Harry and Louis

Harry and Louis live in their own flats in a supported living scheme for young people with learning disabilities. They each have support workers visiting twice a day. On more than one occasion, support workers have found Harry and Louis in bed together in Harry's flat, at times kissing.

The support worker believes that neither Harry and Louis have capacity to consent to sex and raises a safeguarding concern with the local authority.

The social worker conducting the enquiry completes mental capacity assessments with both Harry and Louis separately and concludes that neither have the capacity to consent as they were not able to explain the risks of sexually transmitted infections (STIs) though they both clearly expressed their understanding of the nature of their relationship and the need for them both to agree to sexual contact on each occasion. The social worker works with the support staff on a plan to educate Harry and Louis on STIs and to monitor their relationship to ensure that if either wanted the relationship to cease they would be supported.

Reflective questions

- Consider your own views and values on sexual relationships between adults you work with. What impact might your values have on your attitudes to risk in these relationships?
- Consider the legal threshold set out in the case law set out in the following section on capacity to consent to sex. What are your views on what is considered relevant and not relevant in coming to this judgement?
- How might you work with Harry and Louis to ensure their relationship becomes consensual?

Case example adapted from Pilkington (2012, p 6).

In our view decision making about Harry and Louis should involve the practitioner being self-aware about any prejudices they have regarding sexual relationships between people with learning disabilities and same-sex relationships. It is important to recognise and prioritise what is important about intimate, sexual relationships to people no matter their disability, such as comfort, warmth, intimacy, relaxation and sexual release.

Open and frank discussions with both Harry and Louis – separately and together – about their relationship and key issues regarding their rights to give and withdraw consent at a level appropriate for each of them as well as maintaining health in sexual relationships are all important to consider. Training of staff on supporting dignified and healthy sexual relationships is also important.

Since the implementation of the MCA, guidance has arisen from case law judgments and become more refined on how to conduct mental capacity assessments, particularly on what information is relevant or irrelevant to making certain key decisions (Ruck Keene et al, 2017). From the *CC v KK and STCC* (2012) judgment, the term 'salient points' has become commonly used to describe the key information that a person could reasonably be expected to understand about a decision. The mental capacity assessment set out in the case study focuses on capacity to consent to sexual relationships. This is one of the decisions that case law has built around, as a measure of the importance of considering consent to sexual activity where mental capacity is in question as a result of a person's mental health or cognitive abilities.

Ruck Keene et al (2017) set out the following factors as relevant (and irrelevant) when assessing a person's mental capacity to consent to sex.

Relevant to general assessment of ability to consent to sex:

  a The mechanics and nature of the sexual act.
  b The risk of sexually transmitted infections ….
  c The potential that sexual activity between a man and a woman can give rise to pregnancy, although note that where it is clearly established that the person is homosexual, it is ordinarily unnecessary to consider this since pregnancy is not a foreseeable consequence of homosexual sex.
  d A basic understanding of contraception.
  e That one has a choice whether to have sex and can refuse. (p 15)

Not relevant:

  a The identity of the sexual or marriage partner. In other words, capacity to consent to sexual relations is act-specific, rather than person-specific.
  b An understanding of what is involved in caring for a child (should a protected person become pregnant) ….
  c The risk that may be caused to herself through pregnancy, or the risk to future children ….
  d The fact that the opportunity for sexual relations with a specific partner will be limited for some time to come into the future.
  e The ability to understand or evaluate the characteristics of some particular partner or intended partner. (pp 15–16)

Overall it was noted that consent to sex for a capacitated person must be considered as acting 'from a more intuitive than cerebral set of factors' (p 15) than other decision making as a result of the nature of decision making about sexual activity. This guides those assessing capacity not to set a higher standard for decision making in this area, where there is a query about the person's capacity to decide, than with a person where there is no mental impairment causing concern about the person's ability to decide.

It is worth noting that it could be assumed that those in a gay male relationship could be reasonably expected to have some knowledge of STIs considering the prevalence of public health education and resources focused on these relationships. It is possible to consider the threshold for understanding this within a lesbian relationship may be different. For example, it may be less reasonable to expect that a person whose mental capacity is being assessed is aware of risk factors arising from sexual contact between women as there are far fewer resources and public health information available regarding this potential route of STIs.

▶ ESSENTIAL INFORMATION: SERIOUS CASE REVIEW

Mr C was a 61-year-old man who died in a fire in his flat in September 2014 after involvement with housing, police, fire service, adult social care and mental health services in Bristol. He had a long history of mental ill health, though he had been discharged from mental health services in 2012 as a result of long-term disengagement despite being entitled to section 177 aftercare under the MHA.

After this, concerns about Mr C tended to be treated as anti-social behaviour and the risk he may pose to others from lighting fires in his flat, rather than about his mental health state. His behaviours (for example, using barbecues in his flat for heating and candles for light because his power supplies were cut off, refusing support, losing weight, keeping his flat in a cluttered state that attracted flies, inviting sex workers and drug dealers into his home and so forth) were considered to be choices that he was making and a mental capacity assessment concluded that he had capacity to make these decisions. During this assessment undertaken by adult social workers he had engaged appropriately with the assessor and convinced them that he was vulnerable but willing to engage. Mr C refused services offered as a result of a Community Care assessment and it was decided that the state of his flat was a 'lifestyle' choice.

The serious case review that followed Mr C's death included among its conclusions the view that:

> Mr C's mental capacity was formally assessed but despite his history of serious mental illness, and current behaviours and rationalisations, he was assumed to have capacity. The BCC [Bristol City Council] social worker assumed capacity on the basis of Mr C's verbal reassurances and the Housing Officer noting that his flat was tidier than on a previous visit, and did not take into account the context of Mr C's serious mental health history. (p 12)

Summarised from Heaton, 2016

In Mr C's case, the significant nature of the risk that he posed to himself through his desire to avoid involvement from statutory services, the untreated nature of his mental health condition and the fire risk present in his flat did not appear to have been fully considered within the context of the mental capacity assessment completed by the social worker. The nature of risk as understood and weighed up by the person is fundamentally what is being considered during a mental capacity assessment, although this is not always explicitly recognised in how capacity assessments are conducted. From our practice experience, it is not unusual for mental capacity assessments to conclude that the person has capacity to make a decision while also noting concern about the adult's ability to manage the risk. This suggests that the assessor has not fundamentally grasped what is being assessed and may not have addressed the risks directly with the person during the assessment. Sometimes it can take a courageous practitioner to start a conversation about issues the adult does not want to acknowledge or consider.

Mr C was articulate and persuasive at times in conversation which may have given the assessing social worker the impression that Mr C was able to act on his estimation of his ability to deal with the risks in his life. As with those with acquired brain injuries (Acquired Brain Injury and Mental Capacity Act Interest Group, 2014), where people are more articulate about their decision making, it can be more challenging for assessors to question whether the person's explanations of their understanding and risk-weighing process is an accurate depiction of what they would actually do. Insight into the impact of the adult's mental impairment on their decision making may not be present and can mislead the assessor into giving the person's expressed views greater weight than is needed. It becomes essential in these circumstances to triangulate the views given by the person about their responses to the risks involved in the decision with others involved in their care to check out the consistency of their expressed views with the realities of their behaviour. NICE (2018a) suggest that, where executive functioning could be impacting on decision making, 'structured assessments of capacity for individuals in this group (for example, by way of interview) may therefore need to be supplemented by real-world observation of the person's functioning and decision-making ability in order to provide the assessor with a complete picture of an individual's decision-making ability' (para. 1.4.19).

This approach can be challenging in the context of respecting individual autonomy that is inherent in the principles of the MCA. It is essential to recall that the presumption of capacity is not absolute – there are clearly areas where reasoning about risks to the person is inhibited by mental impairment, when intervention is legally sanctioned and professional judgement may require safeguarding practitioners to act in the face of the adult's articulate and apparently well-reasoned disagreement. However, it is essential that practitioners achieve a balance between acknowledgement of the risks identified and the rights of the adult to act freely according to their own will.

The assessment of mental capacity also requires that there is a connection between the two stages of the test for mental capacity (the diagnostic and functional elements); a connection labelled the 'causative nexus' (*PC v City of York Council*, 2013). If there is no evident connection between the adult's mental impairment and their inability to make the decision in question (for example, there is no mental impairment evident or the person's decision–making ability is affected by something else) then the MCA cannot be used as a legal framework to safeguard their decision making or to act lawfully in their best interests. Coercion, pressure from others or the complexity of decisions are some ways that affect a person's ability to make decisions that are not related to their mental capacity and those involved in caring for the person cannot use the MCA to act on their behalf. In these circumstances there may be limited options, though the inherent jurisdiction of the High Court could possibly be used when no other legal safeguard is available.

REFLECTIVE ACTIVITY

Case study: Charlotte

Charlotte is a 21-year-old woman who lives with her mother, Anne, in a commuter town. She was diagnosed with a mild learning disability while at school and received support while studying, though she is no longer in contact with any services regarding this. Charlotte did not have many friends while she was at school and was bullied and depressed at times. Charlotte has worked in a fast food restaurant in the nearby city since leaving college at 18 and concerns have been raised by her mother about the relationships she has been forming with men whom she met in the restaurant. Charlotte started by catching a bus to her job and after a few months she is getting lifts to and from work from a range of men who her mother does not know.

Anne has contacted the local adult safeguarding team and reported Charlotte being dropped off at home after work evidently drunk and finding drugs and new make-up in her room. She says that she thinks that Charlotte is having a, possibly non-consensual, sexual relationship as she often comes home dishevelled and bruised. Anne tries to speak to Charlotte about her concerns but Charlotte refuses to speak about the drinking, drugs or her appearance. Charlotte will talk about how much she likes her new friends and how much they care for her when she has never had proper friends before.

The safeguarding team explain to Anne that, as part of the section 42 enquiry, they have decided to assess whether Charlotte has the mental capacity to make decisions about her relationships. A social worker comes to Anne and Charlotte's home to discuss Anne's concerns and assess Charlotte's mental capacity about sexual relationships. Charlotte confirms that she has had a sexual relationship with more than one of the men who work in the restaurant. The social worker asks about Charlotte's understanding of what sex involves, the chances of becoming pregnant or getting a sexually transmitted infection, her understanding of contraception and that sex is a choice that she can refuse. From their discussion, the social worker is confident that Charlotte has capacity to consent to a sexual relationship as she is able to explain the risks and how she deals with them. Charlotte talks about knowing she can say no to sex if she wants to. The social worker gives advice to Anne and Charlotte about sources of advice for sexual health and information on reducing the risks from drug and alcohol use. Anne remains concerned about Charlotte and is unhappy that the social worker is refusing to intervene as Charlotte is now legally an adult and therefore make her own choices about sexual relationships.

Reflective questions

– What is your view on the mental capacity assessment carried out by the social worker? Consider the salient points for consent to sexual relationships established in the case law listed earlier in this chapter and the nature of the risks involved.

– What indicators of harm can you identify in this case study? What other risks might you want to explore with Charlotte?

– What impact might the nature of exploitation and coercion have on Charlotte's ability to make decisions about sexual relationships in this situation? Would any different legal or practice responses be needed in this situation? If so, why?

Our thinking is that we question whether the social worker in this instance has covered everything necessary for a mental capacity assessment in Charlotte's case. As well as deciding whether Charlotte has mental capacity to consent to a single sexual relationship related to the act-specific nature of this decision, it is also important to consider the sexually exploitative nature of the situation that Charlotte is alleged to find herself in. The allegations of Charlotte being plied with drink, drugs and gifts and controlling her for sex meet the criteria for sexual exploitation. In the same way that the MCA cannot be used for substitute decision making for sex it cannot be used to consent to something illegal, such as sexual exploitation.

The social worker needs to complete a further capacity assessment regarding the circumstances that are putting Charlotte at risk of sexual exploitation by multiple people. This allegation will also require a multi-

> agency response to enquire whether other children and adults are at risk in this situation and to address these risks. If coercion is established and legal measures are required to make decisions on Charlotte's behalf in the assumption that she continues to show mental capacity, the inherent jurisdiction of the High Court could be considered.

Prior to the implementation of the MCA, *inherent jurisdiction* was the only legal means of acting on behalf of mentally incapacitated adults. The legal principle of inherent jurisdiction means that 'a superior court has the jurisdiction to hear any matter that comes before it, unless a statute or rule limits that authority or grants exclusive jurisdiction to some other court or tribunal' (Szerletics, 2011).

The High Court continues to be able to consider cases where coercion, pressure or control are affecting the decision making of those who have mental capacity but are considered vulnerable for other reasons and are at significant risk from their decisions. For example, in the case of *Southend-on-Sea v Meyers* (2019), the High Court considered whether Mr Meyers could be lawfully deprived of his liberty in a care home that he objected to remaining in and was assessed to have mental capacity to do so. The placement was arranged to prevent harm coming to him from his son. Mr Meyers' son resided, with his father's agreement, at his parents' home where he had been considered by the local authority to be causing harm to his father through abusive behaviour towards carers commissioned by the local authority in accordance with a Care Act assessment of Mr Meyers' care and support needs. The question of whether Mr Meyers was deprived of his liberty in accordance with ECHR Article 5 when he is not considered to be of unsound mind as he has no mental impairment within the meaning of the MCA has been considered during the progress of this case and differing views reached by different judges. The case is awaiting an appeal court hearing at the time of writing (June 2019).

Where the power for the High Court rules in these cases, other legal structures and principles such as the Human Rights Act 1998, proportionate response and best interests still apply. Other legal safeguards of the Mental Capacity Act, such as the right to advocacy, are not available when the inherent jurisdiction of the High Court is used so other means of supporting or representing the person's views within the legal process should be considered, such as a litigation friend.

▶ KEY MESSAGES

- Law and policy ask you to balance the adult's autonomy and self-determination with your duty of care and the adult's right to life. Attention to just one of these will distort your decision making and may leave the adult at unnecessary risk from either a lack of protection or overly restrictive intervention.

- Deciding that a person has mental capacity to make a risky decision does not mean you no longer have a safeguarding responsibility to that person. Maintaining a relationship where risk can be openly managed and addressed remains essential to positive preventative practice.

KNOWLEDGE REVIEW

- HOW can assessment and decision making using the MCA aid clarity around the adult's risks and rights to autonomy?

- WHAT support is available to an adult within safeguarding if they may have difficulty being involved in the process?

- WHAT other legal safeguards are available where the MCA does not apply and what is their purpose?

FURTHER READING

- 39 Essex Chambers publish (and regularly revise) brief guides to carrying out mental capacity assessments and making best-interests decisions that can be accessed, along with newsletters giving updates on mental capacity case law in England and Wales at: www.39essex.com/resources-and-training/mental-capacity-law/.

- This practical guide to using the MCA is useful for practitioners and supports the rights and principles in the Act: Graham, M. and Cowley, J. (2015) *A Practical Guide to the Mental Capacity Act 2005: Putting the Principles of the Act into Practice*, London: Jessica Kingsley.

- For guidance on conducting capacity assessments within DoLS (which can offer good practice principles for wider assessment of mental capacity within the MCA) read pp 96–100 in Hubbard, R. and Stone, K. (2018) *The Best Interests Assessor Practice Handbook*, Bristol: Policy Press.

5

Definitions
in adult safeguarding

Chapter aim

In this chapter we will explore how and why the statutory duty to undertake an enquiry under section 42 of the Care Act 2014 only applies to a small section of the population; those defined as 'adults at risk'. We begin with a discussion of how the legislation and guidance concerning 'adults at risk' is applied. We will explore the challenges faced by different groups in protecting themselves and claiming the right to protection.

Categories of potential harm have been detailed in section 14 of the statutory guidance. Although the guidance omits references to adults at risk who are harmed through forced marriage, female genital mutilation or exploitation in terrorist activities, these forms of harm are usually included in Safeguarding Adults Board local policies and will be explored in this chapter. We will examine how each type of harm is defined and how harm may be identified if it is not disclosed. This chapter includes:

- why definitions are useful;

- adults at risk who may be overlooked by adult safeguarding services;

- identification of harm: general themes;

- identification of harm: locations;

- identification of harm: types of abuse.

Why definitions are useful

Commonly agreed definitions can help to provide a coherent understanding of a subject like adult safeguarding, which means that people from a range of settings and professional backgrounds can discuss the issue with the confidence that they share the same meaning. This encourages inter-agency awareness, the growth of partnership working through a common understanding and the development of effective and consistent responses to the harm described, as well as resources being more readily focused on a defined population or area.

Definitions can risk simplifying complex situations. For example, if an adult is physically assaulted, they are very likely to be psychologically damaged as well as physically hurt. In addition, if the adult has been assaulted because their assailant hates disabled people this can also be defined as discriminatory abuse, and if the responsible agencies do nothing about their plight the adult may also be experiencing discriminatory abuse and potentially organisational abuse. One label will not fit all, but the clarity of defining what harms we are talking about does help to shape our response to a concern. Understanding to whom the statutory duty to enquire applies helps us to focus resources on those who are unable to protect themselves and supports the multi-agency understanding needed for effective adult safeguarding work.

Adults at risk who may be overlooked by adult safeguarding services

Certain groups are regularly not considered to meet the criteria for the section 42 duty, potentially because of practitioners' beliefs about 'lifestyle choice' which disguises the true nature of the adult's inability to protect themselves.

People who are street homeless or staying in direct access hostels

Studies (Homeless Link, 2014) report that between 25 and 30 per cent of the homeless population have severe mental health problems including severe depression, schizophrenia and bipolar disorder. Around 62.5 per cent of homeless people in the study abused substances. There are many adults in the homeless population who cannot protect themselves as a result of their care and support needs: 'longer-term trends have seen disproportionately rising numbers with mental health or other complex needs. Many homelessness managers believe such patterns partly attributable to cutbacks in local services for these groups' (Fitzpatrick et al, 2019). Adults at risk may be identified in a variety of ways, through contact with health, police or outreach services, but it can be hard to establish a regular pattern of engagement which can dilute enquiries and safeguarding planning. It is vitally important for practitioners to understand which agencies are involved with people who are homeless and to also adjust their own working patterns if necessary, to facilitate multi-agency working with this group. You may only be able to catch someone early in the morning before leaving their sleeping place or late at night at a regular soup run stall.

REFLECTIVE ACTIVITY

Case study: James Long

James Long was 62 years old; he was physically frail and had problems with his memory, potentially related to long-term alcohol use and poor nutrition. His previous coping strategies on the street and in hostels no longer worked to keep him safe: he had the possessions he needed for survival stolen, was too weak to sit outside for long and was increasingly disorientated. James was seen by a social worker in the hospital emergency department having been beaten up in a local car park by a group allegedly targeting homeless people for a 'laugh'.

Reflective questions

–   Does the section 42 statutory duty to enquire apply to James Long?
–   What type of harm is he at risk of or actually experiencing?

Our thoughts are that we consider that the statutory duty to enquire under section 42 is met. James's care and support needs will need to be assessed as part of the enquiry, but at the moment he appears to have some cognitive and physical health issues that make it hard for him to protect himself and prevent further harm. James has experienced physical harm, he has been assaulted and, because his usual coping strategies are no longer working, he is at risk of self-neglect and further harm on the street. The risk of harm is imminent and the impact on his well-being potentially severe.

People with addictions

Addiction to a substance alone does not lead to a person meeting the criteria for the section 42 duty, but people who have addictions may also have disabilities, including mental health issues, which make it hard for them to protect themselves from harm. Substance use may lead to the development of mental health issues. Coping with the symptoms of mental ill health may lead people to use substances to mask voices or cope with intrusive thoughts, and in turn the substances themselves worsen existing mental ill health. Physically disabled people may use substances to escape chronic pain or other difficulties caused by their disability or the discriminatory social attitudes towards them. In turn substances may increase an adult's disability, and long-term use can lead to physical damage and disability, including brain damage. People who misuse alcohol can be more vulnerable to trauma, head injury, accidents and violence from others. Older people may use substances to cope with isolation or grief at the loss of those close to them, increasing the risk of falls, confusion, malnutrition and depression. It is important for practitioners to understand the harm the adult is experiencing, which will be masked if the addiction and the behaviour around the addiction are the only elements of the situation considered.

REFLECTIVE ACTIVITY

Case study: Nancy Wright

Neighbours complained about **Nancy Wright** who lives alone. Nancy was often heard shouting late at night and could be threatening to others in the block of flats. Neighbours believed she was a 'drug addict' and was associated with one of the dealers on the housing estate. The housing association who let the flats were considering applying for an anti-social behaviour order to tackle Nancy's behaviour. A housing officer persuaded Nancy to let him into her flat to discuss the situation. Through conversation with Nancy he noted that she appeared to be experiencing auditory and visual hallucinations, talking to someone and shouting out in distress for them to get away from her. She was unable to hold a coherent conversation or answer questions. She wanted the housing officer to leave her alone. There was no food in the flat and Nancy had no bedclothes, the electricity was not working, and the flat was cold. There was no sign of drug paraphernalia but there were some empty alcohol bottles about. Nancy herself looked thin and smelt strongly of urine.

Reflective questions
- Does the statutory duty to enquire under section 42 apply to Nancy Wright?
- What type of harm is she experiencing?
- What initial actions will you take?

Our thoughts are that we consider that the statutory duty to enquire under section 42 to be met. Nancy Wright is exhibiting very concerning signs of self-neglect which appears to be long-standing. Her current mental health, physical health and potential lack of mental capacity to make and act on decisions about her well-being are all indicators of a person in need of urgent care and support. An assessment of her physical and mental health can be arranged via her GP, while an enquiry plan is made to engage her further and develop a multi-agency approach to ensure that her well-being is maintained while an enquiry is undertaken.

Identification of harm: general themes

Harm comes in many forms: it can be something that is done to an adult, or something that should have been done but was not – an act of omission. Harm can result from an adult neglecting themselves to a life-threatening extent. Harm can sometimes be unintentional; the actions of the carer are misguided and have resulted in harm. The emphasis of adult safeguarding is on the impact on the adult, and what can be done to resolve or reduce risk in the situation.

REFLECTIVE ACTIVITY

Case study: John and Max

John Stanley cared for his partner **Max**. Max was very frail – he could not manoeuvre himself without assistance. In helping Max to move from his bed to a chair John pulled him and dislocated his shoulder. It is not the first time that John has unintentionally injured Max, but it is the most serious. John was distraught, and very ashamed of causing such pain; Max was upset and wishes John would give in and ask for help; both of them were exhausted.

Reflective questions
- Does the statutory duty to enquire under section 42 apply to Max?
- What type of harm is he experiencing?
- What will help to resolve or reduce risk in this situation?

Our thoughts are that Max has been physically harmed by John. The harm was unintentional but there is a risk of further harm to Max if John does not agree to get support to care for him. Max is dependent on John to help him at the moment and because of this will not be able to protect himself from further harm. Max could be offered a care and support needs assessment while using hospital services, but if John or Max decline this further enquiries under section 42 will be needed. A carer's assessment for John may also give him some time to reflect on what he needs to be able to continue with his caring role.

There are ten types of harm detailed within section 14 of the Care Act 2014 Care and Support Statutory Guidance (DHSC, 2018a). In general, all UK adult safeguarding legislation and policy covers similar types of harm, including the principle that lists of types of harm are not exhaustive, that is, that lists do not contain all potential types of harm to which adult safeguarding may be relevant.

Remember that to define something means that there can be a common understanding and focus on it, but you need to look further than the type of harm that you are focusing on; you must also understand the circumstances of the adult and the impact of the harm on them. A conversation with the adult at the heart of the concern, visiting them to see their circumstances and talk with others who know them, will help you to understand the extent of the impact on the adult's well-being and what they experience or consider as harmful.

REFLECTIVE ACTIVITY

Case study: Vera Jones

Vera Jones lived in a care home; she was visited regularly by her sister who reported that Vera was regularly subjected to racist abuse from another resident. The care home believed that Vera was not affected by such abuse, potentially because she had Alzheimer's dementia which led to memory loss and difficulty in communicating her thoughts and feelings. Her sister was very concerned that the care home permitted such abuse to happen – the adult who was identified as the source of harm also had dementia and "didn't understand" what he was saying. You visited the care home with Vera's sister and both of you noted that Vera became tense when taken into the dining area, the place where the abuse occurred. Vera kept asking to be taken back to her room, and the care staff told you that she had recently stopped eating so well and seemed more relaxed when on her own.

These signs tell you that Vera is distressed about something. It may well be the racist abuse or some other factor, but you are clear this needs to be explored and resolved.

Reflective questions
–   Does the statutory duty to enquire under section 42 apply to Vera?
–   What types of harm is she experiencing?
–   What will help to resolve or reduce risk in this situation?

Our thoughts are that Vera cannot protect herself because of her care and support needs and she is being subjected to psychological and discriminatory abuse. The section 42 duty applies. A range of options may be considered, from planning ways of reintroducing Vera to areas of the care home and arranging for the other adult not to be present, finding activities Vera might enjoy, or that the other adult enjoys, finding ways to communicate with Vera, educating the care home on challenging

> discrimination and supporting diversity, and on the impact of harm on people with cognitive impairments, exploring how her sister can be her advocate and whether she wants further support to do this.

Section 14 of the statutory guidance on the Care Act 2014 picks out exploitation as an overarching theme across many types of harm.

What is meant by 'exploitation'?

In the context of adult safeguarding exploitation means to use or treat an adult unfairly in order to gain an advantage. The advantage may be material – money or resources – or may be an emotional or physical advantage. The person who gains advantage, who exploits, is more powerful than the adult who has care and support needs. Understanding power, and how it is used in harm and exploitation, is essential to skilled practice as we discuss in Chapters 2, 5 and 6. Power over the adult may be derived from position, for example that of an employee paid to care for the adult; or from emotional significance to the adult, such as that of partner or adult child, or simply because the powerful person is stronger, more capable, has more resources and has deliberately set out to exploit. We will explore themes of exploitation under the types of harm set out in the remainder of this chapter.

In each of the sections that follow we will take an overview of the definitions of types of harm that can happen to an adult with care and support needs. Do refer to Chapter 3 to remind yourself what criminal offences may be involved in all types of harm: the abuse of adults at risk is frequently a crime as well as an infringement of human rights. You will find that the local procedures you use in practice contain lists of 'indicators' of harm, and you will add to these indicators using your own experience and lessons gained from learning events, SARs and research. The purpose of an indicator is to alert you that the adult may be experiencing harm. Indicators can relate to a wide range of issues and behaviours, for example the adult who cannot communicate verbally and who is unusually withdrawn and flinches when approached may be being physically harmed or may have a very bad toothache that they are unable to tell you about. Rather than jumping to conclusions, careful exploration of the context of the indicator is needed.

Identification of harm: locations

Adults are harmed in a range of locations, but most frequently in their own home or community, or in an institution, which is most often a care home although hospital settings may also be a location of harm. NHS Digital data on section 42 enquiries in England during 2017/18 shows that the adult's own home was the most recorded location of harm (43.5 per cent) and that 35.6 per cent of adults were allegedly harmed in care homes (NHS Digital, 2018).

Location of harm: home or community

Abuse in domestic settings can be most often typified as domestic abuse and/or violence.

> ▶ **ESSENTIAL INFORMATION: LEGISLATION**
>
> The statutory guidance (section 14.20) notes:
>
> The cross-government definition of domestic violence and abuse is: any incident or pattern of incidents of controlling, coercive, threatening behaviour, violence or abuse between those aged 16 or over who are, or have been, intimate partners or family members regardless of gender or sexuality. The abuse can encompass, but is not limited to:
>
> • psychological
> • sexual
> • financial
> • emotional

Family members can be defined as: mother, father, son, daughter, brother, sister and grandparents, whether directly related, in-laws or stepfamily. Other family members – cousins, aunts, uncles and so on – can also be included. Domestic abuse is most often described as involving people over 16 years old.

Disabled parents can be harmed by their younger children but may not disclose this for fear that their child may be removed from them. Home Office (2015a, 2015b) guidance stipulates that these children must be referred to children's safeguarding services. Partnership working with children's services is important in getting help for both parent and child and must be agreed between children's and adult's services through face-to-face contact between practitioners and with the adult and child. It is important to use principles of building relationships with other safeguarding agencies described in Chapter 6 as children's services may not be familiar with the duties and role of adult safeguarding. The phenomena of children under 16 harming their parents is not well documented and the invisibility of such abuse compounds the harm for both children and adults. The Home Office has issued guidance (2015b) on responding to adolescent abuse of parents, the guidance does not reference partnership working with adult safeguarding but does contain some useful principles to inform practice.

The law on domestic abuse, coercive control and forced marriage in Chapter 3 includes the legal definitions.

The definition of domestic abuse within the Care Act 2014 also encompasses *honour-based violence*. Honour-based violence can be described as a collection of practices used to control behaviour within families or other social groups to protect perceived cultural and religious beliefs and/or honour. Such violence can occur when the perpetrators think that a relative has shamed the family and/or community by breaking the honour code. Concepts of coercive control can be useful in identifying honour-based violence. There is no specific criminal offence of honour-based violence; the term encompasses various offences covered by existing legislation and is dealt with under these, for example assault, stalking and harassment, kidnap, rape, threats to kill and murder (CPS, 2017).

Forced marriage is not mentioned in the Care Act statutory guidance (DHSC, 2018a) but can be considered as domestic abuse if a person unable or unwilling to enter into marriage is forced to do so by family members or others. Honour-based violence may include forced marriage if this is undertaken to reinforce an honour code. In arranged marriages both parties are free to change their mind at any point and not go through with the marriage. Forced marriage is different, and sometimes can involve coercion and violence, or may involve people who do not have the mental capacity to consent to marriage. The pressure put on people to marry against their will may be physical (for example threats, physical violence or sexual violence) and/or emotional and psychological (making someone feel like they are bringing 'shame' on their family, for example). Financial abuse (such as taking someone's wages) may also be a factor. Adult safeguarding practitioners may well encounter adults who lack the capacity to understand what is involved in 'marriage' and will not be able to consent to marriage.

▶ **ESSENTIAL INFORMATION: LEGISLATION**

Case law: capacity to understand marriage

Re E (An alleged patient): Sheffield City Council v E (2004) sets out the approach to be taken to evaluating capacity to marry. In summary, 'it is not enough that an individual appreciates that he or she is taking part in a marriage ceremony or understands its words. He or she must understand both the nature of the marriage contract and the duties and responsibilities which normally attach to marriage.'

In 2017, 12 per cent (125) of cases of forced marriage known to the Home Office Forced Marriage Unit involved people with a learning disability. Women with a learning disability made up 47 per cent of these cases, and 53 per cent were men. Some 60 per cent of the victims recorded as having a learning disability were adults under 30 years old, 20 per cent were aged over 30 (Home Office and Foreign and Commonwealth Office, 2018). These are cases of forced marriage that are known about, but we cannot be confident about how many unknown cases there are. These can involve disabled adults of any gender or at any age. There may be some dilemmas for practitioners – the families who have arranged these marriages may not have used any coercion, but have arranged for the adult to be married in order to obtain a carer for the adult, or financial security for them, or for a culturally relevant reason, perhaps seeing marriage as a rite of passage for all, or simply because to be married is the only option for an adult. Families may argue that mental capacity has no relevance in their culture but that their actions are intended to preserve a sound future for their child. However, the experiences of an adult who has been forced to marry can include abandonment once their spouse realises their disability, financial and sexual exploitation; prosecution of the spouse who will be committing a criminal offence in having a sexual relationship with an adult who cannot consent to this; or may themselves experience violence or coercion if trying to leave the marriage. Practitioners cannot be complicit in forced marriage and must take careful and skilled action to either prevent the marriage or solve the consequences of the marriage. The Nottingham University 'My Marriage My Choice' project (Clawson, 2017) has produced some helpful practice guidelines on working with families and adults; these include a detailed guide on assessing mental capacity and advice on approaches to be taken to avoid the real risk of the adult being removed from the country.

Indicators that a forced marriage may be planned for an adult with learning disabilities can include the adult talking about marriage, jewellery or wedding clothes; they may appear happy about being married or anxious; a family member may raise concerns that a relative may be/has been forced into marriage or may inform a professional that their relative is to be married or ask the practitioner to sign a visa immigration or passport application; the adult may be removed from services or leave the country without explanation or warning.

Forced marriage is a criminal offence under the Anti-Social Behaviour Crime and Policing Act 2014. See Chapter 3 for more detail on this offence.

Female genital mutilation (FGM) is not mentioned within the Care Act statutory guidance but is important to recognise as a form of domestic abuse. FGM is a term for procedures which involve partial or total removal of the external female genitalia for non-medical reasons. FGM is usually carried out on girls between the ages of 1 and 15, but younger babies, older girls and women can be victims too. In some areas the practice is carried out just before marriage or after the birth of the first baby. The health risks to adult women who have undergone FGM are severe and include high risk of infections, damage to other organs and difficulty in urinating, multiple problems relating to both penetrative and non-penetrative sex or giving birth. Women may experience post-traumatic stress disorder, anxiety and depression. They may need further surgery to open the vagina for sex and childbirth.

There is no requirement for mandatory referral of an adult women who has had FGM to adult social services or the police. Each woman's situation must be carefully assessed at the woman's pace, and a safeguarding adult referral made for any woman who is also an adult at risk. An adult woman who has had FGM may also be an indicator that others in the family, including children, may be a risk of FGM. There is a mandatory requirement to make a child protection referral for under 18-year-olds who are at risk of, or have had, FGM.

What might indicate domestic abuse?

Indicators of domestic abuse will include all of the indicators of other harms described here. These will include unexplained injuries or implausible explanations for those injuries, sexual assault, financial difficulties, depression, anxiety and/or low self-esteem. The presence of a third party or parties who are overly intrusive in conversation, or who control whom the adult sees or speaks to should also raise concern. Coercive behaviour can include isolating the adult from sources of support, including health and social care agencies. The adult being harmed may express shame and be quick to blame themselves for any harm, particularly if the harm is being perpetrated by their (adult) child or has been going on for some years.

Remember: domestic abuse can happen to anyone, no matter their age, sexuality or gender. While women remain the largest group in all data relating to domestic abuse it is also evident that male adults at risk are also subject to domestic abuse and violence. Domestic abuse can occur in same-sex relationships and between family members, including parents and children. Only small and limited surveys of domestic abuse perpetrated against transgender people are currently available in the UK. A survey of 60 transgender people carried out in Scotland (Roche et al, 2010) found that 80 per cent of respondents had experienced some form of abuse by an ex or current partner.

Mate crime or *disability hate crime* is another useful concept to use in recognising abuse in a community setting.

Mate crime is defined as the befriending of people who are perceived to be vulnerable, for the purposes of taking advantage of, exploiting and/or abusing them. The term 'mate crime' is contentious, and the Crown Prosecution Service uses the term 'disability hate crime' (CPS, 2018a) while recognising that some disability organisations (Association for Real Change, 2013) use the term 'mate crime' as a way of raising awareness and focusing action.

Landman (2014) has argued that the definition of hate crime (see Chapter 3) has led to a perception that hate crimes are perpetrated on the street by strangers and are bullying in nature (for example name-calling, throwing objects, spitting). A range of SARs (Flynn, 2007; Spreadbury, 2018a) contradict this perception. The Crown Prosecution Service's current advice is that disability hate crime perpetrators:

are often partners, family members, friends, carers, acquaintances, or neighbours. Offending by persons with whom the disabled person is in a relationship may be complicated by emotional, physical and financial dependency and the need to believe a relationship is trusting and genuine, however dysfunctional. Where perpetrators are partners or live with the disabled person and are either members of the same family or have previously been partners, the offence of controlling or coercive behaviour may apply. (CPS, 2018a)

Some campaigners (Landman, 2014) emphasise the incidence of mate crime committed against people who have learning disabilities or autism, but the phenomenon can be observed in other groups, in particular people with mental health issues and/or addictions or simply any adult at risk who may be perceived as being vulnerable to exploitation by so-called friends. McCarthy (2017) describes how domestic abuse, hate crime and mate crime are connected, for example in 'cuckooing', a crime in which drug dealers take over an adult's home in order to use it as a base for drug dealing. The home of an adult can also be taken over by 'friends' who are homeless or wishing to hide. Control over the adult is maintained via physical and verbal threats and humiliations regarding disability or frailty.

Hate crime encompasses a range of criminal offences. If the offence can be shown to be motivated by hostility or prejudice based on the victim's disability or other characteristics, section 146 of the Criminal Justice Act 2003 imposes a general duty on criminal courts to treat any offence more seriously when sentencing.

Indicators of 'mate crime' or exploitation by friends/acquaintances, and disability hate crime include the source of harm presenting as the adult's carer or caring friend. The source of harm isolates the adult by alleging that other friends or paid carers are not trustworthy. They involve the adult in activities where alcohol or drugs are used and exert control through withholding/using alcohol or drugs and playing on any guilt or shame the adult feels. The source of harm exploits the adult, initially in minor ways which then increase in severity. These can include financial or sexual exploitation; making the adult commit minor criminal offences such as shoplifting; and using or selling the adult's medication. Control over the adult is maintained by public accusations of the adult being a paedophile or another untrue and socially despised identity, by threats and intimidation, or public and private displays of power over the adult. There can be increasingly cruel and humiliating treatment of the adult, often related to the nature of their disability: for example, blindfolding someone who is deaf or destroying mobility aids. The adult's accommodation may be taken over by the source of harm and their associates, to have somewhere to live, and/or use to take or sell drugs, hide stolen goods and encourage under-age drinking or sexual activities. Other adults at the same property may also be at risk, for example adults in sheltered housing or supported accommodation. Individuals, couples and groups can perpetrate crimes against adults, and can encourage each other by filming cruel treatment and sharing with each other or on social networking sites.

Adults can be wary of reporting crimes committed by friends, through fear of these so-called friends, or being afraid of statutory agencies, especially the police. Sin (2013) notes that some disabled people may experience regular unkind and discriminatory behaviour from others, finding such behaviour so endemic to their lives that it becomes internalised and normalised. Other adults may have such low self-esteem after experiences of institutionalisation and marginalisation through the life course that such acts of unkindness do not appear to be abusive to them, but an expected part of their lives.

Location of harm: institutional settings, including care homes and hospitals

Harm that occurs in an institution, for example a care home, hospital, day care or supported living, or harm that is caused by a member of an organisation providing a service to an adult, can be described using any of the types of abuse listed here.

When the institution or service itself is so dysfunctional that there are risks to all living in the setting or using the service, this is defined as *organisational abuse*. The statutory guidance (section 14.17) defines organisational abuse as:

> Including neglect and poor care practice within an institution or specific care setting such as a hospital or care home, for example, or in relation to care provided in one's own home. This may range from one off incidents to on-going ill-treatment. It can be through neglect or poor professional practice as a result of the structure, policies, processes and practices within an organisation.

The statutory guidance definition can confuse: is organisational abuse about poor practice, or a one-off incident involving individuals who live in a care setting, or is it about the organisation itself? The key phrase is that harm has occurred 'as a result of the structure, policies, processes and practices within an organisation'. Harm has occurred because of a feature of how the organisation is operating, not because of the action of one member of staff. The case study may help to clarify the difference.

REFLECTIVE ACTIVITY

Case study: Mr Greene

Mr Greene has been assaulted by a member of staff at Blue Skies care home. She shouted at him when he threw his meal onto the table and she rubbed his face into the food. The care home manager immediately suspended the staff member, called the police and reported the matter to adult safeguarding. The member of staff has a recently updated

Disclosure and Barring Service check, is a long-standing member of staff but has recently been exhibiting some out of character frustration with other staff, but until the incident with Mr Greene, no concerns have been reported about conduct towards the people who live at Blue Skies. Mr Greene is reported to be upset and frightened. The manager has taken measures to reassure him and is requesting a review of his support needs and an advocate to support him during the police investigation.

Reflective question
–   Is this 'organisational abuse' or physical and psychological abuse perpetrated by a person with power over Mr Greene?

Our thoughts are that the care home manager is responding appropriately to the incident and is focused on Mr Greene's current and future well-being.

If the indicators of organisational abuse were present, we might see a different scenario:

Mr Greene's mother reports that he has been assaulted by a member of staff at Blue Skies care home, the assault happened in the last week. Mr Greene says that the staff member shouted at him when he threw his meal onto the table and rubbed his face into the food. When you contact the Blue Skies manager, she confirms that this happened but said that Mr Greene did not seem unduly upset. The incident has been recorded as 'Mr Greene was challenging at mealtime yesterday and told off by X'. The staff member is long-standing and nothing like this has happened before; the staff member cannot be suspended from duty as the home is already short-staffed. The manager cannot see any purpose in investigating further and is horrified by the thought that this is viewed as an assault against Mr Greene.

Reflective question
–   What concerns do you have about how the care home manager is responding to Mr Greene being harmed?

Our thoughts are that, at best, the care home manager has minimised any impact on Mr Greene. She has not put his needs at the centre of her concerns but is preoccupied with the running of the home. We might be concerned that the home does not take a person-centred approach to the care of the adults living there.

Indicators of organisational abuse are explored in research by Hull University. Marsland and White (2012) observed six areas where early indicators of concern about the practice of organisations working with older people could be identified. This was preceded by research into early indicators of concern in organisations working with people who have learning disabilities. These areas have been considered and developed by adult safeguarding practitioners over the years and form a simple framework that can be used for a variety of purposes, including risk assessment. We will revisit this framework and how to use it in risk assessment in Chapter 6.

▶ **ESSENTIAL INFORMATION: PRACTICE GUIDANCE**

Early indicators of concern in organisations

Examples are given under each heading.

1. *Concerns about management and leadership*
   - Managers are not leading the service; they do not make decisions and do not appear to be able to change the culture or working practices.
   - The service/home is reactive to crises but has no structured plan on how to improve matters.
   - Managers appear unaware of serious problems in the service.
   - The manager has left and there are no practical interim arrangements.

2. *Concerns about staff skills, knowledge and practice*
   - Staff appear to lack the information, skills and knowledge to support the needs of the people using the service.
   - Members of staff are controlling of residents/service users.
   - Members of staff use negative or judgemental language when talking about residents.

3. *Concerns about residents' behaviours and well-being: one or more adults using the service*
   - Have lost weight or have deteriorating physical or mental health with no documented explanation.
   - Show signs of injury or harm through lack of care or attention.
   - Moods or psychological presentation have changed, including anxiety, depression, anger, fear.

4. *Concerns about the service resisting the involvement of external people and isolating individuals*
   - Available external health or support services are not considered or referred to.
   - Managers/staff do not respond to advice or guidance from practitioners and families who visit the service/are dismissive or hostile towards advice.
   - The service does not consider or make applications for Deprivation of Liberty authorisation.
   - The service is not reporting concerns or serious incidents to adult safeguarding, regulators, families, advocates or attorneys, external practitioners or agencies.

5. *Concerns about the way services are planned and delivered*
   - There is a lack of clarity about the purpose and nature of the service.
   - The service is accepting adults whose needs they appear unable to meet.
   - Adults' needs as identified in assessments, care plans or risk assessments are not being met.

6. *Concerns about the quality of basic care and the environment*
   - The service is not providing a safe or clean environment.
   - There are a lack of activities or social opportunities for residents, the service does not support a good quality of life.
   - Equipment is not being used or is used incorrectly.

Marsland and White (2012) suggest that indicators across two or three of the themed groupings should be considered significant. Our practice experience has taught us that any indicators in the first grouping, 'concerns about management and leadership', are a significant early indicator; other indicators will follow if this indicator is present.

Identification of harm: types of abuse

The types of abuse described here may occur in any setting, including the adult's own home, hospitals, care homes and the community.

Physical abuse

Physical abuse is defined in the statutory guidance as including offences against the person, for example assault, hitting, slapping, pushing, misuse of medication, restraint and inappropriate physical sanctions, including unlawfully depriving an adult of their liberty. Although the list of behaviours that constitute offences against the person looks straightforward, there are several factors to consider. The Care Act guidance does not differentiate using ideas of 'significance' or impact of harm. Using the person-centred Making Safeguarding Personal approach enables consideration of the meaning of the behaviour to the adult concerned. Is a push part of a playful interaction with another or is it part of a pattern of threats and intimidation? If the push results in no harm, but is part of a pattern of intimidation, is it physical abuse? If the playful push which the adult was enjoying results in an injury, was that abuse, or an unfortunate and one-off accident? Understanding the context of the harm helps to understand the experience of the adult.

Sexual abuse

Sexual abuse is defined in the statutory guidance (section 14.17) as including 'rape, indecent exposure, sexual harassment, inappropriate looking or touching, sexual teasing or innuendo, sexual photography, subjection to pornography or witnessing sexual acts, indecent exposure, sexual assault, sexual acts to which the adult has not consented or was pressured into consenting'.

Sexual abuse and exploitation can be perpetrated by one individual, or by an exploitative group who target individuals or a group of adults who have care and support needs; children may also be targeted as part of organised sexual exploitation. The sexual exploitation of adults with care and support needs involves exploitative situations, contexts and relationships where adults with care and support needs receive affection or inclusion or some type of 'reward', for example food, accommodation, drugs, alcohol, cigarettes, gifts or money, as a result of performing sexual activities, and/or others performing sexual activities on them. Sexual exploitation can occur through the use of technology, for example being persuaded to post sexual images or videos onto social media or being sent images by the person causing harm. In all cases those exploiting the adult have power over them by virtue of their age, gender, intellect, physical strength and/ or economic or other resources. Sexual exploitation can also be part of modern slavery and human trafficking. Any sexual relationship that develops between adults where one is in a position of trust, power or authority in relation to the other (for example support worker/social worker/therapist, nurse, doctor, other health or care worker and so on) will constitute sexual abuse and is likely to be a criminal offence.

There can be challenges for the practitioner when receiving concerns about sexual abuse. In some situations, the adult may perceive sexual exploitation as a relationship that is valued and wish to continue despite the harmful effect on them. Others may report an adult's consensual and much enjoyed sexual intimacy as harmful simply because of their own prejudices about age and sex, or the way in which the adult is expressing their sexuality. It is important to reflect on and understand your own values and prejudices and ensure that you are comfortable about discussing sex and sexuality in your everyday adult safeguarding practice.

Psychological abuse

Psychological abuse can be seen as a single type of abuse but can also occur as part of all other types of abuse. The statutory guidance (section 14.17) defines psychological abuse as constituting 'emotional abuse, threats of harm or abandonment, deprivation of contact, humiliation, blaming, controlling, intimidation, coercion, harassment, verbal abuse, cyber bullying, isolation, unreasonable and unjustified withdrawal of services or supportive networks'.

Psychological abuse involves the use of humiliation and fear, and can range in intensity from the daily coercive control exercised in the adult's own home by an intimate partner through to regular teasing of an adult with learning disabilities by a member of staff enjoying a joke at the expense of a less powerful person. The impact of psychological abuse can be damaging and long-lasting, from loss of self-esteem to depression, self-harm and suicide. Any type of abuse can contain an element of psychological abuse or be intensified by the psychological impact of abuse. For example, if an adult is physically assaulted, they will often feel intimidated, or if financially abused the adult may experience strong feelings of humiliation and shame.

Indicators of psychological abuse can be observed in three areas:

1. *Changes in the adult's behaviour*
   They may appear depressed and lack energy, be sad or anxious, particularly in the presence of the source of harm; the self-esteem of the adult changes, they express feelings of worthlessness; there may be changes in their sleeping patterns or continence. The adult harms themselves or their possessions.

2. *The adult's circumstances*
   The adult is allowed only restricted contact with the outside world. Visitors and phone calls are restricted, they might be locked in their room or in their home. There is a punitive and controlling approach to the adult's daily needs, in particular continence and personal hygiene, sometimes access to aids or equipment, or the features of life that give happiness and support identity and relationships.

3. *Observed behaviour towards the adult*
   Threats to abandon or 'put away' the adult; verbal abuse including teasing, threats and intimidation; talking about the adult as if they were a child or object; use of racist, ageist, disablist, sexist, homophobic or transphobic language. Bullying via social networking internet sites or via mobile phone communication.

Financial abuse

The statutory guidance gives more detailed guidance on situations of financial abuse than any other form of harm (sections 14.24–14.32). Financial abuse can be fairly simple to identify but removing the risk of further abuse or mitigating its impact can be complex. In 2017/18, 66 per cent of adults at risk who were the subject of a section 42 enquiry into alleged financial abuse were being abused by someone they knew – a family member, friend or neighbour (NHS Digital, 2018). The dynamics of these relationships can make it difficult for the adult themselves to decide on criminal prosecution, even when large amounts of money have been stolen from them. There are many different forms of financial abuse, and good partnership working with banks, the police, the Department for Work and Pensions (DWP), Trading Standards and the Office of the Public Guardian (OPG) is key but agreed pathways do not always exist. The statutory guidance (section 14.24) reminds us that: 'Financial recorded abuse can occur in isolation, but as research has shown, where there are other forms of abuse, there is likely to be financial abuse occurring. Although this is not always the case, everyone should also be aware of this possibility.'

Financial abuse can take a number of forms:

1. Theft

Money or property taken from a person without their knowledge, and/or without their consent. This can be prosecuted under the Theft Act 1968.

2. Fraud

The act of gaining a dishonest advantage, often financial, over another person. Fraud offences can be prosecuted using the Fraud Act 2006. The Crown Prosecution Service (CPS, 2018b) reports that it is now the most commonly experienced crime in England and Wales, with an estimated 3.4 million incidents in the year ending March 2017. More than half of these were cyber-related. The incidence of these crimes does not show much variation across age groups or for particularly vulnerable groups. The number of fraud and forgery cases dealt with by the CPS has risen by almost a third since 2011. Types of fraud include:

- **Rogue traders:** being charged over the acceptable rate for household repairs, which may not exist or be over-exaggerated.
- **Online fraud:** any type of fraud committed using the internet. Examples may include fraudulent sales of goods, romance scams, or any other type of fraud facilitated online.
- **Investment fraud:** can occur online but also involves cold calls, emails or direct approaches encouraging investment in something which is either worthless or does not exist.
- **Identity fraud:** bank accounts or shopping accounts are opened in the name of the adult at risk.
- **Fraud by abuse of position:** where a person abuses a position of responsibility in which they are expected to safeguard the financial interests of another person or organisation.

3. Coercion regarding wills and property

Coercion is a strong word which implies intimidation. Although this can occur, a frequent presentation is one of strong persuasion or pressure, using emotional connections and the portrayal of oneself as in need. Behaviours include being continually asked for loans which are not repaid, being asked to sign over property or give a large sum of money as a gift. Prosecution of these offences is difficult; the adult has given over money and property willingly and charges of theft and fraud may be hard to prove.

The impact of financial abuse on the well-being of an adult at risk can be profound. Being unable to afford food, heating or rent damages physical health while the emotional impact can profoundly affect the adult's mental health. Davison et al (2015) summarise research on the emotional impacts on older people: 'These can include feelings of betrayal, feelings of distress, especially if a house or other assets need to be sold, embarrassment, loss of self-esteem and confidence in one's own judgement, denial, fear, self-blame, social isolation, and the loss of confidence to live independently' (p 7).

Neglect

While the types of harm already listed are about what is done to another person, *neglect and acts of omission* are about what should have been done but was not. Adults who are neglected can be those most dependent on others to meet their care and support needs. Neglect was the most common type of harm in section 42 enquiries concluded during 2017/18, comprising 32 per cent of all enquiries undertaken (NHS Digital, 2018). Neglect can mean failing to ensure the adult has enough to eat and drink, is warm or comfortable and has the correct medical support for any physical needs. The impact of neglect is damaging to the well-being of all adults at risk. Neglect of basic needs can be fatal to those who are frail. Heath and Phair explain frailty as:

> a weakened state of being in which a person's reserve capacity is reduced to an extent whereby health, functioning and well-being are compromised. In the precursor stage a range of indicators can identify people who are vulnerable to frailty. Advanced frailty threatens life. Complications of frailty occur when care delivered fails to compensate for the effect of frailty and other medical conditions on the person's physical, psychological or spiritual health, resulting in harm to the person. Complications are mostly avoidable. (2009, p 126)

Heath and Phair (2011) point out the risk to frail people of neglect of their basic needs as 'immobility, insufficient fluid intake or untreated pain, even within a short time span, are potentially sufficient to trigger the domino effect resulting in death' (p 51).

Examples of the neglect of physical care and support needs include not treating pressure areas, not providing the correct diet for an adult who has diabetes, and leaving an adult in soiled clothing. Other indicators include ignoring call bells, or not arranging dental or medical care. Neglect of emotional and social care and support needs creates despondency and despair. Remember that harm can sometimes be unintentional, for example denial of an adult's emotional and social needs can be based on a mistaken idea that people who are cognitively impaired do not experience bereavement, trauma or loss in the same way as others. This is profoundly untrue but can result in no emotional support being given during times of grief or fear.

The inclusion in the Care Act 2014 of *self-neglect*, or harm which the individual's behaviour has created, was welcomed by some with relief as responses to people who were self-neglecting were inconsistent, lacking a framework or confident partnership working between agencies. The definition of self-neglect within the initial Care Act statutory guidance was broad and led to confusion about when to refer and when section 42 enquiries were needed; for example, self-neglect 'covers a wide range of behaviour neglecting to care for one's personal hygiene, health or surroundings and includes behaviour such as hoarding' (statutory guidance, 14.17). To try to resolve the confusion an additional sentence was added to subsequent versions of the statutory guidance:

> It should be noted that self-neglect may not prompt a section 42 enquiry. An assessment should be made on a case by case basis. A decision on whether a response is required under safeguarding will depend on the adult's ability to protect themselves by controlling their own behaviour. There may come a point when they are no longer able to do this, without external support. (Statutory guidance, 14.17)

The guidance lacks any meaningful definition of either self-neglect or the rationale for involvement. The use of the phrase 'adult's ability to protect themselves by controlling their own behaviour' implies that a value judgement needs to be made: is the person choosing freely to live like this? Braye et al offer a more detailed picture of the impact of severe self-neglect, gleaned from research undertaken with practitioners working with people who are neglecting their own well-being:

> There is no clear point at which lifestyle patterns become 'self-neglect', and the term can apply to a wide range of behaviour. At one end of the spectrum, the stories featured individuals who sometimes showed an almost total lack of attention to personal hygiene, by not washing or bathing, not changing clothes and bedding, not cutting hair or nails, or incontinence and soiling. There might be no food in the adult's home and little evidence that they were eating, or the food they consumed might be mouldy, rotten or composed of leftover scraps. Combined, these factors often led to malnutrition, skin breakdown and pressure

sores and dehydration, requiring hospital admission, sometimes on a repeated basis. Neglect of their own health care often made things worse. A number of people also lived in extremely dirty and sometimes infested conditions, which had often built up over many years, during which cleaning had not taken place. (2015, p 6)

Hoarding of found objects, consumer goods, animals or, in extreme situations, bodily waste, may occur in addition to self-neglect. Equally people may also live in very sparse surroundings, with little or no possessions.

Discriminatory abuse

The definition of discriminatory abuse in the statutory guidance is short, such abuse includes 'forms of harassment, slurs or similar treatment because of race, gender and gender identity, age, disability, sexual orientation, religion' (section 14.17).

As we explored in Chapter 2, discriminatory abuse is prevalent throughout the lives of adults at risk of abuse and neglect. The indicators of discriminatory abuse may take the form of any of those listed under any of the other categories of abuse. The difference lies in that the abuse is motivated by discriminatory attitudes, feelings or behaviour towards an individual. The adult may change their behaviour and become withdrawn and isolated, they are fearful of going out or of certain places. The adult may be refused access to services or be excluded inappropriately or, because of past experience of discrimination, resist or refuse to use the services that are required to meet assessed needs. From our experience, safeguarding enquiries are often disinclined to engage with the discriminatory elements of abuse, preferring to deal with concrete examples of abusive behaviour rather than the discrimination that the adult at risk is experiencing. It is important to engage with the adult's experience of discrimination and explore the impact of current and historical discrimination on their sense of identity and well-being.

Modern slavery

The statutory guidance includes modern slavery as a type of harm that adults at risk may experience. Kidd and Manthorpe (2017) cite examples of people with learning disabilities being used in domestic servitude and examples of homeless people used in forced labour. Craig and Clay (2017) describe the impact modern slavery has had on the people caught up in it, including physical injuries or the development of addictions as a coping strategy. They highlight the possibilities of carers being victims of domestic servitude, either bought into the family home to care for free or working in care homes.

Children and adults from vulnerable groups may be exploited by organised drug groups who use them in the supply of drugs, the movement of cash proceeds

(Home Office, 2018) and who use their homes to store and supply drugs. The former practice is often known as 'County Lines' and the latter practice as 'cuckooing'. Both are forms of modern slavery. The National Crime Agency (2017) reports that 74 per cent of 100 UK police forces noted exploitation of vulnerable people within the modern slavery definition; 37 per cent of these forces reported exploitation of people with mental health issues and 12 per cent exploitation of people with physical health issues. Modern slavery offences can be addressed under various pieces of legislation, including the Sexual Offences Act 2003. The Modern Slavery Act 2015 consolidated and updated criminal legislation on human trafficking, slavery, forced labour, cannabis farming, organ harvesting, forced begging and domestic servitude. Public authorities, including local and health authorities, have a duty to cooperate with the Independent Anti-Slavery Commissioner.

Terrorist activity

Prevent is the government policy designed to prevent people being drawn into terrorist activity. The statutory guidance does not reference the Prevent duty contained in the Counter-Terrorism and Security Act 2015, but many SABs include the Prevent duty in their overarching policies and procedures. The Act requires specified authorities, including local authorities, to have 'due regard to the need to prevent people from being drawn into terrorism' (S26(1)). Other authorities include educational provisions, the health sector, police and prisons. Most SABs will have policies that include adults at risk and exploitation into terrorism. The Prevent Strategy (Home Office, 2011) is the governmental initiative that aims to work with vulnerable individuals who may be at risk of being exploited by radical groups and/or being drawn into terror related activity.

Indicators that an individual may be being groomed into extremism can be:

- they may possess or search for extremist literature online;
- they may express feelings of anger, grievance, injustice;
- using language that supports 'us and them' thinking;
- they have a new group of friends who have an extremist ideology;
- people becoming withdrawn and stopping participating in their usual activities;
- they may go missing from care, home or school setting.

▶ KEY MESSAGES

- **Shared definitions support multi-agency working, but risk simplifying complex and unique situations.**

- **Exploring the adult's situation with them or those close to them can help us decide whether the statutory duty to enquire has been met.**

- Harm may be unintentional – the emphasis of adult safeguarding must be on the impact of the harm on the adult and what can be done to resolve or reduce risk in the situation.

KNOWLEDGE REVIEW

- WHAT does 'exploitation' mean in adult safeguarding?

- WHAT are the two useful concepts to help you understand the dynamics of harm in domestic or community settings?

- HOW does organisational abuse differ from one-off incidents of harm or neglect in an institution?

FURTHER READING

- There are plenty of good practice guides to help you extend your knowledge and skills in working in particular situations of harm. Do develop your own library. Here are some resources to start you off. Do always check who you can ask for advice in your organisation and with contacts in your local safeguarding adults team. Some situations can be unusual but there may be a practitioner who has developed their practice in a particular area, for example forced marriage. The local authority adult safeguarding team or similar may be able to point you in the right direction.

  - A wealth of resources on coercive control can be found at Research in Practice for Adults (RiPfA) at: https://coercivecontrol.ripfa.org.uk/.

  - SafeLives have a range of resources to use with people experiencing domestic abuse who may also have care and support needs such as: www.safelives.org.uk/knowledge-hub/spotlights/spotlight-2-disabled-people-and-domestic-abuse.

  - A useful toolkit on forced marriage by Clawson is available at: www.nottingham.ac.uk/research/groups/mymarriagemychoice/documents/toolkit.pdf.

  - There are a number of toolkits to help with financial abuse work on the Bournemouth University website. Start with Brown and Lee's (2017) 'Financial Scamming and Fraud' which is available at: https://ncpp.co.uk/publications/financial-scamming-and-fraud/.

Part 2
Good adult safeguarding practice

6

Relationships, values and ethics

Chapter aim

Adult safeguarding practice demands that you are able to build a working relationship with an adult at risk and those who are close to them including, at times, the person who has caused harm. In this chapter we outline the competencies that practitioners need to build relationships and work with confidence in adult safeguarding. We will explore the ethical and communication challenges of working with people experiencing harm, abuse and discrimination as well as working alongside other professionals.

This chapter includes:

- definitions and descriptions of relationship-based adult safeguarding;

- what meaningful professional relationships have in common;

- the importance of understanding power and oppression through the life course;

- ideas for extending relationship-building skills;

- building relationships with colleagues from other agencies;

- understanding your own values and how these interact with professional ethics.

Definitions and descriptions of relationship-based adult safeguarding

Contemporary approaches in adult safeguarding, for example Making Safeguarding Personal, are predicated on the practitioner being able to make a relationship with the adult and the people and agencies around them. Guidance may refer to person–centred procedures or practice, but these are not to be confused with the person–centred approaches advocated by theorists such as Carl Rogers (1951) which are based on the notion of self-determination and the value of the relationship in itself in effecting change. While the relationship in itself between the practitioner and adult may well enable the adult to make changes in their lives, our focus is also on how building a relationship will support the adult to be involved in their own protection, by exploring their situation, identifying potential outcomes and recovering from harm.

You may need to build a relationship quickly in a crisis situation, for example during a mental health crisis or when an adult needs to leave a dangerous situation. These relationships need to be effective in the short term but may not be sustained beyond the initial crisis. Relationships can take longer to develop with people who have experienced abuse over a long period, or who are self-neglecting, or for whatever reason find it hard to trust others. These relationships can sustain the adult through the ups and downs of change. Whether short- or long-lived, helpful relationships have a number of important elements in common. These elements may be present after one meeting or may take several meetings to build up.

> ▶ **ESSENTIAL INFORMATION: PRACTICE GUIDANCE**
>
> Important elements of relationships to think about when planning to meet a person:
>
> 1. **Preparation:** what do I need to know before I contact or meet this person? Are there records of previous contacts, and/or anything the referrer says I should note? If meeting the person, is the meeting place safe for them, and me, is it accessible, comfortable? When is the best time of day to meet with them?
> 2. **Engagement:** how will I communicate with the person? Do I need any help to do this? How will I explain clearly and in plain language who I am and why I am contacting or meeting with them? How will I encourage the person to talk with me, to begin to trust me and engage with the possibility of change?
> 3. **Listening:** what is the person's perspective? What is their story about the situation they are in? What are they afraid or worried about? What are their hopes? Listening and responding continues throughout the relationship.
> 4. **Collaboration:** sharing mutual understanding of problems and options. What has the person tried previously, what worked and didn't, what is an acceptable option and what is not?
> 5. **Working together:** clarity about what needs to happen and what can happen now, who will do this? How will we know what has helped?
> 6. **Creating a shared plan:** by planning the next steps together with clarity about who does what and when.

Being able to communicate with an adult is fundamental to being able to create a relationship with them. Practitioners often struggle to convey the reason for contact without using bewildering professional jargon. For example, how do you describe adult safeguarding? Do you use this term or another such as safeguarding adults or adult protection? Do you try to explain what they mean in everyday language?

REFLECTIVE ACTIVITY

"I have received a concern regarding financial abuse in which your son was named as the alleged source of harm. I am from the Blankshire adult safeguarding team. Following information gathering, we have determined that we have a duty to undertake a section 42 enquiry and I need to meet with you to discuss your desired outcomes."

–   Try to rephrase this sentence in everyday English.
–   Think about the jargon you use – is there anything you think it important to include and explain?

People cannot be involved in their own safeguarding if they cannot understand what we are saying or doing. Only using professional language or jargon is alienating and will create unhelpful barriers between you, the adult and the people supporting them. It can be empowering at times for people to understand what jargon is used so they can connect with and explain the systems they are involved with – jargon should only be used when explained and contextualised.

When a person has been harmed, or has been harming others, they may feel at their lowest ebb, and have low self-esteem and energy. It is important to convey respect in the way you communicate with people whose self-esteem is low, use respectful language and observe their pace of communication. Don't rush because you are busy. If you need help to communicate with a person, do plan ahead where you can. Is there someone who already knows the adult who can support you to understand what they are saying? How can you quickly access translation services? Is it possible for a colleague from speech and language therapy to attend or offer guidance to you on how to communicate with a person with specific communication needs?

What meaningful professional relationships have in common

Ingram (2013, p 994) has collated over 40 years of social work research to identify the practitioner behaviours that adults who are experienced in working with social workers value:

- practitioners who understand and value their perspectives and views and who are good listeners;
- having personal uniqueness valued;
- involvement that is purposeful and supportive;
- being asked to define problems and goals – leading to a mutual understanding;
- practitioners who adopt a friendly approach, showing warmth, empathy and genuineness; and
- practitioners who demonstrate respect, honesty and reliability.

Adults identify empathy, or the ability to be sensitively aware of another's perspective, as a valued skill in the practitioners who work with them. How can you continue to develop empathy for another's experiences, feelings and situation?

▶ **ESSENTIAL INFORMATION: PRACTICE GUIDANCE**

How to develop and nurture empathy

- Be curious – ask how the person felt and thought, hear the whole story – "What happened next?"
- Listen – without interruption or preconceptions. Allow yourself to absorb the person's experiences, feelings, values and hopes; resist any thoughts of interrupting with problem-solving ideas. This can be hard but is the way to understand the other's perspective without putting your own interpretation onto their lives.
- Try to see things from the perspective of the other person – put yourself in their shoes and focus on how that feels.
- People may be able to talk about their feelings by telling stories about their lives.
- Listening with empathy and curiosity helps to build trust, while sharing the experiences of the past is important in understanding the meaning of harm and risk to the person.
- It is important to understand the dynamics of harm in specific situations, and how a person feels about these, in order to explore the sometimes conflicting or unspeakable emotions experienced which may prevent the person or their family moving forward.

Some of the more commonly encountered emotional responses to being harmed, or to harming others, may be found in the Reflective Activity.

REFLECTIVE ACTIVITY

Consider how your approach will take account of the person's emotional response in these case studies:

Shame – a feeling caused by the person's belief that they are, or that others think they are, inferior or unworthy of affection and respect because of their thoughts, actions, lifestyle or past experiences.

- **Mrs Gill** did not tell anyone about her daughter stealing from her. She thought that if people knew they would think she was a bad mother. She must have been a bad mother to be in this position.
- **Amanda Gill** hated herself. She could not think about how much money she had taken from her mother over the last year. She tried to keep up being a caring daughter – she did love her mum, but she knew that if anyone found out what she had done she would be seen as the nasty woman she really was.

Fear – a feeling of distress, apprehension or alarm caused by impending danger or pain, or a belief that danger or pain is likely.

- **Mr Roberts** grew up in a hospital for children with learning disabilities. He was very afraid at night when the lights were put out and no staff were around. Another child would bully him, and sometimes others joined in. One of the staff nurses on duty would make fun of him being afraid of these boys. These days Mr Roberts is still afraid at night. He now lives in a residential home and one of the night staff called him a "cowardy custard" on one occasion, apologising afterwards. He is now terrified of going to bed, the home manager is unsure what to do or why Mr Roberts is suddenly so afraid.
- **Ms Joliffe** cares for her father. She lives with him and, since her mother died, the pair have been close companions. She has recently had to acknowledge that her father is dying; his doctor says that his cancer is now terminal. Ms Joliffe feels terrified – separated from her father, she will be lost. The fear feels overwhelming. She has stopped any professional coming into the house and hopes that if she continues to watch him carefully, he may not leave her.

Guilt – while shame is about how you think you may appear to others, guilt is about recognising that your thoughts or actions have violated your personal moral code.

- **Ms Rose** was sexually assaulted by another resident in the supported living house she lives in. She hasn't told anyone about this as she allowed him into her room, against the agreed rule of the house that separates men and women into different corridors of flats. She also let him bring alcohol into the flat, although she doesn't drink and knows what alcohol can do. She feels that she only has herself to blame for what happened.

- **Nurse James** gave Mr Brown the wrong tablets. This happened because he was the only nurse on shift and was completely overwhelmed by all the events that day. He feels terrible, he has started to worry that he will be struck off or something bad will happen to him. He is not going to say anything about what happened.

Sadness – a feeling of disadvantage, loss, despair, grief, helplessness, sorrow. At its most severe, sadness will manifest as depression.

- **Mr Smith** is neglecting himself to a dangerous extent. He might eat once a day and he does not wash or change his clothes. He has stopped taking his medication. When his father died, he felt that his heart stopped working and that he cannot keep going any more.

- **Mrs Jones** didn't mean to scold her disabled sister. Some days she just doesn't seem to be able to think straight. Since her husband died it's hard to get out of bed in the morning and she wonders what's the point in keeping going. No one seems to care about her life and nothing will ever change.

Anger – a hostile response to perceived provocation, hurt or threat. Anger can occur when a person feels their personal boundaries are being violated. Some people have a learned tendency to react to anger through retaliation as a way of coping. Others use anger as a protective mechanism over sadness, fear or pain.

- **Mrs Peters** gets angry and hits out at staff when they are giving her personal care. Staff are now avoiding taking care of her needs and she is being neglected.

- **Mr Michaels** hit his wife today. It's the first time in their 50-year marriage that he has ever done this. The district nurse says he is experiencing 'carer stress' but he doesn't think it's that. It's more that she isn't his wife anymore, just some woman he looks after. He feels so angry about it all.

Shame is a particularly powerful emotion that impacts on the individual, their family networks and community. Frost (2016) details some of the individual responses to being shamed which include feelings of incompetence, inferiority, powerlessness and self-harm. People can also numb their feelings with alcohol or drugs, or take dangerous risks with life in response to the need to deny, hide or escape. The person may become submissive or compliant, or angry and violent.

Individuals may also belong to a social group that is labelled as inferior in some way, for example people receiving benefits being called 'scroungers'. Being labelled in this way leads to an internalised feeling of being ashamed. People who feel shame are less likely to ask for help. For example, older women experience a range of barriers to identifying and reporting domestic abuse and can struggle with a sense of shame in tolerating abuse which may have lasted for over 40 years (SafeLives, 2016c). Shame can cause identity damage, which can be mitigated through being listened to and valued within a relationship of trust and respect. The process of telling your story and being accepted for who you are can begin to reduce the power of shame.

The importance of understanding power and oppression through the life course

How much power or agency do people have in the circumstances they are living in? This consideration enables us to understand how people view their situation and the options for improving their well-being. We consider oppression and anti-oppressive practice in Chapter 2. Stories of oppression and how this has affected an adult's self-esteem and identity need to be understood as part of the process of relationship making. An adult may have spent their life as a member of a marginalised group and developed mechanisms for living well with this status. All this may change if they are now in a situation of dependency on the goodwill of others.

REFLECTIVE ACTIVITY

Case study: Mr Ray

Mr Ray is 85 years old. In his early youth expressing his love for other men was illegal and in his middle years many of his friends died in the UK AIDS crisis. Throughout much of his life he has actively campaigned against prejudice and violence, for better healthcare and for an open and respectful society. His husband visits him in the care home he now lives in, but they have been asked not to hold hands or kiss in public areas, "or the other old people might be offended". Mr Ray is devastated, saying

"I know how to tackle people like these, but I am just too ill to stand up for myself and others yet again."

Reflective question
— How can you work with Mr Ray to put a stop to this abuse?

Our thinking is that you should consider his wisdom and experiences as a campaigner, what expertise he could teach you about standing up to prejudice and use these to inform your anti-oppressive safeguarding practice and how you will tackle this situation.

Others may have lived most of their lives in circumstances where other people have power over them. This may mean that people are prevented from expressing their identity and feelings because those caring for them have prejudices against certain groups or behaviours.

Family relationships may also change as previous coping strategies are no longer possible. The impact of disability on a person can mean the end of previous coping strategies:

'When he got angry and shouted at me, I used to go round to my friend, but now the Parkinson's is so bad I can't get out by myself so I have to put up with it.'

Or those who were once powerful are now diminished, causing ambivalence in those caring for them:

'I used to watch my dad beat my mum up. He terrified me as a child and being near him still makes me feel afraid. He can't move or speak since the stroke. I have power over him now, and I don't let him mess me about, he has to watch himself with me.'

By listening to their experience of power and oppression you can begin to understand the person's history, their triumphs and sadness, what strengths they had in the past and how these might be drawn on in the present, and what support they may need to make changes in their lives.

Ideas for extending relationship-building skills

Relationship-building adult safeguarding practice skills can be extended with some of the suggestions in this section. Training in using these approaches is recommended.

Using tools from systems thinking

Every individual is part of a wider system. Even the most isolated of us have connections in the present to others in our community, including neighbours and professional services. We may also have strong connections to past systems, which can have relevance to understanding our current dilemmas. The systems around us can act as facilitators or blocks to making change. It is important to understand who is part of an adult's system when understanding current and historical relationships, assessing risk of recurrence of harm, or drawing up a safeguarding plan together.

You can use a *genogram* to explore and understand family connections. Genograms look like a family tree but have many functions. As the genogram is drawn you can talk about the people within it, their connections to the adult, and the adult's feelings about them. Drawing genograms together can help people talk about historical abuse within a family, as well as the sources of strength available to them. There are particular symbols used within genograms. There is a link to further information on how to compose a genogram at the end of this chapter. You don't need special software, just a big piece of paper, a pen and time with the adult or their family.

An *ecomap* can be used to define who else is relevant in the system around the adult. These are useful in exploring meanings, experiences and options to address the current situation. Ecomaps depict the adult's relationships and the positive and negative factors in their life. The adult is represented by a large circle in the middle of the chart. Smaller circles around the large circle represent different relationships – friendships, services, groups – and other relevant factors in the adult's life.

These smaller circles are connected to the adult's circle by different types of line. The line provides information about the nature of the relationship. Positive and consistent relationships are identified with a double line, a dashed line shows the relationship is distant. A wavy line can indicate a stressful connection. Line thickness can also be used to show the intensity of the relationship. Arrows at the ends of the lines show which way the influence goes. If a relationship is mutually positive and strong, the line has arrows on both ends. If the influence flows only one way, the arrow is on one end; there is a link to further information on how to compose an ecomap at the end of this chapter.

As a relationship-building exercise, using these tools provides opportunity for practitioners, the adult and their family to discuss and reflect on the current situation. Systems tools are also helpful in risk assessment – who can help, who might hinder – and in formulating a safeguarding plan that may utilise the people and resources the adult has in their lives.

Motivational interviewing

Motivational interviewing is a person-centred approach that supports and guides adults to explore and resolve the ambivalence they feel about making changes in their lives.

Prochaska and DiClemente (1982) developed the motivational interviewing approach while working in addiction services. Practitioners are now using the principles of motivational interviewing across many fields. You may be keen to problem solve and suggest changes in others' lives, but this tendency will reduce the chance of people making changes. People are often ambivalent about change; they may not believe change is possible or are fearful of the consequences. The practitioner trained in motivational interviewing accepts that ambivalence is to be expected, and that the desire to make change comes and goes but that we can influence this by paying attention to 'readiness' for change. Motivational interviewing is underpinned by the values of collaborative partnership with acceptance of the adult, their expertise and goals, while acknowledging their absolute worth and autonomy to make their own decisions. This approach is valuable when working with people who are self-neglecting as well as other adult safeguarding scenarios, for example domestic abuse.

Adult attachment theories

Adult attachment theory explains how attachment styles developed in childhood manifest themselves in adulthood and will help in understanding the relationships between people, their responses to harm and their perception of options available.

Attachment styles and the behaviours these generate are described as:

- **balanced:** a positive view of self and others – a 'secure' attachment style;
- **preoccupied:** a negative view of self and a positive view of others; anxiety over abandonment;
- **dismissing:** a positive view of self and a negative view of others; discomfort with closeness;
- **fearful:** negative views of self and others coincide. Both anxiety over abandonment and discomfort with closeness are evident. (Adapted from Shemmings, 2000)

The adult's attachment system is activated when they are, or perceive themselves to be, under threat or in distress. Loss, from a partner or parent changing role or the anticipation of separation through death or disability, activates the adult's attachment style. Shemmings (2000) has explored adult attachment theory in relation to violence in later life, and how attachment styles may influence all relationships that adults make with each other. The attachment styles of older people and their intimates can create barriers and conflicts when changes occur;

for example, a person with a 'fearful' attachment style may behave in angry, anxious and 'needy' ways when they feel the older person is abandoning them through illness, residential care or death. At best, this results in difficulty in resolving problems, at worst, in abuse.

Building relationships with colleagues from other agencies

Relationship-building skills are also vital in creating and maintaining working relationships with colleagues from other agencies or teams, whether these are temporary or part of a regular working partnership. The values of respect and valuing each other, communicating clearly and taking time to listen to the concerns, challenges and successes of a partner practitioner are invaluable starting places.

Adult safeguarding work is a cause of anxiety for practitioners in all agencies who work with adults at risk. Practitioners are concerned to do the right thing, and worried about the consequences should they miss a warning sign. One voluntary sector worker says that:

> 'We spend the majority of the staff meeting debating whether this is an adult safeguarding concern and if we should refer on.'

Time pressures can reduce opportunities to talk with other practitioners in partner agencies. In order to control workflows, some agencies may use overly bureaucratic approaches to communication, for example asking colleagues to fill in a form and await contact. Practitioners can become resentful and dismissive if one agency is perceived as offloading work, feeling that an agency 'refers everything and then doesn't want to know'.

Adult safeguarding approaches are reliant on the ability of multi-agency partners to work together to enable the adult concerned to get the best possible outcome. All agencies are experiencing the pressures of an increasing volume of work against diminishing resources, so how can you create partnerships around an adult at risk that are effective and efficient in time and resources?

▶ ESSENTIAL INFORMATION: PRACTICE GUIDANCE

Top tips for building positive relationships with colleagues in other agencies

- **Make sure you clearly understand the other agency's role, responsibilities and powers.**
  For example, a practitioner may record feeling stuck with a case of financial abuse and record 'the police won't do anything', meaning that the police

are not bringing a prosecution against the source of harm. However, an understanding of the police role and powers may result in a fuller picture of the situation: "The police spoke with Mrs Green who did not wish to press charges but has said that she will ring 101 if the man returns. A PCSO will look in on her next week and report back any concerns."

The second recording reflects an understanding of the police position and the details of a plan which Mrs Green and the practitioner can work with.

- **Be clear with other agencies about your role, responsibility and powers.**
  Other agencies can also be mistaken in what the role of an adult safeguarding practitioner involves. Be clear in your own mind and make sure you can clearly communicate your role, responsibility and what powers you do and do not have.

- **Understand and appreciate the invaluable skills and knowledge of colleagues from other agencies.**
  Acknowledge the assistance of other colleagues.

- **Reflect on the pressures other agencies are experiencing, find out about the working lives of staff in other agencies.**
  Use empathy. How would you feel in their position?

- **Discover the best way of communicating.**
  You will have your preferred method of communicating, but how does this work for colleagues in other agencies? Is there any point in emailing a practitioner who is focused on clinical work in the community and never opens their email? Do they have a mobile where you can leave a message? If a vital practitioner is currently on night shift, contact them when their shift starts. The inconvenience of having a ten-minute conversation in your non-work time will be outweighed by resolving an issue which would otherwise be protracted by a lack of appreciation of others' work patterns.

- **Understand the partner organisation's culture and values. What is most important to them?**
  Patient safety? Public protection? What do they worry about? What do they pride themselves on doing well?

- **Express appreciation and always get back to colleagues who refer concerns or ask for advice.**

Understanding your own values and how these interact with professional ethics

Most safeguarding practitioners work to professional codes of ethics, standards or codes of conduct, whether they are police officers (College of Policing, 2014), nurses (Nursing and Midwifery Council, 2015), social workers (BASW, 2014) or any registered health or social care professional, including social workers in England (at the time of writing), occupational therapists, physiotherapists and so on (HCPC, 2016). Ethical codes are moral codes of conduct or statements of behaviours that are considered professionally correct. Any judgement made of whether a practitioner's behaviour is acceptable or unacceptable will be based on the relevant code of ethics. Ethical codes will contain statements about professional values and guiding principles. Values describe what is important to a profession, an organisation or an individual.

▶ **ESSENTIAL INFORMATION: PRACTICE GUIDANCE**

Codes of professional ethics and conduct

These excerpts are about similar areas but are not all exactly the same: they express each profession's principles and values, explaining how individual practitioners will behave according to the ethical standards of their profession. They are taken from codes of conduct used in England. Other professional standards with similar emphasis apply for social workers in Wales, Scotland and Northern Ireland.

Police
Code of ethics: Standard 3 of professional behaviour: equality and diversity (College of Policing, 2014, p 7)

> I will act with fairness and impartiality. I will not discriminate unlawfully or unfairly.

According to this standard you must:

- uphold the law regarding human rights and equality
- treat all people fairly and with respect
- treat people impartially.

Nurses

The code: Statement 1 – prioritise people: treat people as individuals and uphold their dignity (Nursing and Midwifery Council, 2015, pp 6–7)

To achieve this, you must:

- treat people with kindness, respect and compassion
- make sure you deliver the fundamentals of care effectively
- avoid making assumptions and recognise diversity and individual choice
- make sure that any treatment, assistance or care for which you are responsible is delivered without undue delay, and
- respect and uphold people's human rights.

Social workers

Code of ethics: Human rights principle 1: upholding and promoting human dignity and well-being (BASW, 2014, section 2.1)

Social workers should respect, uphold and defend each person's physical, psychological, emotional and spiritual integrity and well-being. They should work towards promoting the best interests of individuals and groups in society and the avoidance of harm.

Health and Care Professions Council registrants

Standard 1: Promote and protect the interests of service users and carers: challenge discrimination (HCPC, 2016, section 1.5)

- You must not discriminate against service users, carers or colleagues by allowing your personal views to affect your professional relationships or the care, treatment or other services that you provide.
- You must challenge colleagues if you think that they have discriminated against, or are discriminating against, service users, carers and colleagues.

Ethical dilemmas occur for many reasons. Dilemmas can relate to a lack of alignment between professional ethical frameworks and values, organisational policies and your personal values. Personal values contain the guiding principles used throughout life. They guide the way we live our lives and the personal decisions we make. Personal values are derived from a variety of sources, our family, life experience, education, religion, political group, peer group or the culture of the society we live in all influence us and make us unique. You are also influenced by your professional values and must be guided by these when working. However, it is not always easy to align personal and professional values.

REFLECTIVE ACTIVITY

Case study: Mr Short

Mr Short is 83 years old, very ill and frail. He is currently on Ward 20 in the local general hospital. It is hoped he will be able to go home for his last days. Your team has received an adult safeguarding concern. The ward manager reports that Mr Short's daughter assaulted him yesterday, while his other daughter was verbally abusive to him. Security were called and the police will visit Mr Short later today to ask if he wants to discuss the matter. On further enquiry you discover that Mr Short sexually abused both daughters for many years when they were children, but neither daughter had really discussed this until now. They feel angry and outraged that their father had brought such pain to both of them. Mr Short's partner would like him to die at home, but ward staff are concerned that this may be risky for him as his daughters are now threatening his safety.

You have worked with the survivors of sexual abuse for years and have a close friend who was raped by her uncle and is still traumatised. You have thought of the men who perpetuate such crimes as less than human and not worthy of your respect. You do not wish to spend any of your energy on a man who has sexually abused his children. The BASW social work code of ethics tells you that you must 'respect, uphold and defend each person's physical, psychological, emotional and spiritual integrity and well-being. You must work towards promoting the best interests of individuals and groups in society and the avoidance of harm.' You cannot treat Mr Short as if he were exempt from this principle.

Reflective question

–   What will you do?

Our thoughts are that we have encountered similar dilemmas and are sure you have too. Adults at risk have many life experiences and not all people have made choices in their lives that we agree with. If an aspect of working with an adult is challenging to your personal values then it is very important to seek support, either through formal supervision or mentoring to ensure that your practice meets ethical professional standards and that you are not discriminatory in your decisions and actions.

Being aware of your own values, and how these have developed, is an important exercise to undertake early in any professional career. It is also important to keep reflecting on these as your life and work experience develops.

- How do your personal values affect your approach to practice?
- What biases do you have?
- How might those biases affect your decision making?

REFLECTIVE ACTIVITY

Identifying my personal values

Reflect on the following questions:

- What are my values?
- What do I think is right or wrong?
- Fair or unfair?
- What is important or valuable to me in life?

To guide you further you might want to think about the following areas:

- Life: what do I think is a life worth living?
- Gender: what do I think is acceptable and unacceptable behaviour between men, women and others?
- Abuse: what do I think are the root causes of the abuse of certain groups in my society?
- Family: how important is family to me? Are there behaviours that would cause me to cut off contact with my family?

There may be other areas that occur to you in the course of your work, for example your values about your culture, religion or social justice. It is important to make time to reflect on your own values – write them down or discuss them with a peer.

Where did these values come from?

- How did you formulate these values? From your cultural background? Your family or friendship group? From your life experience? From a social, political or religious group?
- It is interesting to reflect on your values throughout your career. You may keep some strong core personal values but increasingly identify with the values of your profession.

How might my personal values affect my professional judgement?

Consider each of the personal values you have identified: how might they emerge during your work with others, what impact could they have on your attitude or on the decisions you make? Write down what the consequences may be.

For example, you may find it so intolerable that an adult child exploits their parent that you do not explore with the adult whether they want the child who has harmed them to remain in their life. Conversely, family may be so important to you that you do not fully explore their wish to report the matter to the police. You may find the control an older man has over his wife's finances so unreasonable that your start to worry that he is controlling her, rather than explore the cultural expectations of the era in which the couple were married.

Becoming aware of your personal values and how these may affect your working life does reduce the risk that these will create bias. Now you have identified your personal values, and the history of their creation, are there areas you need to further reflect on in order to relearn values that are out of step with your professional code of conduct? Listen carefully to what the people you work with are telling you about their values, find out about their culture and ask them what is important in their lives.

Dilemmas between professional ethics and values and organisational values are also common. Organisational constraints may lead to the breach of ethical codes, particularly in the areas of human dignity and well-being. Stacey et al (2011) undertook research into ethical conflicts between mental health nurses and their employing organisations, describing three reactions to these types of ethical conflict:

- **Acceptance:** the nurses acknowledged that their values were challenged at times but had chosen not to raise this. They accepted they would continue to work within the constraints, despite the personal conflict they were experiencing.
- **Rejection:** the nurses questioned the organisational philosophy and the limitations this placed on expressing their values in practice. The personal difficulty this conflict produced appeared to result in them considering leaving the organisation.
- **Innovation:** the nurses worked to initiate change, despite resistance, potential separation and hostility from others. Some of these nurses had been promoted and were engaged in finding ways to keep to their professional values in harsh environments.

These reactions are common in public and third sector organisations. It is important to recognise and discuss organisational values that challenge your professional ethics. Do raise your concerns in supervision or at staff meetings, or there may a forum to discuss professional issues in your organisation, for example a social work board or forum, or you can approach the principal social worker in your organisation to discuss and start to find a way through. Sometimes understanding another perspective will help you find an ethical route through these dilemmas and sometimes you can engage with others to initiate changes in practice.

(▶) KEY MESSAGES

- Relationships underpin all aspects of adult safeguarding work, from working with individuals and their networks, to working with individual agencies and multi-agency partners. These relationships have common elements that can be developed through practice and reflection. Empathy is a valued and useful skill that can be developed.

- Listening to the stories that people tell us helps us to understand the meaning of harm and risk to the adult, the emotional impact of harm and the experience the adult has of power and oppression.

- Ethical dilemmas occur for many reasons. Dilemmas can relate to a lack of alignment between professional ethics and your personal values, or to a conflict between the values of the organisation that employs you and your professional ethics.

KNOWLEDGE REVIEW

- WHAT are the vital components of relationship-based adult safeguarding?

- WHAT do all professional relationships have in common?

- HOW do your personal values influence your professional decision making?

- IDENTIFY the core values of the organisation you currently work in. Are there conflicts with your professional values?

FURTHER READING

- Find out more about motivational interviewing in Rosengren, D.B. (2017) *Building Motivational Interviewing Skills: A Practitioners Handbook* (2nd edn), London: Guilford Press.

- Shemmings (2000) gives a clear account of the impact of adult attachment styles in later life in 'Adult Attachment Theory and Its Contribution to an Understanding of Conflict and Abuse in Later-Life Relationships', *The Journal of Adult Protection,* 2(3): 40–9.

- See www.genopro.com/genogram/ for a practical guide to composing genograms. Why not try it out using your own family first? You can get a practical example of an ecomap at: http://barefootsocialwork.weebly.com/uploads/3/9/7/4/39743910/ecomap_activity.pdf.

- For further reading and thought-provoking exercises on ethics and values read: Beckett, C., Maynard, A. and Johnson, P. (2017) *Values and Ethics in Social Work* (3rd edn), London: Sage.

7

Assessment of risk

Chapter aim

In this chapter we will consider how assessment and management of risk are central to the adult safeguarding process. This includes how to ensure that risk assessments are informed by the adult wherever possible and responses agreed to changes in the level and nature of risk. We will consider carrying out risk assessments in a range of situations and environments, such as where people live in their own homes or in care settings, where risks to others are present – to other adults and children in the same environment or similar circumstances as well as risks to workers in these settings.

This chapter includes:

- working with risk: the practitioner's perspective;

- principles of best practice in risk assessment;

- approaches to risk assessment;

- risk assessment as a part of an adult safeguarding process;

- examples of risk assessment tools, with individuals and in organisational settings.

Safeguarding means protecting an adult's right to live in safety, free from abuse and neglect. It is about people and organisations working together to prevent and stop both the risks and experience of abuse or neglect, while at the same time making sure that the adult's wellbeing is promoted including, where appropriate, having regard to their views, wishes, feelings and beliefs in deciding on any action. (Statutory guidance, DHSC, 2018a, 14.7)

Working with risk: the practitioner's perspective

Situations where there is a risk to an adult with care and support needs can promote anxiety in all involved. The adult will be experiencing the impact of being harmed, and also the worry of statutory agencies being involved in their life. Although the intention of the practitioner is to improve the quality of the adult's life, the power that practitioners are perceived to have can be stressful and alarming for the people at the centre of any adult safeguarding concern. The adult's family and friends may be anxious about risk and may well have a preference for a course of action that will completely remove risk from the life of the adult but damage their independence and well-being irrevocably. Partner agencies involved can be anxious about risk and may also have a preferred course of action. In Chapter 6 we talked about understanding partnership agency cultures and how this can help in discussing risk together. There may be expectations that risk will be completely removed from an adult's life, but a lack of understanding of the potential cost to the adult's well-being of doing so.

The adult safeguarding practitioner will be aware of all these different anxieties while bearing some of their own. When we talk about risk with practitioners, some feel excited and interested in the dilemmas and challenges involved, while others are concerned about getting it wrong and worry about a blame culture in their organisation or society at large:

- "I might get it wrong and then lose all my professional confidence."
- "What if I get it wrong and the adult dies?"
- "I will be on the front page of the newspaper."
- "It may all go wrong, and there will be a Safeguarding Adults Review."
- "I will lose my job, and my professional registration, at the end of the day the finger will point at me."

Working with risk can feel risky for the practitioner; public servants are very aware of demands for public enquiries and media reports on who is to blame. SARs focus on the systems around practitioners that help or hinder, rather than the performance of the practitioner themselves, but SARs still create anxiety in practitioners and are focused on learning from the failure of multi-agency systems, rather than learning from multi-agency successes.

Organisations employing adult safeguarding practitioners can also feel anxious about how working with people in situations of risk impacts on their reputation and their culpability if things go wrong. Managerialist approaches may be employed to reduce the impact of risk on the organisation; for example, using tick boxes rather than professional expertise and demanding complex recording of risk assessments. The LGA and ADASS (Lawson, 2018) urge SABs to lead the change in the culture around risk taking and blame:

> The SAB and partner organisations must provide the necessary context for effective working with risk in front line practice. This includes an emphasis on the importance of, and support for, a culture of positive risk taking that helps practitioners to work in risk enabling ways, where

the adult is 'at the centre'. It includes leadership and a culture that supports front line staff in balancing sometimes conflicting principles (for example empowerment and protection). ...

Support for a learning culture and a 'no blame' culture. ... This should be reinforced in communications with front line staff. These should openly support staff who have made and documented transparent and defensible decisions, even where these do not go to plan. There must be clear acceptance that there is responsibility at organisational level not just with front line staff. These messages should also be communicated to stakeholders and residents. (Lawson, 2018, p 8)

Practitioners should expect support from their organisations in their day-to-day work, and need to be provided with ready access to peer and managerial consultation, access to legal advice as needed, and regular reflective supervision together with the time to create engagement with people and the systems around them to enable positive risk assessment.

The UK law courts support the view that all risk cannot, and should not, be removed from a person's life. During a case in the Court of Protection concerning contact between MM and her partner (*Local Authority X v MM and Anor*, 2007) Justice Munby made the now famous statement:

Physical health and safety can sometimes be bought at too high a price in happiness and emotional welfare. The emphasis must be on sensible risk appraisal, not striving to avoid all risk, whatever the price, but instead seeking a proper balance and being willing to tolerate manageable or acceptable risks as the price appropriately to be paid in order to achieve some other good – in particular to achieve the vital good of the elderly or vulnerable person's happiness. What good is it making someone safer if it merely makes them miserable?

Anxiety about risk is often associated with the idea that the practitioner must be an expert on such matters and if only the right approach or tool is used then the risk will be successfully managed or contained. However, this way of thinking ignores the importance of the adult's expertise in their own life. The adult brings their own assessment to the process of sharing, what the meaning of the risky situation or behaviour is to them, the impact of the risk on their well-being, what strategies they have tried, what worked and what didn't, and what options are acceptable and unacceptable to them. A practitioner must bring their understanding of the circumstances that may indicate risk of harm, or knowledge of options that may reduce or increase a risk in the adult's circumstances. Risk is ideally assessed mutually, as a process of gathering, sharing and considering information, thoughts and wishes.

Principles of best practice in risk assessment

Exploring the risk with the adult

A key principle to build into all of your risk assessment work is that good risk assessment is built on exploration with the adult or adults experiencing that risk. The meaning of different types of risk is unique to each individual. Some attitudes may change through the life course as experience of life is collected. Furedi (2011) interviewed 14 older people who used care services. He reports that they did not seem interested in any right to take risks but were very concerned that their views should be taken seriously, that they should be listened to and respected.

Younger people who use care services may be keen to take risks, and to fully explore their own potential and limitations. In order to build life experiences, we take risks and learn from them. However, we should not rely on stereotypes, there are older people who feel most alive while risk taking, and younger people who prefer caution.

Some people may have limited experience of decision making about risk: they have been protected from life experiences and have not been able to learn about their own attitudes and responses to risk; or they may be unused to the process of weighing up the advantages and disadvantages of potential options.

Attitudes to risk can be influenced by how the adult perceives themselves and maintains their identity, the important aspects of their lives, which can include place, family and friends, and religious or moral principles.

Decisions are often made by professionals about risk in care settings without the adults who live there being consulted or made aware that a risk assessment is being undertaken. Those making decisions may justify the lack of individual involvement on the basis that the risk assessment is about an entire population using a service, not just one individual. People are not only experts in their own lives, but in the experience of living in a particular care setting. The experience of living in a care setting can contribute to a feeling of powerlessness, so it is essential that people in all settings are able to share their assessment of their own situation, and their perception of risk to themselves and to others in the same service.

REFLECTIVE ACTIVITY

Case study: Brownstone Nursing Home

The local adult safeguarding team were enquiring into concerns about organisational abuse in **Brownstone Nursing Home** for older people.

The enquiry began with a visit to the premises by two members of the team and later the commissioning of two advocates to represent adults living at the home who had 'substantial difficulty' in participating in the adult safeguarding process. Adults were asked what their experience was of living there and whether they were concerned for themselves or any other adult at the home.

Initially adults generally said that they were all right but expressed concerns for others, particularly those on a 'dementia floor', and regarding the general conduct of the night shift which they had observed being neglectful and unkind. Adults living at Brownstone were consulted throughout the enquiry and had updates on the progress of the subsequent action plan as often or as little as they wished.

The nursing home later commissioned independent advocates to run regular sessions in the home to facilitate the identification of good quality or poor practice and to build partnerships between the people living at the home and the staff and management there.

Reflective questions

- What might make residents of Brownstone Nursing Home wary of expressing concerns about their care?
- How could advocacy promote the involvement of residents and families in improving care at the home?

Our thoughts are that power relationships, such as relative powerlessness and fear of retribution, can impact on the ability of residents to raise concerns about the risks in the nursing home environment. Building the role of independent advocates in this setting can aid the confidence of residents and families to speak out and the organisation to be more open to scrutiny.

The role of the practitioner is to act as facilitator in conversations about risk, not to be the expert; in addition to promoting mutual risk assessment, such conversations can also have an empowering impact on the adult. The practitioner can ensure the adult is respected, given time and space to make choices and is supported to act on their decisions. A discussion about harm, rights and how to get help if needed leaves an adult informed and aware that there are avenues of advice and support available to them.

The adult's well-being must be at the centre of decisions we make with them about risk

This includes promotion of the adult's human rights. In Chapter 2, we have considered how the well-being principle (Care Act 2014, S1) corresponds to the promotion of human rights, giving a sharper focus to ideas about duty of care, self-determination or autonomy. Remember that certain human rights are absolute, meaning that public bodies have a duty to take steps to observe these.

▶ ESSENTIAL INFORMATION: PRACTICE GUIDANCE

Human rights to bear in mind during risk assessment, from the ECHR

Article 2: Right to life
- Do I have the food, drink, shelter and medical treatment I need to stay alive?

Article 3: Prohibition of inhuman and degrading treatment
- Am I being physically or sexually assaulted, verbally abused, left in soiled clothing or having my dignity regularly disregarded?
- Does my own self-neglect lead to me living in degrading circumstances?

Article 5: Right to liberty and security
- Am I unable to leave where I am currently living and are people always aware of where I am and what I am doing?
- Is there no legal framework in place to make these restrictions lawful?

Not having these rights will have a negative impact on any person's well-being. The role of adult safeguarding is to enable people who are unable to do so to claim their own civil and human rights.

We will sometimes work with people who do not wish to engage with the adult safeguarding process but are living in high-risk situations; for example, with domestic violence or self-neglect. The practitioner must be able to weigh their duty of care towards the adult and others, with the adult's right to self-determination. Focusing on these absolute human rights can help us to start unpicking these dilemmas.

REFLECTIVE ACTIVITY

Case study: Michael Downes

Michael Downes has neglected his own health needs, nutrition and hygiene for many years. He is currently living in a bedsit which is unheated and cold, there is no food and the toilet is blocked. Michael has no bedclothes and does not appear to have washed for a long time. He is thin and his hair and fingernails are long and dirty.

Neighbours have called an ambulance as they helped him home after he collapsed in the street and are worried about his physical and mental state. Michael refused to be conveyed to hospital so the ambulance crew assess his mental capacity to make a decision about having a medical assessment. They conclude that Michael does have capacity but appears to be making a very unwise decision. They are not sure about any underlying medical condition, but Michael may be experiencing the symptoms of malnutrition. The crew are very aware of their duty of care to Michael and must balance his right to life with his right to autonomy. They cannot simply leave him as he wishes them to do.

They contact his GP surgery, explaining the situation and make a direct referral over the telephone to adult safeguarding, explaining the urgency of the situation. The crew stay with Michael for the next hour. He is enjoying their company although still declining to go to hospital, until the GP and duty social worker appear. Michael agrees to emergency help with food, heat and bedding as an alternative to going to hospital. He also agrees to a daily visit for the next week from a support worker who will convey him the next day to the GP surgery for further tests and discussion with the GP. The social worker will visit again to undertake an assessment of his care and support needs within the next week. She is aware that support offered to Michael must be acceptable to him, and that a proportionate focus on his survival and access to health assessment in a place that is acceptable to him is a good start. He may retreat back into himself tomorrow, but he has the necessities of life for a while longer and hopefully a positive experience of getting support.

Reflective question

–   How do you use your awareness of human rights in thinking through dilemmas about self-determination and autonomy where these may conflict with your duty of care?

Our thinking is that dignity plays a key part in human rights-based adult safeguarding practice. Through sensitivity to Michael's views and right to autonomy, a dignified and sensitive relationship can be built with Michael that is likely to offer more successful long-term and low-key intervention than removing him from his home to the hospital would have.

Using the Mental Capacity Act 2005

Many of the adults we work with do not have the capacity to make crucial decisions about their own safety and well-being. The Safeguarding Adults Collection Annual Report for 2017/18 (NHS Digital, 2018, p 23) notes that 31% of adults who had a section 42 enquiry in that year lacked the capacity to contribute to making decisions about their protection, including their participation in the safeguarding enquiry (p 23). Practitioners should be regularly asking themselves 'How can we involve adults who lack capacity in assessing risk?'

The second principle of the MCA (do not treat people as incapable of making a decision unless all practicable steps have been tried to help them) sets the expectation that every effort must be made to encourage, assist and support the adult to make the decision for themselves. It can help to have in mind that you are 'supporting this person to make a decision' rather than 'I am assessing this person's capacity to make this decision'. When decisions must be made on behalf of the adult because they have been assessed as lacking capacity at that time, you must take account of their past and present wishes and feelings, as well as considering whether it is possible to decide or act in a way that would interfere less with the adult's rights and freedoms of action, including whether there is a need to decide or act at all (MCA Principle 5).

The provisions of the MCA are often misunderstood or misused in two key ways during assessment and decision making about risk in adult safeguarding:

1. Assessments of capacity to make decisions about a specific risk are not conducted correctly. For example, too much weight is put on what the adult is saying rather than what they are doing or able to do. Social workers are prone to place an emphasis on verbal evidence. It is often more telling to ask the adult to demonstrate what they can do – "Show me what you do as well as tell me." An adult's *executive capacity*, meaning their ability to implement or deal with the consequences of a decision, is not always explored. In addition, emphasis may be put on the individual verbally communicating that they understand and can retain information, but less on whether they can use the information to weigh up the alternative options and to see the potential consequences and the impact of these on their well-being. Preston-Shoot (2017) reminds us that 'practitioners need specifically to consider whether someone's executive capacity may have been impaired by their physical and mental ill-health, or the dynamics of their lived relationships ... and to weigh in the balance the relationship between a person's autonomy and a professional's duty of care' (p 27).
2. Practitioners may also fail to use *professional curiosity* once they have assessed that an adult has capacity to make decisions about risk. What is the adult's motivation for what appears to be an unwise decision? So many factors influence decision-making ability, and we fail in our duty of care to the adult if we do not continue to engage them in a dialogue to explore these factors

or make meaningful attempts to support them. An adult may be acting under duress from others or may be exploited or controlled to the degree that they cannot exercise a free choice and have lost their free will. They may be heavily influenced by past experiences and coping behaviours that they have not yet discounted as ineffectual.

REFLECTIVE ACTIVITY

Case study: Rhiannon Jones

Rhiannon Jones's son-in-law exploited her financially. He visited regularly to do her shopping, taking £100 in cash each time but coming back without any change from the money. He sold her various useless items that she did not want including a broken TV set and charged her a good deal of money for each.

You visited Rhiannon after a report from the district nurse who was concerned that Rhiannon had little money for heating or food and said that she was afraid of her son-in-law and wanted him to stop visiting her. Rhiannon told you that the nurse was mistaken, she didn't mind giving money to her son-in-law and liked to help her daughter and grandson who was at university. She might hand over £150–£200 per week to her son-in-law but 'didn't mind'. You wondered how the nurse could have got so confused and asked Rhiannon to tell you about her daughter and family, and how they fitted into her life.

Over the next hour Rhiannon began to trust you and understand that she was in control of the conversation and whatever happened next. She explained that her son-in-law coercively controlled both Rhiannon and her daughter for many years. He was a frightening man who also had a gambling addiction. He controlled when she saw her daughter and if she alienated him, she might also lose contact with her daughter. Both mother and daughter have coped for years by keeping him calm.

Reflective question

– What course of action might you consider next?

Our thoughts are that it is important that you continue to work alongside Rhiannon at her pace, considering with her what is and isn't safe for her and what will support her quality of life. Make sure that she has and understands information about domestic abuse and coercive control and has clear explanations about how an IDVA and other domestic violence services, including the police, may help her and her daughter think through the risk in their lives and what they are and are not willing to continue to cope with.

Clarity about the balance of the practitioner's duty of care and the adult's self-determination/autonomy is vital to all risk assessment activities

Risk assessment and management processes that involve careful consideration of the adult's perspective, capacity, abilities and strengths, and how these can be supported, will help professionals avoid overly simplistic approaches that emphasise either a purely self-determining or overly protective approach. Approaches must be balanced to ensure that adults can exercise their rights to choice and control over their lives while ensuring that they also enjoy their right to a life free from harm, exploitation and mistreatment. Duty of care is described in UK tort law as 'the obligation to exercise a level of care towards an individual, as is reasonable in all circumstances, by taking into account the potential harm that may reasonably be caused to that individual or his property' (*M'Alister (or Donoghue) v Stevenson*, 1932).

If an adult is unable to protect themselves from a risk which may cause their death or serious injury, we have a duty of care towards them and must respond to prevent a profound loss of human rights. Braye et al (2011) explore how practitioners approach concerns about adults who self-neglect but can make capacitated decisions about their own well-being. The principle of beneficence – the idea of kindly concern about another's welfare and the wish to promote another's well-being – acts as a counterpoint to any tendency to accept a capacitated adult's initial refusal of help. Respect for an adult's autonomy and self-determination does not, and should not, mean disengaging from continued involvement with them.

Dong and Gorbien (2006) advise practitioners working with adults who refuse help to think of decision-making capacity as a spectrum rather than a dichotomy, and to consider what factors may influence the adult's decision, including all contextual and cultural issues that may affect their capacity. When working with people who are in situations that threaten their absolute human rights, but refuse or are ambivalent about help, remember:

- Relationship – to allow the adult's story to unfold and to develop an understanding of their context and perspective. Options to promote well-being may emerge from these understandings.
- Start with solutions to small problems and build from there.
- Collaboration with colleagues from partner agencies can maximise choice for the adult, as can be seen in the Michael Downes case study, earlier. Work with multi-agency colleagues on the least restrictive options that can be offered.

Use the recording and supervision methods within your organisation which support defensible decision making

Defensible decisions are decisions that can be judged as well-considered and evidenced decisions, regardless of any outcome, and are taken with the full involvement of the adult and, where appropriate, their network of support, other agencies and professionals.

Kemshall et al (2013, p 19) describes defensible practice as practice that 'intertwines' aspects of professionalism with procedural compliance, noting that procedure should support professional judgement, and not limit the practice application of skills and knowledge. Decision making must be evidenced, in order to be accountable to the adult and to your organisation, and to provide a rationale for the decision you have reached.

Recording well will also provide an accurate picture of the nature of the risk and the responses made to other practitioners. Risk assessments can influence future decisions about an adult, and badly made or recorded decisions will risk unfair and unjust treatment of the adult or misunderstanding of their true situation in the future.

Top tips for evidencing defensible decision making

- Make sure that all reasonable steps have been taken to respond to the concern and risks described.
- Use reliable assessment methods to inform decisions.
- Collate and thoroughly evaluate all the information available.
- Record how you have arrived at the decision. Communicate this to others and keep reviewing with the adult and evaluating the need for further decisions.
- Follow your local policies and procedures and make sure you have considered your legal responsibilities.

Approaches to risk assessment

Positive risk taking

The word 'risk' is often seen as synonymous with danger or harm in adult safeguarding. Risk assessment can become unbalanced if we only look at the negative impact of risk on an adult's life. Positive risk taking is a process that starts with the identification of the potential benefit as well as harm in continuing with a risky behaviour or in a situation where there are risks. An emphasis on the positive aspects of risk taking aims to encourage and support people to take risks in order to achieve personal change or growth.

We need to understand the adult's perspective of what they will gain from taking risks, and understand what they will lose if they are prevented from doing so.

REFLECTIVE ACTIVITY

Case study: Simon Grant

Simon Grant's daughter, Jemma, was addicted to heroin. She started seeing Simon again after two years of absence. He was initially delighted and, when she said that she had moved back to the area and was looking for accommodation, he invited her to sleep on the sofa in his sheltered housing flat. Jemma moved in, but so did her partner, and after a week various friends also began to frequent Simon's flat and use drugs there.

The sheltered housing landlord supported Simon to tell his daughter to leave and she did so, but Simon was heartbroken; he wanted to stay in touch with Jemma and help her all he could. Jemma was his only family and Simon wanted her to be part of his life.

Reflective question

– It is important for Simon to have his daughter in his life. He hopes that she will fulfil his need for family and relationship. What can you do to support Simon to take this risk?

Our thoughts are that the relationship between Simon and his daughter is very important to him. A risk management plan that ignores or sidelines this key part of life is likely to fail as he is not likely to follow it. A plan that minimises the actual, not presumed, risks to Simon from his daughter and maintaining contact in a considered way is likely to be more successful for him.

A *strengths-based approach* will support shared conversations about risk between practitioners and adults. A strengths-based assessment focuses on the adult's situation and identifies the factors that get in the way of living without harm and those who can help the adult to protect themselves. Strengths-based approaches underpin the idea of Making Safeguarding Personal.

Contrast these two statements:

1. Jane has a learning disability and is vulnerable to exploitation from men. She is in need of protection against exploitation.
2. Jane has a wide social circle and attends two social clubs a week. She would appreciate some support around understanding relationships as she has never had the opportunity to do this, and an opportunity to plan ahead what she will do should an abusive man try to exploit her. Jane would like to involve her two closest friends in the planning activity as they are her frequent companions when she is out enjoying her life.

In a strengths–based conversation:

- The **practitioner** brings their knowledge and understanding of the factors that can increase or reduce risk and their knowledge of options that may help.
- The **adult** brings their knowledge and understanding about their own life and well-being:
  - What does well-being mean to them? What do they think is important now in supporting their well-being and what isn't important? What kind of life do they want to lead?
  - What solutions they have tried? What worked, or didn't work? What have they concluded from this?
- What gets in the way of the adult being able to use their strengths and make changes in their lives? These factors can include being in an institution with no access to representation or advocacy, their own feelings of depression, fear or previous experiences.
- What are the formal and informal systems around them? What supports and resources are available for them to use? What helps the adult – for example family members, friends? Are there positive risk-taking opportunities, or opportunities to develop a supportive social network?

These conversations can begin to shape a safeguarding plan that will protect the adult while enhancing their well-being.

Key areas to think about in risk assessment

Every individual, and every situation is different. However, there are key areas that can be usefully explored when talking about, and thinking through, risk and the assessment of risk:

- *Power relationships*:
  Is the adult dependent on others to provide for their basic needs, such as food, drink, heating, clothing, safety and so on? How much can they influence how they are supported? Dependency on others can limit the adult's ability to self-protect. Needing support with basic needs can be used as a tool for exploitation and control by others, for example threatening to withhold food or care, or using the relationship to control an adult's finances.
- *Family dynamics, current and historical*:
  What is the story of relationships within the family? Has the adult at risk previously abused or been abused by family members? Is there a family history of domestic abuse? Did the adult have a particular role within the family that they can no longer fulfil, leaving others feeling frustrated or angry? Is the adult being subject to coercion or control by another family member?
- *The adult's history*, including historical abuse, and how the adult is affected by experiences now:

Has the adult experienced abuse while in an institution? Have they had any significant life trauma, or childhood abuse? How does this affect their self-esteem and identity now? How does it affect their ability to self-protect? Are there services they will not engage with through fear of loss of independence or because of previous experiences?

- *Addiction*:

  Does the carer or carers, and/or the adult have an addiction to a degree that their everyday lives are affected? Substance misuse can impair the adult's ability to self-protect and leave them more vulnerable to exploitation. Carers, family members or friends who misuse substances or gamble may find it difficult to focus on the adult's care or may exploit in order to fund their habit.

People who say go away: risk assessment where risk is high

Despite all of the practitioner's relationship-building skills there will be occasions when risks to the adult or others are reported as being high but it is impossible to engage the adult in any conversation about this. If other adults or children are affected, or if the person's right to life ('vital interests') or other absolute human right is reported to be at risk, we must continue to enquire and try to mitigate risk.

When working with risk where there is difficulty engaging with the adult you should consider:

- How imminent is the risk and how severe is the potential impact on the adult or others? If the risk is imminent – the situation occurs daily and the consequences of the risk could happen soon or now – and the impact on the adult or others will be serious, you may well need to convene an urgent multi-agency strategy meeting with agencies who know the adult, or who can contribute to a plan to engage them.
- Agencies such as primary health teams, fire and rescue, police, environmental health and, as appropriate, the adult's housing provider or third sector groups will be able to problem solve together and find a way forward to engage and work with the adult.
- Look again at the information you have. Is there an agency or person who is able to help you engage with the adult? Is there someone who can begin engagement or help you get in through the door and help to facilitate a conversation?
- Try to understand the adult's beliefs, fears and previous experiences. Why are they refusing to see you? Is there something that can be done to reassure the adult?

Ultimately, there may be adults who decline to engage with any offer of support but are still in high-risk situations. Your local authority may have a forum in which to discuss cases where it is difficult to engage the adult but risks to their well-being or that of others is high.

> ▶ **ESSENTIAL INFORMATION: PRACTICE GUIDANCE**

Practice example: Plymouth Creative Solutions Forum

Services and commissioners in Plymouth saw an increase in the numbers of people presenting with highly complex pictures of substance misuse, physical and psychiatric co-morbidities. In addition, the Care Act 2014 required a more integrated response to people with issues of self-neglect and who present a risk to themselves or others.

The Creative Solutions Forum developed from the need to establish a way to support individuals, staff and agencies to understand and manage risk fluidly. The aim of the forum is to provide an additional multi-agency, multidisciplinary response, which includes commissioners who can agree bespoke packages of care, enable better risk sharing and risk management between agencies, and facilitate improved outcomes for people than could be achieved with a 'usual care' approach. The Forum members work as partners to consider creative options for people with highly complex needs and presentations that require a multi-agency response and where other single or multi-agency processes have been exhausted.

The Forum meets monthly and is chaired by a safeguarding adult's independent officer. Accountability for the individual person remains with the referring agency; however, where the level of risk or complexity demands multi-agency intervention or escalation the Forum will identify appropriate actions, agencies or resources to reduce the level of risk. The Forum considers two or three referrals per month, ordinarily allowing one hour to discuss each referral. The agency making the referral will present a case summary for no more than 15 minutes, followed by focused consideration of risk, options and solutions for 30 minutes, and finally 15 minutes to conclude and agree actions with a review date. At the beginning of each Forum meeting a short review/update of the previous month's referrals is made to monitor agreed outcomes. The Forum representatives or agencies agree to take responsibility for delegated actions and principally support the referring agency with managing risk. Referring agencies agree to return to a future Forum as appropriate to update on progress towards outcomes.

The Forum has had an impact on partnership work across strategic and operational teams, agencies no longer feel alone with high-risk situations, the existence of a safeguarding partnership is tangible and is being built on across the Plymouth safeguarding system.

Plymouth Safeguarding Adults Board, 2019

Risk assessment as a part of adult safeguarding processes

Assessing risk is particularly pertinent at different intervals in any piece of adult safeguarding work. Here we give an overview of relevant questions you could ask about risk at each interval.

On receiving a concern from a third party

- Has the referrer taken any immediate action needed to protect the adult if they are reported to be at high and imminent risk of harm? If not, what immediate action needs to be taken and by whom?
- Has the harm already created an unsafe situation for the adult which needs to be addressed urgently? For example, are they in need of accommodation or urgent financial support?
- Will the risk to the adult be increased by contact with a safeguarding adults practitioner? Is a plan needed to ensure the adult can be seen in a safe location, and how any safety risks will be minimised? Are there any risks to the visiting professional?

Gathering the initial information to support a risk assessment about the concern and way forward

Primary information comes from talking with the adult, or adults, concerned. Information also needs to be gathered from the person referring the concern – what do they believe the risks to be, and what have they done so far to mitigate risk?

You could also talk with other agencies involved with the adult as proportionate to the reported concern. If risks are reported as life-threatening or others are at imminent risk of harm, other agencies can be contacted without the adult's permission. Otherwise, do wait until you have the adult's consent to contact others. There may be agencies who have specialist knowledge of relevance to the concern, for example tissue viability nurses, primary care nurses, and doctors, including psychiatrists.

Do look at your agency's existing records. Have there been previous concerns about the adult? What helped or hindered? Is the situation getting worse? If the adult uses a care service, or is in a hospital or social care setting, have there been previous concerns about the provider? When were the adult's care and support needs last reviewed? What were the outcomes?

REFLECTIVE ACTIVITY

Case study: Delores Wilson

Delores Wilson lives with her daughter, Michele. Delores is 50 years old and a wheelchair user. She has a diagnosis of secondary progressive multiple sclerosis (MS) and is also partially sighted. Delores' sister, Evelyn, has contacted the adult social care front door service as she is concerned that her sister is being kept away from her and has said that she is frightened of Michele, who shouts at her.

An adult safeguarding practitioner follows up this conversation with Evelyn who is worried as Michele will not let her into the flat and thinks that she is intimidating Delores. Delores has telephoned her and says she is very down at the moment as she is feeling weaker and the symptoms of MS are progressing. Delores says that Michele has been shouting at her and leaves her in bed on the weekends so she "doesn't get in the way". Evelyn does not want Michele to know that she has contacted social services and explained that Michele was mentally unwell 15 years ago and was sectioned and taken to hospital. If she knows that social services have been contacted, Michele may prevent all access to Delores.

The social worker contacted Delores' GP who had a different view of Michele. The GP explains that Michele had always seemed supportive of Delores and has a good relationship with the GP and MS consultant.

The social worker looked up both Delores' and Michele's records and noted that there was a concern six months ago when Delores said that Evelyn was continually asking to borrow money and she suspected was stealing from her. Part of the safeguarding plan was that Evelyn no longer saw Delores alone but only when Michele was present. On balance the social worker decided to telephone Delores and ask if she could visit to talk about her current well-being as she had received a report from a 'concerned person' that Delores was struggling.

Reflective questions
- What different views of the nature, level and type of risk to Delores are present in this case?
- What should you do to ensure that all alleged risks are considered?

Our thoughts are that Delores' views of both Evelyn and Michele are crucial to understanding the nature and level of risk in this situation. Building Delores' trust in the safeguarding practitioner is essential to ensure that she feels safe to explain her views.

When planning an enquiry

You need to consider known risks and explore the need for an interim safeguarding plan to promote the well-being of the adult or adults involved while enquiries are undertaken. Any planning discussion should also consider how risk will be assessed with the adult or their representative, and how to mitigate any risks caused to the adult concerned by the enquiry itself.

In our example of Dolores Wilson, the social worker had a discussion with her team manager before going out to see Delores. They decided that it was important that the social worker saw Delores alone and if this was not going to be possible, decided to reassess the risk to Delores from enquiry activities. This allows the practitioner to consider other possibilities for seeing Delores alone, for example when Michele is out or at any external venue Delores might attend. Delores can then be told about her sister's concern. The social worker will also talk with Michele about her well-being as the carer of a parent who is becoming more disabled, and find out how she is feeling about her life.

During the section 42 enquiry

A central activity within any enquiry is establishing facts and assessing risk with the adult and the system around them. We may be able to have a full discussion with an adult, but if they have 'substantial difficulty' in being involved we need to make sure that they are supported by an advocate or representative who knows them well. If the adult does not have the mental capacity to understand information about risk, we can still follow the steps below as part of a best-interest decision-making process, ensuring that we get the fullest picture possible of the adult's previous history and wishes and current situation. We present a framework for gathering information about risk from individuals. It is adapted from a framework presented by White (2017, p 118).

> ### ▶ ESSENTIAL INFORMATION: PRACTICE GUIDANCE
>
> *Talking about risk with individuals*
>
> **Step 1: Understanding the adult's wishes and feelings in relation to the risk identified by the concern**
> Listen to what the adult says about the situation; gather information about the history of the situation and the relationships and networks around the adult. Who is important to the adult? Who do they think knows and understands what is happening? Do they have a network around them, or are they isolated? Do they have someone they can count on? Gather information about their life, what is

important to them, their wishes and feelings, and the outcomes they want from their work with you.

This will begin to develop a sense of shared responsibility for safety as well as trust and shared understanding.

- What has happened previously?
- What works, what didn't and what can be learned?
- What are their views on the risk, and the benefits and drawbacks of the situation?
- Explore other aspects of well-being: what about physical, social and psychological well-being?

Speak with others who are identified as important to the adult, with their permission.

Work with the adult to put their wishes and needs in order of importance to them.

Step 2: Understanding and clarifying the impact of risks on the adult
After listing wishes and needs, set out the risks and the impact of these, including benefits and drawbacks, in written or another accessible summary form. This will provide a good basis for further discussion with the adult, their family or other representatives and other professionals as well as providing a means of sharing information and challenging perceptions. The adult may change their view after seeing information set out like this. If there are limited benefits but serious negative impacts identified and the adult remains unable to see the risk, further exploration of what is happening to lead the adult to this conclusion is needed. Are they under duress, or counting on previous history and coping mechanisms, or is there some impairment of the adult's ability to understand, retain, use and weigh information?

When listing the risks with the adult you can apply the simple tests of likelihood and impact to understand the extent of perceived risk. List how much the identified risks contribute to the adult's desired quality of life and well-being. Identify what strengths or positive factors are present that may mitigate risk. Consider what recovery and restorative actions are needed. A full risk assessment will be available at the end of the enquiry.

Step 3: The safeguarding plan: enabling and responding to risk
We will explore how steps 1 and 2 inform safeguarding planning in Chapter 8. These key steps are:

- Use multi-agency meetings, or strategy discussions with multi-agency partners, or reflective or peer supervision to support you to consider the range of concerns, opinions, experiences, culture, perceptions, risks and legal responsibilities. These aspects may also be shared with the adult as helpful in agreeing a response to risk.

Key questions to consider:

- How can safety be promoted without damaging the adult's human rights, or other benefits from the situation?
- Are there ways of supporting the adult to change the situation to reduce risk while still respecting choice and promoting the quality of life they want?
- What could go wrong – what contingencies are needed?
- Does everyone involved have a joined-up understanding of the adult's situation, what is important to them and what the risks are?

The safeguarding plan is made either during the enquiry or after it has concluded. The safeguarding plan brings all the previous steps together into an agreed plan. This will summarise the adult's wishes, views and feelings, the agreed risk assessment, enablement solutions and agreed actions to respond to residual risk and contingency planning, plus how the plan will be considered successful and reviewed.

Useful questions to think about may be:

- Does the adult feel safer? If they are concerned, who will they contact?
- How are their identified outcomes being met?
- When will you both agree that the need for the plan has ended?
- If the adult cannot tell you themselves, how will you assess the success of any plan? Who will tell you, how often?

The impact of existing risk on the adult's well-being must be considered with the adult at every *review* of the safeguarding plan, if one needs to be in place.

Examples of risk assessment tools, with individuals and in organisational settings

Now we present some examples of risk assessments, with individuals and in organisational settings. Remember that tools are there to support your professional judgement; they must be used to focus and support your thinking rather than give you an outcome or formula that tells you what to do.

Simple risk assessment tools are usually based on the idea of likelihood or imminence and degree of harm. *Red Amber Green* (also known as *RAG*) ratings are often used to denote the degree of likelihood or harm. An example template for simple RAG rated risk assessment may be found in Figure 7.1.

Figure 7.1: Risk assessment RAG rating template

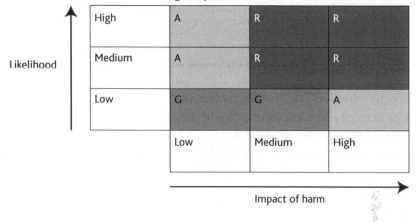

- If the likely imminence of harm is low and the impact of the harm is low or medium, risk may be considered low or 'green' (G).
- If there is a high or medium likelihood of the harm occurring or recurring, and the impact is low then the risk is medium or 'amber' (A), if the impact is medium or high then the risk is high or 'red' (R).
- If there is a high likelihood that the harm will occur or recur and the impact of the harm is medium or high then the risk rating is also high or 'red' (R).

There are more complex versions of RAG ratings, sometimes with numerical values attached. However, understanding the concept of RAG rating will help you understand how a number of agencies, in particular the police, will rate and present risk information.

Specific risk assessment tools are used by agencies working with people who are experiencing domestic abuse

The tools available through SafeLives (previously known as Coordinated Action Against Domestic Abuse) are widely used by multi-agency partnerships. The 'domestic abuse, stalking and "honour"-based violence' (*DASH*) risk checklist is a tried and tested way to understand risk between intimates in domestic settings. SafeLives have produced some additional guidance about older people and disabled people (2016a, 2016b) to accompany the more generic DASH assessments. Older or frail people may not always score as high risk on DASH (Bartley, 2015) and the DASH checklist used in some areas needs to be adjusted to account for a serious risk of injury when an older or frail person is pushed over, something that can be as serious as using a weapon. 'High' or 'medium' risk from harm from domestic abuse may also present differently for older or disabled adults; there may be no weapon involved but the threat of or actual disconnection or removal of medical equipment or medicines can be life-threatening. The DASH risk assessment is used to ascertain whether a referral should be made to a Multi-Agency Risk

Assessment Conference (known as *MARAC*), where agencies will work together to make a plan to address further harm to the adult. As well as MARACs to address domestic abuse you may also have specific MARACs in your area that focus on sexual exploitation or anti-social behaviour.

Multi-Agency Public Protection Arrangements (known as *MAPPA*) are risk-assessment meetings to support multi-agency working with people who present a significant risk to the public. Through this mechanism, various agencies, led by the police, probation and prison service, can assess, plan and work together to manage the risks posed by violent and sexual offenders. The police, probation and prison service are 'responsible bodies' for the MAPPA process; local authorities are one of the 'duty to cooperate' bodies, that is, they must cooperate with the MAPPA arrangements to manage the risk posed by an offender (MoJ, 2018). It is worth considering a MAPPA referral for individuals who are controlling and exploiting vulnerable groups, including adults at risk. MAPPA enables agencies to share information and cooperate to manage the risk posed by such individuals. Do find out who the MAPPA coordinator is in your area who can discuss potential referrals with you.

Risk assessments in organisations

We first explored Marsland's work in Chapter 5. While the research (Marsland and White, 2012, Marsland et al, 2015) was developed to support external practitioners to identify concerns, the six themes are also useful in identifying areas of risk for the people who live in or use a service. While the authors suggest concerns spread across a range of the thematic groups are a cause for concern about an increased risk of abuse, harm and neglect, our practice experience is that a concern about management and leadership alone can indicate the possibility of a failing service where people may be harmed, if not imminently then at some point in the future unless remedial action is taken.

The thematic areas are:

- concerns about management and leadership;
- concerns about staff skills, knowledge and practice;
- concerns about residents' behaviours and well-being;
- concerns about the service resisting the involvement of external people and isolating residents;
- concerns about the way services are planned and delivered;
- concerns about the quality of basic care and the environment.

An example of how the themes can be used in assessing risk to adults using a residential service is presented in the Reflective Activity.

REFLECTIVE ACTIVITY

Blueskies Care Home – initial risk assessment

Evidence has been gathered via a contract compliance visit, complaints from residents and relatives and the accounts given by Blueskies staff (see Table 7.1).

Using Table 7.1 can enable you to spot individual as well as group risk. You can also easily see where actions need to be taken.

Reflective question

- What actions can be taken to try to stabilise the situation while further improvements are made?

Our thoughts are that an urgent discussion with the provider regarding the need for the manager to be present and urgent attention to the need to improve staffing to manage the morning shift and address staff and resident morale. We must also identify all who live at Blueskies who require time-specific medication, have a low Waterlow score (an indication of high risk of pressure areas), who require lifting, who must have specific daily health support or who are distressed. We need to prioritise these individuals for a health and social care review of their needs with a view as to how to further mitigate risk, including distress.

There also needs to be a discussion with the provider and commissioners – and potentially no new admissions until the home is adequately staffed.

Table 7.1: Risk themes in organisations

Theme	Evidence	Who affected
Concerns about management and leadership	The responsible manager is covering two other services. No plans have been made regarding low levels of staffing on the morning shift.	All who live at Blueskies.
Concerns about staff skills, knowledge and practice	Staff are cutting corners to try to get people up and washed in the mornings. Residents report that their dignity and that of others is being compromised. There are two complaints of staff being rough and short-tempered and one incident when correct manual handling procedures were not used.	All who live at Blueskies, and particularly people who need assistance to move (60% of current residents).
Concerns about residents' behaviours and well-being	People are being left in soiled beds for two hours into the morning shift. One observation of a person crying. One incident when medication missed. One injury reported through poor lifting practice.	All who live at Blueskies and particularly those who rely on time-specific medication (such as Mrs X who has diabetes, Mr G and Ms P who have Parkinson's). People who need assistance to move.
Concerns about the service resisting the involvement of external people and isolating residents	No reports made to adult safeguarding or CQC regarding these incidents. People left in their rooms for long periods. Advice of physiotherapists sought but not acted on.	All who live at Blueskies and particularly Miss V and Mr T who have new physio post cerebrovascular accident plans.
Concerns about the way services are planned and delivered	Insufficient staff on morning rota. No plans to recruit or use agency. Home is still admitting people who are not mobile or have dementia and cannot self-care.	All who live at Blueskies and particularly newly admitted people, whom staff do not have time to get to know.
Concerns about the quality of basic care and the environment	Staff cannot support people in the morning so that people are left at risk of not getting meds on time; no one to assist with eating; injuries through poor lifting practice; loss of dignity and resultant distress; increased risk of pressure area and other injury through being left in soiled bedding. Emotional harm as some staff are short-tempered and poorly led.	All who live at Blueskies and particularly all those already mentioned plus people with existing pressure areas or low Waterlow scores.

(▶) KEY MESSAGES

- An adult is the expert about their own life, about the risks they personally face and the risks in the service they are using or living in.

- Practitioners bring expertise about indicators, resources and options and can facilitate discussions about risk.

- Risk assessment tools are not a substitute for professional judgement.

- Remember that decision making about risk must be well evidenced and defensible.

KNOWLEDGE REVIEW

- WHAT is the principle of beneficence?

- WHAT do we mean by strengths-based assessment?

- HOW can you assess the risk of harm in organisations?

FURTHER READING

- It is worth reading Emily White's chapter to help you reflect further on how strengths-based approaches inform an MSP approach to risk assessment: White, E. (2017) 'Assessing and Responding to Risk', in A. Cooper and E. White (eds) *Safeguarding Adults Under the Care Act: Understanding Good Practice*, London: Jessica Kingsley, pp 110–27.

- It is important to have training on how to safely use the SafeLives DASH checklist, but in the meantime find out more at: www.bava.org.uk/wp-content/uploads/RIC_with_guidance.doc.

- You can read more about professional curiosity and adult safeguarding at https://www.norfolksafeguardingadultsboard.info/assets/NSAB-GUIDANCE/NSAB-Professional-Curiosity-Partnership-VersionSEPT2018FINAL02.pdf — guidance drawn up by Norfolk Safeguarding Adults Board on professional curiosity.

8

Decision making in adult safeguarding

Chapter aim

In this chapter we will discuss decision making in adult safeguarding, when decisions are made and who makes them. Barriers and supports to effective decision making are reviewed. We will look at how some of the agencies who are involved in adult safeguarding make decisions and what factors and information are used to do this.

In this chapter we will explore:

- making a referral about a concern;

- decision making about the section 42 duty;

- concerns that do not meet the criteria for the section 42 duty;

- quality and adult safeguarding;

- decisions about advocacy;

- decisions about what happens as a result of an enquiry;

- decisions made by other agencies.

Making a referral about a concern

A set of decisions have to be made before making a referral to the local authority about a concern. The vast majority of referrals are made by professionals or care workers rather than the adult or their family and friends. A self-referral has the advantage of the adult consenting to and wanting help to protect themselves. In order to decide to refer themselves, the adult must know that adult safeguarding exists and how to get in touch, and have the means to do so, such as access to a telephone or the internet. The adult must be able to quickly and simply make contact with an adult safeguarding service and have trust that the social workers or contact centre workers they are talking to will listen to them and help rather than make their situation worse. Adults at risk need to know that adult safeguarding is the right service for them to speak with.

REFLECTIVE ACTIVITY

Self-referrals

How easy is it for adults at risk in your area to self-refer for help from adult safeguarding? What can be done to increase their awareness and access to contact with the adult safeguarding service?

Here are some ideas:

- Accessible leaflets and other materials which highlight the 'right number' to ring.
- Local awareness raising events – some local authorities and SABs support and promote adult abuse awareness week or World Elder Abuse Awareness Day on 15 June every year.
- Mini awareness events in groups or one-to-one with service users and carers linked into provided services.
- Support from other professionals and providers to self-refer, rather than making a referral on the adult's behalf. In this way the adult will be involved in their own safeguarding from the initial point. Or, if this does not increase risk to the adult, the professional could consider contacting adult safeguarding services while still with the adult; in this way the adult can inform how the concern is expressed and give information for themselves.

Professionals or care and support staff may be referring because the adult has disclosed harm to them, or they have witnessed abuse or a set of indicators of potential harm. The referring professional should make an assessment of risk with the adult in order to decide what steps are needed to address any immediate safety issues. The emergency services may need to be called if there is a threat of or actual violence or injury.

The adult may need support if they wish to call the police. In considering this decision with the adult it is important to appreciate the implications of not doing so for any future prosecution. Although the adult and those supporting them must strive to retain evidence of harm where there is a likelihood of the need for an investigation of a crime, the police are best at advising how and taking action to do so. If, for example, a sexual assault has occurred, the adult will want to wash at some point and may be unsure initially whether they want to speak to the police. Forensic evidence will be lost unless it has been secured via a specialist sexual assault forensic service. Sexual assault referral centres (SARCs) can offer the opportunity for evidence to be secured and allow the adult to think through the decision to speak to the police at their own pace. SARCs can provide support and advice as well as the facilities to report the assault to the police. The Survivors Trust (2018) offers further details on SARCs across the UK.

▶ ESSENTIAL INFORMATION: PRACTICE GUIDANCE

Consent to make a referral

If the adult is unable or unwilling to make the adult safeguarding referral themselves, it is important that the professional concerned asks for the adult's consent to make a referral. If the adult lacks the capacity to consent to a referral the professional must be sure that they are making the referral in the adult's best interests. It is very helpful if the referrer can give information about the adult's mental capacity with regard to adult safeguarding. For example, can the adult make a decision about whether a referral should be made or not? Are they able to engage in discussions about their own safety, including an understanding of the potential for longer term harm as well as immediate effects? If an enquiry is initiated later, it will be the responsibility of the agency undertaking the enquiry to assess the adult's capacity to make the relevant decisions as they will be the decision maker at that point, but an early indication that there may be a need for support with decision making is very useful.

To give meaningful consent to a referral, the adult needs to have enough information to understand what making a referral to adult safeguarding entails, and what is likely to happen next. That means that the referring professional must also have a good understanding about what a referral entails and what the response is likely to be, and to be able to explain this in a way that is honest and supportive.

It may not be safe to see the adult to ask for their consent before referral, in which case the referral must go ahead with the safety concern information highlighted so that the local authority is aware of the risk. Remember, if children are present and at risk of harm then a referral must be made to child protection services.

If the adult decides not to consent to a referral, one can still be made in the circumstances detailed here. It is important that the adult knows a referral has been made and, although their lack of consent has been overridden, that they can still be involved or kept informed as much or little as they wish. Referrals can be made without the consent of the adult if there is a public interest (when others are also at risk) or a vital interest (when the adult may die or be injured). Reasons for making a referral without the consent of the adult can be:

- There are other adults at risk from the same source of harm.
- The adult is subject to duress or coercion to prevent them consenting to a referral.

- There is a high risk to the health and safety of the adult at risk (their 'vital interests' or ECHR Article 2 right to life is endangered).
- The adult does not have the mental capacity to decide to consent or not to a referral and a decision has been made that a safeguarding referral should be made in their best interests.
- A serious crime has been committed or it is believed is about to be committed. A 'serious crime' can be defined as in Schedule 1 of the Serious Crime Act 2007, which lists a number of serious offences that:
  - involve the use of violence, including the use of weapons and firearms;
  - are sexual assaults;
  - result in substantial financial gain;
  - cause substantial financial loss to the victim;
  - are conducted by a large number of persons 'in pursuit of a common purpose', for example gang intimidation, sexual exploitation or modern slavery.

What should I do if the adult refuses to consent to an adult safeguarding referral?

It is important to consider what prevented consent being obtained. Does the referrer need to return to the adult to obtain their consent? In situations where there appears to be an imminent risk of harm to the adult's vital interests this may not be appropriate. In other situations, as already noted, it will be important for the referrer to explain to the adult that they want to refer to adult safeguarding, explain their concern and ask the adult what their initial views and wishes are. Some professional referrers report feeling uncomfortable about doing this. They may fear there will be an impact on their relationship with the adult; however, it is not unusual to discuss referral and potential outcomes with the adult only to be told 'this is not safeguarding' at the initial point of contact and that there will be no involvement from the local authority. Such situations need to be explored carefully with the referrer, as you'll need to find out what the adult's expectation is, and discuss the next steps the referrer can take if the concern does not meet the criteria for the section 42 duty.

Decision making about the section 42 duty

The section 42 duty on the local authority exists from the point at which a concern is received (ADASS, 2019). It is helpful to divide the section 42 duty, as the Care Act 2014 does, into two parts, sections 42(1) and 42(2). The first decision on receipt of a concern relates to section 42(1) of the Act, meaning does the concern meet the criteria for continued action under section 42?

► **ESSENTIAL INFORMATION: LEGISLATION**

Section 42 duty: section 42(1)

Once a referral expressing concern is made, the local authority decision maker needs to gather enough information in order to ascertain whether there is:

Reasonable cause to suspect that an adult in its area (whether or not ordinarily resident there)—
(a) has needs for care and support (whether or not the authority is meeting any of those needs),
(b) is experiencing, or is at risk of, abuse or neglect, and
(c) as a result of those needs is unable to protect himself or herself against the abuse or neglect or the risk of it.

Care Act 2014, S42(1)

We have stressed 'reasonable cause to suspect' as the decision maker only needs to gather enough information to establish this. Part of that information gathering should be talking with the adult to ascertain their views on the alleged harm, how they are experiencing the harm, the risk to their safety and well-being, and what they think will help to remove or mitigate those risks. It may be that it is unsafe to have these conversations at this point. The focus of any subsequent enquiry or action must therefore be to identify how and when the views of the adult will be ascertained. Conversation with an adult who does not have care and support needs will provide an opportunity for them to discuss their thoughts on preventing harm, any support they need to be safe and where they can get information about other options available to them.

Do remember to also look up any local authority records that can contain relevant information and to return to the referrer to ascertain relevant current circumstances. Sometimes a concern can appear to be a repeat of a long-standing situation, a useful question to ask the referrer is '*Why refer now?*' What has changed in the adult's situation, what new risks have occurred, why are existing approaches no longer working?

If the criteria for further action under section 42 are not met there are a range of other routes that can be used to support the adult. If the adult appears to have care and support needs, but there is no indication of harm at present, a care and support needs assessment (Care Act 2014, S9) or carer's assessment may be indicated to prevent harm. Do consider how and whether referrals into care management processes are followed up. Adults with urgent need can wait for some time for an assessment, but how will this impact on the potential for harm that you are trying to prevent?

In other instances the adult may have no care and support needs. Support and action may need to be considered using different routes. Decision-making teams need to be very clear about who to contact and how to refer to other services in the local area.

- Do you know how non-urgent referrals into mental health services are made in your area?
- If there are concerns about radicalisation into terrorism, how do you make an urgent or non-urgent referral into Prevent teams?
- If you have enough information from the adult or referrer about domestic abuse can you complete a DASH assessment which will indicate if a referral should be made to MARAC (see Chapter 7)? Do you have the contact numbers for local domestic abuse services?

If you have advised a referrer to contact a different service it is important to ask them to check back with you for further advice. Do contact the referrer again to make sure they have been able to take matters forward with another service if the adult is experiencing a risk of harm. Referrers can remain unclear about next steps, believing that now they have told the local authority that the onus on them has somehow been transferred. This is not acceptable in any case, but particularly so if the risks discussed indicate that there may be a serious outcome if concerns are not addressed by other agencies.

It may be difficult to ascertain enough data during information gathering, particularly about whether an adult is experiencing, or is at risk of, abuse or neglect and what their views are. The decision might be to initiate an enquiry under section 42(2) in order to gather more information. If it is later established that the adult is able to protect themselves or is not experiencing harm the enquiry ends, and the section 42 duty will cease.

▶ **ESSENTIAL INFORMATION: LEGISLATION**

Section 42 duty: section 42(2)

If there is reasonable cause to suspect that the concern relates to an adult whose circumstances meet the criteria we have set out, the next decision is about whether an enquiry, or some other course of action, is needed.

> The local authority must make (or cause to be made) whatever enquiries it thinks necessary to enable it to decide whether any action should be taken in the adult's case (whether under this Part [of the Act] or otherwise) and, if so, what and by whom. (Care Act 2014, S42(2))

A range of actions can be taken under section 42(2), including a care and support needs assessment under section 9 or under section 11 of the Care Act. Section 11 applies if the adult refuses but is not capacitated to make this decision and it is in their best interests to be assessed, or the adult refuses but is experiencing, or is at risk of, abuse or neglect.

It may be that the local authority decides not to undertake an enquiry or indeed any other action at that time because to do so may cause harm to the adult. In the example in the Reflective Activity, Mr Winford is dying, and the alleged harm will not have an impact on his safety or well-being; however, undertaking an enquiry may adversely affect him. We will detail adult safeguarding enquiries further in Chapter 9.

REFLECTIVE ACTIVITY

Case study: Mr Winford

Mr Winford has two sons, Eric and Sean. Eric alleged that Sean had taken money from Mr Winford's bank account. Before Mr Winford was approached as to his wishes he was rushed into hospital. He was not expected to live. Both sons stayed with him and supported each other to say goodbye to their father at the end of his life. Mr Winford was seen by a hospital social worker, but he was very confused and slipping in and out of consciousness.

Reflective question
— What actions are needed to protect Mr Winford in his current circumstances?

Our thoughts are that we can decide to do nothing. If Mr Winford recovers we can ask him what he wants to do, but at the moment his greatest need is to have the support of his family, and an enquiry is likely to disrupt Eric and Sean's current relationship and the process they need to go through to support their father as well as each other.

Who has a duty to make decisions under section 42?

The decision as to whether the section 42 duty exists and whether an enquiry needs to be undertaken is that of the local authority. The decision to undertake an enquiry cannot be made by the adult or their representative as it is a local authority statutory duty: only the local authority can decide. The decision can be informed by the adult, but it is not their decision.

The No Secrets (Home Office and Department of Health, 2000) concept of 'significant harm' to an adult, which would mean that the harm to an adult reached a threshold for an adult safeguarding process, no longer exists within the Care Act 2014. Instead, if an adult meets the criteria for the section 42 duty, any subsequent enquiry or further action needs to be proportionate to the impact of harm and degree of continued risk. It may well be that the harm that has been discussed with the adult appears to be a one-off occurrence with minimal harm to the adult, who does not think any actions need to be taken. After these enquiries are conducted then the section 42 duty can be considered as ended.

An adult may be subject to the risk of actual and continual harm by a member of their family or a friend who they feel afraid of. The adult may be under duress from the source of harm but wish any enquiry to end. The local authority still has a section 42 duty towards the adult and must consider and decide whether the risk to them is harmful enough for enquiries to continue and/or a contingency plan to be made with them.

Multi-agency information gathering and decision making

Multi-agency information gathering and decision making can be more effective if a multi-agency safeguarding hub (MASH) is used. The first MASHs were developed in 2011 in response to the communication failures identified in serious case reviews about children and highlighted in the Munro Review of Child Protection (2011). MASH models vary greatly: some are based on the co-location of the police and local authority social workers, sometimes with health or probation input; others may have virtual or regular meetings. They will have the following features in common:

- a core group of professionals working collaboratively within an integrated unit;
- the core group usually has access to many other services and agencies that might be able to contribute to a picture of an individual's history;
- while intelligence gathering and information sharing are vital responsibilities of the MASH, the most effective models are those that are able to make timely and appropriate decisions about the information analysed;
- joint risk assessments underpin the decision–making approach. Whatever model is developed, all MASH models require good leadership and clear governance to create a shared operational culture and focus on outcomes (Centre of Excellence for Information Sharing, 2017).

MASH models were often initiated with children's services with an adult MASH being bolted on. The outcomes of an adult MASH can be harder to demonstrate, although this may be because of the early stages of development of these MASHs or because of the lack of certainty about their core business, such as which group of adults needs to go to the MASH. The concept of seamless information exchange between agencies, and a shared understanding of common risk assessment, is desirable, though that may be a desired aim rather than reality at present.

What else gets in the way of making decisions about section 42?

For decisions makers, the sheer volume of adult safeguarding concerns and decisions to be made can be exhausting and lead to a blunting of professional curiosity and increase in non-reflective, labelling practice. The unique features of each case may be lost in the rush to keep up with the urgent decisions that have to be made. Such teams and individuals need access to regular reflective supervision and responsive advice and guidance. Sometimes, using the reflection strategy in the Practice Guidance box, we can step out of busy activity to reflect in a few moments.

> ▶ **ESSENTIAL INFORMATION: PRACTICE GUIDANCE**
>
> *Reflecting alone*
>
> Keeping a reflective journal can extend into a regular habit of making time to reflect. Sicora (2017) suggests that material for reflection can be generated in only a few minutes each day, recording an event by giving it a title followed by a very short summary. By keeping such a record over a month or so themes for further reflection can be identified and extended. A safeguarding adult practitioner's collection could look like this:
>
> Title: Legality does not mean action
>
> Summary: Older woman assessed as lacking capacity to make a decision to stay in her home without care, but what happens now? Admit did MCA assessment to force decision on move – whose decision was I forcing?
>
> Title: A bed is not a necessity for all
>
> Summary: Ambulance staff concerned that man has no bed and sleeps on the carpet, referred as self-neglect, man explains that his back is better since he got rid of his bed. So – absence of bed opposite of self-neglect in this case?
>
> Such snapshots can be used to develop thinking about all our adult safeguarding activities – how we are making decisions, or using legal provisions, or any theme that you can pick out of your daily musings.

Some decision-making teams report a feeling of obligation to resolve as much as possible at the front door or on first contact in order to relieve pressure on other teams. These feelings are often observed when adult safeguarding is passed onto non-specialist teams who are also undertaking a range of other Care Act duties. The feeling of obligation may be created by feedback from receiving teams; for example, complaints that the cases being put through to them are inappropriate or could have been resolved if the first-contact decision makers undertook small actions. Pressure on services often creates a lack of empathy or understanding of the role and pressures both within and between agencies. Sometimes there is an agreed pathway in place that relies on first-contact decision makers resolving a large number of cases before passing them on. Operational risks of these models include creating a backlog of cases at the start of the process as practitioners attempt to resolve issues before passing them on, or if there is insufficient resource in the receiving teams, long waiting lists.

Recent research (Dixon, 2018) indicates that decision makers try to assess the motivation of referrers in referring a concern, focusing on the referrer's perceived intent to avoid blame, or trying to access services via a faster route. Referrer motivation was used alongside case details to assess whether there was a risk of, or actual, harm. Such attempts to assess motivation can mean that the decision is biased by the decision maker's assumptions and might not reflect actual risks or the impact of harm.

REFLECTIVE ACTIVITY

Case study: Robert and Pamela Stone

Mr Wolfe was **Robert and Pamela Stone**'s solicitor. He was undertaking the conveyance of a house that belongs to the couple. Mr Wolfe telephoned the local authority first-contact service to ask for advice. He reported that Robert and Pamela had had an altercation and Robert had moved into a summer house in the garden of the house that was to be sold. Robert appeared to be mentally unwell and indeed Pamela said she could not be close to Robert anymore and had left for the couple's holiday villa in France. The property to be sold was worth over a million pounds. Mr Wolfe was extremely concerned about Robert who did not appear to be eating and had no washing facilities in the summer house. Robert was reported to have had mental health issues in the past and also had a thyroid condition for which he needed daily medication.

Mr Wolfe offered to accompany a social worker to see if Robert could be engaged in conversation – Robert had a reported fear of mental health services. The decision-making team became convinced that Mr Wolfe had an agenda to get Robert evicted so that the house could be sold. They did not understand Mr Wolfe's motive and did not take up his offer to visit Robert. They did contact the GP who said that he had not seen Robert for some time but that he had been well for years. As a result, a response to Robert was delayed by three weeks during which time he had become extremely mentally and physically unwell.

Reflective questions

- Do you make assumptions about the motivation of those referring potential adult safeguarding concerns?
- What is the factual basis for the assumptions you are making?
- How does referrer motivation affect the section 42 duty of the local authority?

Our thoughts about the last question are that referrer motivation does not change the section 42 duty of the local authority. You still need to gather information and, if necessary, undertake an enquiry to find out what the actual circumstances are.

Concerns that do not meet the criteria for the section 42 duty

What if the person does not have care and support needs? A local authority can undertake a non-statutory (sometimes called 'other') enquiry if the adult does not have care and support needs. The only difference should be that the section 42 duty does not apply. A non-statutory enquiry can be used for the same purposes and have the same focus on involving the adult and addressing risk with them. As the section 42 duty does not exist the adult can decide that they do not want an enquiry and stop the process. The only exception might be if there is a vital interest or a public interest involved.

Local authorities appear to use non-statutory enquiries for a number of purposes. Some use this category to make enquiries about carers, people with addictions or people who are homeless, that is, people who have support rather than care and support needs. Others have reported using the category to cover enquiries following the death of an adult, or 'low level' abuse or 'poor quality rather than safeguarding'. It is not clear that these latter uses meet the criteria for a non-statutory enquiry. If the purpose of the enquiry is to assess if other adults are at risk of harm from the same circumstances as the adult who died then surely this is a statutory enquiry. If any harm is experienced or there is a risk of harm to an adult with care and support needs from poor practice, this too is potentially a statutory rather than a non-statutory enquiry.

Quality and adult safeguarding

Decisions about what type of enquiry is to be carried out, what the focus will be and who is best to undertake the enquiry are discussed in Chapter 9. But for now, we will look at a common decision that must be made when an individual is using a provided service: is the concern about the quality of provision rather than adult safeguarding, and is it therefore a matter for quality improvement teams to follow up?

The Care Act statutory guidance (DHSC, 2018a) points out that adult safeguarding cannot be engaged in the quality assurance of services, that it is the responsibility of the provider, the commissioners of the service, for example local authorities and the NHS, and the care regulator, in England, the CQC:

> Safeguarding is not a substitute for: providers' responsibilities to provide safe and high quality care and support, commissioners regularly assuring themselves of the safety and effectiveness of commissioned services, the Care Quality Commission (CQC) ensuring that regulated providers comply with the fundamental standards of care or by taking enforcement action. (Statutory guidance, section 14.9)

Some local authorities have officers who support the promotion of quality in the services commissioned by the local authority. These quality assurance activities can range from visits to providers to check they are compliant with the contract they have agreed with the authority, collating information from various sources to identify themes and trends about quality, or actively working with providers to address concerns about the quality of provision. The range of activities engaged in is usually determined by the size of the resources available, and the relationship between quality assurance and adult safeguarding can depend on what response quality assurance officers can give. In areas where there is little or no quality assurance resource, adult safeguarding practitioners can find themselves engaged in activities that attempt to prevent harm by promoting quality. In areas where there is an effective quality assurance response, there is a risk that concerns that should be addressed via the section 42 duty are not seen and adults are left at risk while a quality improvement programme progresses. The case example in the Reflective Activity illustrates this potential pitfall.

REFLECTIVE ACTIVITY

Case study: Doris Green

Doris Green had type 1 diabetes but during building work at the care home was seen walking about in bare feet. Care staff didn't appear to understand the impact a cut to her foot could have. You were told that only one member of staff had training in diabetic care and another person with diabetes was about to be admitted. The quality team visited the provider who agreed that the primary care diabetic specialist nurse could support them to source the right training for staff and would also speak to Doris's key worker. But no immediate action was taken to ensure that Doris was having her needs met, and was safe, while this improvement action was undertaken.

Reflective questions

- What relationship do you have with your local quality assurance (or contract compliance) team?
- What role can individual safeguarding practitioners play in establishing and maintaining a conversation about quality and safety in provided services?

Our thoughts are that safeguarding practitioners need to form working relationships with colleagues in quality and compliance teams, and must support the assessment of individual risk while quality of service concerns are addressed. Joint visits and attendance at relevant meetings when there is a possibility of risk are all helpful.

Provided services can be found to be short-staffed, but the impact of this on the individuals using the service is not always considered: how does the absence of staff affect well-being? Each individual will have different needs and areas of vulnerability. These must be understood and actions taken to prevent harm to them. Enquiries can be made alongside improvement actions that will maintain the well-being of people using the service while poor practice is addressed. While safeguarding is not a substitute for the activities of providers, commissioners and regulators, those activities are also not a substitute for adult safeguarding. Risks to individuals or groups of adults can be assessed during any large-scale quality improvement work by using the model suggested in Chapter 7 for risk assessment in organisations. These risks can be monitored and reviewed on a regular basis as the improvement work continues.

Decisions about advocacy

Under the Care Act 2014, local authorities must make sure that an adult is able to be involved in their own safeguarding. The Act identifies that if an adult has 'substantial difficulty' in doing so then the local authority has a duty to arrange independent advocacy.

It is important that this 'substantial difficulty' is not confused with a lack of mental capacity, even though the characteristics look similar. An adult may have substantial difficulty in being involved because their distress at a past experience of working with statutory services interferes with their ability to use or weigh information or they may be inexperienced in expressing their views and wishes or making decisions and communicating these. They might also be under such coercive control that they cannot use or weigh information. It is important that these adults have the support of an advocate who can empower them to have control and choice in their lives. The statutory guidance takes a broader view of who may have 'substantial difficulty' in being involved: 'an individual who is thought to have been abused or neglected may be so demoralised, frightened, embarrassed or upset that independent advocacy provided under section 68 to help them to be involved will be crucial' (statutory guidance, section 7.28). All the factors that may impede an adult's involvement should be considered. Our focus must be on how much we can maximise the adult's involvement and what steps we need to take to do this.

It is important to note that the adult needs to consent to the person seen as appropriate to represent and support them, and that if they are unable to consent the local authority must be satisfied that the person's appointment is in the adult's best interests. The person who is allegedly causing harm to the adult cannot act as their representative. In addition, the statutory guidance reminds us that the appropriate person may not be 'suitable' if they live far away or are unable to participate themselves for any reason (statutory guidance, section 7.35). It is the local authority's decision whether the adult should be represented by an appropriate person, whether an advocate should be commissioned, or whether indeed both should happen as the appropriate person is able to carry out some of their obligations well but will struggle with others.

If an enquiry needs to be undertaken very urgently it can begin without an advocate being appointed, but the duty to appoint an advocate under section 68 still exists and an appointment must be made as soon as possible. Conversely, an advocate may have been appointed but an enquiry finds that there is someone who can act as the appropriate person, in this case the advocate can simply hand over to them.

The Care Act statutory guidance (7.9) advises that if a person lacks capacity to make decisions and has been represented by an IMCA, then the same advocate should be used to avoid the person having to instruct and get to know a new advocate.

REFLECTIVE ACTIVITY

Reflective questions about advocacy

- Are you clear about your duty to arrange an advocate?
- Have you been able to create a relationship with your local advocacy services?
- Do you know what their experience has been of providing advocacy to involve adults in their own safeguarding?
- What challenges and barriers do advocates experience?

Decisions about what happens as a result of an enquiry

The key decisions about how an enquiry is conducted and what it focuses on should be made with the involvement of the adult. Although the local authority is the decision maker regarding whether or not there should be an enquiry, all other decisions need to be shared and the adult's views and wishes taken into account. Key aspects of the involvement of adults in enquiries are considered further in Chapter 9. The crucial element that informs the adult's involvement is the mutual exploration of the outcomes the adult hopes for as a result of the enquiry. How do they want their lives to change? What is important to them? What would improve their quality of life?

These desired outcomes strongly influence the decisions made at the end of the enquiry. The statutory guidance reminds us that:

> What happens as a result of an enquiry should reflect the adult's wishes wherever possible, as stated by them or by their representative or advocate. If they lack capacity it should be in their best interests if they are not able to make the decision, and be proportionate to the level of concern. (14.79)

An adult may decide that they want no further action taken. The adult's decision may need to be overridden and further enquiries and actions continue if the adults 'vital interests' or ECHR Article 2 right to life, are at continued risk, or there is a public interest, for example a criminal offence has taken place, which may put others at risk, or regulatory enforcement action needs to be taken by the CQC or other relevant regulator. The adult should be informed that this is happening.

We may need to continue to share information about the adult in these circumstances. The statutory guidance states that:

> If the adult has the mental capacity to make informed decisions about their safety and they do not want any action to be taken, this does not preclude the sharing of information with relevant professional colleagues. This is to enable professionals to assess the risk of harm and to be confident that the adult is not being unduly influenced, coerced or intimidated and is aware of all the options. This will also enable professionals to check the safety and validity of decisions made. It is good practice to inform the adult that this action is being taken unless doing so would increase the risk of harm. (14.92)

Decisions made by other agencies

Decisions made by other agencies will influence how enquires are undertaken, the outcomes of enquiries and how adults are protected. In Chapter 6 we talked about the importance of building relationships with other agencies, and understanding their role, responsibilities and powers. Although local authorities have duties under the Care Act 2014, local authority adult safeguarding practitioners have no powers, they are reliant on other agencies deciding to use their powers to effect change in the lives of adults at risk.

Criminal justice

While it is useful for all practitioners to have some grasp of criminal law it is ultimately police colleagues who will be able to identify that a crime has been committed. We set out a simplified summary of police decision-making processes. Do use it as a basis to ask your police colleagues for a more detailed description when needed; depending on the type of crime that has allegedly been committed, the factors that go into decision making can be complex and are underpinned by a wide range of legislation and police operational procedures.

The police may decide to carry out an initial investigation. Securing forensic evidence is important at this point after any victims have been identified and assisted. 'The first chance to obtain material may be the last. Identifying these actions during the initial investigation stage produces the most effective outcome. A delay in protecting, preserving or gathering material may result in evidence being contaminated or lost' (College of Policing, 2019, section 3).

If further investigation of the facts needs to be undertaken the case may be passed on to another investigating officer who must make a clear plan for further investigation. Once the police have concluded their investigations, they will refer the case to the Crown Prosecution Service (CPS) for advice on how to proceed in all but the most minor and routine cases. The CPS makes the decision on whether a suspect should be charged, and what that charge should be.

Where a person is suspected of committing an offence, the Police and Criminal Evidence Act 1984 Code of Practice, Code C (PACE, 1984, p 41, 10A) requires there to be 'some reasonable, objective grounds, based on known facts or information, which are relevant to the likelihood that the offence has been committed and the person to be questioned committed it' before the person can be charged. Once the person is charged with an offence, the CPS and police are jointly responsible for the prosecution of the case. The CPS will read the case file and the two tests laid down in the Code for Crown Prosecutors, the *evidential test* and the *public interest test*, must be applied in every case.

In the evidential test the prosecutor must decide whether or not there is enough evidence against the defendant for a realistic prospect of conviction. If there is not a realistic prospect of conviction, the case must not go ahead, no matter how important or serious it may be. It is the duty of every crown prosecutor to make sure that the right person is prosecuted for the right offence.

The public interest test is applied after the crown prosecutor decides that there is a realistic prospect of conviction. A prosecution is less likely to be needed if, for example, a court would be likely to fix a minimal or token penalty, or the loss or harm connected with the offence was minor and the result of a single incident (CPS, 2019). The interests of the victim are an important factor when considering the public interest. Crown prosecutors will always take into account the consequences for the victim and any views expressed by the victim or victim's family.

If the crown prosecutor decides that a prosecution should not go ahead, the case will be stopped, usually by what is called 'discontinuance'. If a prosecutor decides not to bring charges against a suspect, discontinues proceedings or offers no evidence in a case, there is a right to appeal under the victims' Right to Review scheme (CPS, 2016).

Care Quality Commission

The CQC has both civil and criminal enforcement powers. The CQC's civil powers focus on reducing the risk to people who use regulated services and their criminal powers are used to hold registered persons to account for serious failures. In some cases, both civil and criminal enforcement powers are used at the same time. It can appear to take time for CQC to take action to use its enforcement powers. The CQC has to base its actions on evidence and will need evidence from third parties, such as adult safeguarding services, to begin to compile a portfolio of evidence that can be used to take legally compliant enforcement action. The CQC uses an enforcement decision tree to guide its decision making on the use of enforcement powers (CQC, 2017). The decision tree has four stages:

1. initial assessment;
2. legal and evidential review;
3. selection of the appropriate enforcement action; and
4. review of enforcement actions taken.

Initial assessment is triggered when the CQC becomes aware of a possible breach of law or regulation which may warrant civil and/or criminal enforcement action. Sources of information to evidence this include notifications by providers, safeguarding alerts, instances of whistleblowing, reportable incident or coroners' reports, complaints, information from the public, and concerns identified during a CQC inspection. At this stage the CQC may carry out an inspection, may gather more evidence or may refer the concern to another public body. The CQC may also progress straight to Stage 2 of the decision tree and consider what enforcement action to take.

Legal and evidential review involves an assessment of the legal and evidential basis to determine whether there is sufficient evidence to substantiate a breach of the legal requirements by a registered person. CQC inspectors and their managers can carry out this function. If the inspector considers that the evidence demonstrates an identifiable breach of a legal requirement and the evidence is sufficient and robust to prove the breach, the case will continue to the next stage.

Selection of the appropriate enforcement action is made using two criteria – seriousness of the breach and evidence of multiple and/or persistent breaches – to decide which enforcement powers can be used. The CQC takes progressively stronger action in proportion to the seriousness of the breach and the potential impact on people using a service as well as the number of people affected. The CQC also takes stronger action where a service is carried out in an inappropriate way without effective management of risk. Depending on the seriousness of the breach, recommendations for civil action can range from cancellation of registration of the service, which closes the service, to a requirement notice for a minor breach with no serious consequences.

Criminal enforcement action is considered in every case where the CQC proposes civil enforcement or identifies a specific incident of suspected avoidable harm. Decisions about the most appropriate criminal enforcement action to take are made in consultation with CQC legal services and must follow the two-stage test as set out in the Code for Crown Prosecutors, mentioned earlier, meaning that the evidential and public interest tests apply. This action is usually considered when a regulation has been breached and an adult has experienced serious and avoidable harm. In April 2015, the CQC assumed responsibility for prosecuting providers for all health and safety related incidents, taking over from the Health and Safety Executive and local authorities.

▶ ESSENTIAL INFORMATION: LEGISLATION

CQC enforcement action: Southern Health NHS Trust

On 12 October 2017, Basingstoke Magistrates' Court heard the prosecution against Southern Health NHS Trust, the first CQC prosecution against an NHS provider. The case related to Melbury Lodge, an acute inpatient psychiatric unit. The CQC's prosecution submitted that despite three inspections of the service, all of which cited issues and potential risks associated with access to the roof of the building, safety measures were not implemented to minimise risks to service users.

Evidence was presented to the court that there had been seven occasions where patients had climbed onto the roof, including an incident involving a patient named as Mr AB in March 2012. He was subsequently re-admitted to the service three years later, and on 3 December 2015 Mr AB managed to get on to the roof of the building again and then fell, suffering severe injuries. Even after this, there were three more reported incidents where patients gained access to the roof.

The service was reinspected in January 2016 and a warning notice was issued. The Trust was sentenced to a fine of £125,000 for failing to provide safe care and treatment and putting people at risk of avoidable harm.

▶ KEY MESSAGES

- It is important to be clear about what decision is being made and who can make it. If a local authority has a duty to make a decision it does not need the consent of the adult involved but must make the decision based on reasonable and proportionate information gathering and without assumptions regarding anything but the known facts.

- It is important to seek the views of adults regarding the decisions to be made, to act on the duty to arrange advocacy if an adult will have 'substantial difficulty' in being involved and to consider best interests if the adult is unable to inform the decision.

- Adult safeguarding practitioners have duties but no powers. It is important to understand the decision-making processes of the agencies we work with who do have powers that they can use to protect adults. We need to have some understanding of the checks, balances and procedures those agencies use in exercising their legal powers.

KNOWLEDGE REVIEW

- WHAT are the local authorities' duties related to adult safeguarding under the provisions of the Care Act 2014? What can impede decision making about how those duties are used?

- IN WHAT circumstances should you arrange advocacy? What should you bear in mind when considering an appropriate person to represent an adult?

- WHAT are the two basic principles that both the CPS and the CQC must bear in mind when considering prosecutions?

FURTHER READING

- More resources on decision making about the section 42 duty can be found at: www.local.gov.uk/making-decisions-duty-carry-out-safeguarding-adults-enquiries-resources.

- This article gives a thoughtful view on what advocacy can mean to older people in the context of adult safeguarding and explores the role of the advocate and meaning of advocacy post the Care Act 2014: Lonbay, S. and Brandon, T. (2017) 'Renegotiating Power in Adult Safeguarding: The Role of Advocacy', *The Journal of Adult Protection*, 19(2): 78–91.

9

Adult safeguarding enquiries

Chapter aim

In this chapter we will look in detail at some of the essential components of an enquiry, whether 'statutory' or 'non-statutory', with an emphasis on practical approaches to involving adults and working with other agencies. Do review the learning from previous chapters to remind yourself about aspects of making relationships, working with risk and decision making. We will focus on resolution and recovery in more detail in Chapter 10.

In this chapter we will explore:

- the essential components of an enquiry;

- involving adults in enquiries and using advocacy;

- who can undertake an enquiry and how to support them;

- making safeguarding plans;

- the importance of escalation.

The essential components of an enquiry

The Care Act 2014 statutory guidance describes a set of objectives which will be achieved in an enquiry.

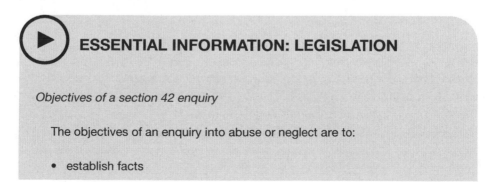

▶ **ESSENTIAL INFORMATION: LEGISLATION**

Objectives of a section 42 enquiry

The objectives of an enquiry into abuse or neglect are to:

- establish facts

- ascertain the adult's views and wishes
- assess the needs of the adult for protection, support and redress and how they might be met
- protect from the abuse and neglect, in accordance with the wishes of the adult
- make decisions as to what follow-up action should be taken with regard to the person or organisation responsible for the abuse or neglect
- enable the adult to achieve resolution and recovery

Care and Support Statutory Guidance, section 14.94 (DHSC, 2018a)

An enquiry does not progress through distinct linear stages but is fluid or dynamic in nature. For practitioners undertaking enquiries, it is important to address the objectives of an enquiry in whatever order meets the needs of the adult and enquiries must be proportionate to the impact of harm or risk of harm and interfere as little as possible in the adult's life. Enquiries should only interfere enough to establish if the adult or others are being harmed or are at risk of harm and if action needs to be taken to help. The statutory guidance describes the proportionate nature of enquiry: 'An enquiry could range from a conversation with the adult, or if they lack capacity, or have substantial difficulty in understanding the enquiry their representative or advocate, prior to initiating a formal enquiry under section 42, right through to a much more formal multi-agency plan or course of action' (section 14.77).

REFLECTIVE ACTIVITY

Case study: Ron Wise and a 'conversation' enquiry

Ron Wise's support worker referred a concern about an 'old friend' taking up residence in Ron's flat and potentially exploiting him. Ron lives in a supported living flat in sheltered accommodation and has learning disabilities.

Ron told the support worker that he did not want this man to stay with him but felt sorry for him. You telephoned Ron, who invited you over to the flat. He told you that he had sorted the situation out himself but would welcome a chat. You visited Ron, and he told you that the old friend left to stay with other friends. He did not want him back; he said that he did not feel threatened by him and did not give him money but the friend ate all Ron's food and made him feel uncomfortable. Ron thought that the friend would return. He wanted to think through a strategy for saying 'no', which he could rehearse with his support workers.

You devised a strategy with Ron that included the following practical steps: Ron will not buzz people through to the flat before hearing who they are, he will tell the friend or any other unwelcome visitor that he cannot see them and will end the conversation quickly. He will be clear with visitors that he does not have people to stay and he will alert his support workers if he needs support to tell a visitor to leave.

Ron's support worker arrived and Ron updated him as to what was agreed. This turned into a wider conversation about how hard Ron found it to stand up for himself. Ron and the support worker identified other opportunities when Ron could practise doing this – beginning with being assertive with his support worker.

Reflective questions

– How could a similar scenario result in a further enquiry?
– What further factors might you see?

Our thoughts are that we would need to undertake a further enquiry if there were signs that the friend was trying to undermine Ron's ability to self-determine – signs of deliberate exploitation. In this case, Ron may say that the friend threatened or demeaned him, or demanded that he would move in to the flat or become Ron's 'carer'.

We may then also consider any public risk. If the friend sounds exploitative and travels between various addresses, are others at risk? We might want to find out more about this friend. Is he known to the police?

In these scenarios Ron will remain in control of how he protects himself, but we would need to review his outcomes with him, including whether he wants to make any complaint to the police about the friend's exploitative behaviour. Ron might want to get to know the local Police Community Safety Officer (PCSO) and we should also consider any other protective and preventative factors in Ron's life. It will be important to arrange return visits to review the safeguarding plan with Ron as needed.

The course of action to be followed is sometimes difficult to predict and can emerge as the enquiry progresses, new facts emerge, circumstances change or the outcomes the adult is seeking alter.

The beginning of the enquiry

Taking time to plan even the shortest of enquiries is important. At this stage of the enquiry we need to take time to plan our conversation with the adult and to think through how we will explain adult safeguarding and the concerns about them. Find out if there is information in your organisation that will help you talk about adult safeguarding with the adult and those around them.

> ▶ **ESSENTIAL INFORMATION: PRACTICE GUIDANCE**
>
> *Literature that supports conversations: Swindon Local Safeguarding Adults Board*
>
> Swindon Local Safeguarding Adults Board have produced a printed booklet to give to adults who are involved in adult safeguarding procedures. It has pages for adults or representatives to record who their adult safeguarding 'link person' is, they are kept informed by the link person and can contact them at any point, and to record who else is involved in the enquiry. There is a page for meetings' date, time and place, a description of what happens at meetings and options for how they can be involved. There is a section to record what the adult wants to happen and how they would like the enquiry managed, and a tear-off page for feedback.
>
> The booklet has clear and accessible information on adult safeguarding, often using the term 'keeping' or 'staying' safe. As well as the adult's human rights, their rights during the safeguarding enquiry are detailed.
>
> See: Swindon Local Safeguarding Adults Board (2015)

During your conversation with the adult you will ask for their perspective on the concern by asking them, "What happened?" Missing this step can have disastrous consequences. For example, Mr Short was alleged by a hospital worker to have disclosed that he was regularly sexually assaulted by night-care staff. The police were contacted and an emergency planning meeting convened. Mr Short was interviewed by a police officer and social worker. He was very embarrassed. He explained that he disliked the night staff attending to his personal needs and so made jokes about it. Mr Short had been joking, but this had been misunderstood by the concerned health worker.

Talking with the adult also gives you an opportunity to seek their consent to you asking other agencies for information about them. If the adult refuses their consent you may have to accept this, but you can share information without their permission if there is a risk to their 'vital interests' (General Data Protection Regulations, Article 6(1)(d), see European Parliament, 2016) or you believe that they are under duress or being controlled by another person, there are others at risk or a 'serious crime' has been committed as discussed in Chapter 7.

Lastly, you will ask the adult what thoughts they have about what they want to happen next. They may wish you to do nothing, but remember the duty to enquire is still there. You may need to decide to continue with the enquiry. If you do need to continue, it is important to tell the adult why you are continuing without their consent and that you will keep them informed as much, or as little, as they wish and that they can still be involved at a later date if they change their mind. The adult may have an initial set of thoughts about what they want to happen next, what kind of life they want and who is important to them. Being harmed, being visited by a social worker and talking about harm may all be stressful for the adult. It can be helpful to go back after the adult has had time to think through what has happened. Being rushed is not empowering, and potentially life-changing decisions take time to make.

What if the adult is prevented from seeing you by another person?

The first essential step when faced with this dilemma is to try to understand why the adult is being prevented from seeing you. We list some common scenarios, but remember that each situation is unique:

- People may try to keep social workers away from the adult because of previous poor experiences, including having children taken into care or being sectioned under the Mental Health Act, or they may have a general mistrust of statutory services.
- People may misunderstand the intention of social workers, fearing that the adult will be 'put into a home', or the house they live in will be sold immediately to pay care fees. They may not understand what we mean by adult safeguarding and what this entails.
- People may prevent access to the adult because they are afraid that some aspect of their own behaviour that they are defensive about will be identified, such as substance misuse or other addictions, mental health difficulties, learning disability or dementia.
- Obstructing may be an aspect of coercive control, the behaviour that underlies domestic abuse. The adult is deliberately isolated and their life strictly controlled.
- The obstructer may know that there are serious problems but want life to stay as it always has been. This can be true of adult children who are now neglecting a frail or incapacitated parent, but do not wish to acknowledge that changes must be made, or they may be protective family members who wish to keep a disabled person 'safe' and away from the possibility of change.

Norrie et al (2018) carried out a study of social workers and service user representatives in three English local authorities, capturing their perspectives about the options they used to respond to the obstruction of entry to older adults. The majority of the social workers interviewed reported that their first action was to try to 'negotiate with the obstructive third party' (p 1079). They tried to develop a rapport with the person obstructing or 'hindering' in order to understand the context for the refusal of access. Social workers also carried out as many checks as possible on the person obstructing in order to understand on what basis they lived with the adult or whether they had a history of domestic abuse or addiction. These factors are important to understand in order to plan the negotiation. If an engagement and negotiation approach failed the social worker might become more assertive, using professional, rather than legal, authority to emphasise the importance of seeing the adult alone and unhindered. Social workers also talked about 'pursuing creative routes' (p 1080). They might plan to meet the adult outside the home in the day centre they attended, via a GP appointment or in another public place. They might try to get another family member to facilitate a meeting. These options, and the 'neutral person' options (see next paragraph), must always be risk assessed to explore the possibility of further serious harm to the adult because they have met with a professional, and disclosed harm.

People who have previously had a bad experience of working with social workers or are fearful of statutory services may be able to relate to a more neutral figure, for example an advocate, to help them understand the concerns and possible outcomes of adult safeguarding. You could also consider if someone from a different agency is more likely to be able to enter the premises and carry out an initial conversation with the adult.

Consider:

- Would a colleague from a partner agency have more success in gaining access to the adult?
- Is there someone who can be considered as 'neutral' by the person who is obstructing access?
- Is there a care agency or district nurse who regularly visits the adult?

Remember that you need to brief and continue to support the person who will talk with the adult, and plan for any increased risk to the adult from this approach. Examples of a 'neutral person' include: primary healthcare professionals including GPs, nurses, community occupational therapists, or other services who know the adult including home care or voluntary sector organisations. Neutral agencies may include Trading Standards, Victim Support, Fire and Rescue, the RSPCA, advocates including Independent Mental Capacity Advocates (IMCAs) or family solicitors.

REFLECTIVE ACTIVITY

Case study: Mrs Swift

Mrs Swift lives in a sheltered housing complex. She is 92 years old. Her son Nigel moved in after his partner threw him out after violence against her and her children. A concern was received from the Ambulance Trust after they were called to the flat: Nigel had pushed Mrs Swift during an argument between them and had later disconnected the oxygen she relied on to help her cope with breathing difficulties.

Mrs Swift used the lifeline alarm after he had left the flat. Mrs Swift did not want to be taken to hospital and did not want Nigel to know she had told anyone about him. She seemed to the ambulance staff afraid of Nigel but determined to 'stand by him', explaining that he had a difficult childhood with a violent father. She does not want a social worker involved; she says that Nigel hates them as they tried to take his children away.

You make some initial enquiries about Nigel and discover that there are recorded concerns about threatening behaviour towards his mother. The police tell you that he was arrested a year ago after assaulting his partner but not charged. Nigel does not venture far from the flats and the GP surgery tells you that he attends appointments with Mrs Swift. The sheltered housing 'floating' warden tells you that Nigel should not be living in the flat and he has frightened Mrs Swift's friends away as well as stopping her attending local clubs as he does not think she is 'safe' outside the flat.

He does not want to help Mrs Swift with her personal care, however, and for the moment a carer goes in every morning and two carers assist Mrs Swift to use the shower twice a week. You want to engage with Mrs Swift to see if she is well and what her views are on taking matters forward. There is not only a risk to Mrs Swift's safety but also a risk that Nigel may stop the home care agency seeing her as he is controlling all other external connections she has.

Reflective question
- How are you going to engage with Mrs Swift without endangering her safety and well-being further?

Our thoughts are that there are a number of options to consider; we need to engage the home care agency and seek their knowledge about the situation and whether they can assess Mrs Swift's immediate safety as

> well as trying to ascertain her thoughts about the situation. Are there any opportunities for them to speak with Mrs Swift alone? When Mrs Swift does attend the GP surgery could Nigel be assertively told to remain outside on a pretext?

Planning an enquiry

After ascertaining the views and wishes of the adult there may be further enquiry planning, especially if more than one agency is to be involved. Good planning will make sure that the adult can benefit from the assistance of the right agencies, and that the activities of those agencies are coordinated and supported by the local authority. The statutory guidance describes some of the activities that may take place during an enquiry:

- Using the wishes of the adult at risk ascertained during the early part of the enquiry, discuss what further enquiries and/or actions they think are required.
- Enable the adult to understand what their options might be and how their wishes might be realised.
- Support the adult at risk to gain confidence and self-esteem to enable self-protection, especially in complex domestic circumstances, involving the police, NHS and others as required.
- Consider actions such as disciplinary, complaints or criminal investigations or work by contracts managers and the CQC to improve care standards.
- Consider both civil and criminal justice approaches that are available as well as ways to improve well-being including therapeutic or family work, mediation and conflict resolution, peer or circles of support. (Adapted from Care Act statutory guidance, section 14.105)

Planning is best seen as a process and not a single event. The process begins, as described, with ascertaining the adult's views and wishes, their 'desired outcomes'. The rest of the planning process can be undertaken in various ways, perhaps as a series of telephone conversations, or by meeting with an individual practitioner, or as a meeting with the relevant people and agencies.

Face-to-face meetings can seem time-consuming to those participating, but are effective mechanisms for gathering information, enabling problem solving, agreeing detailed enquiry processes and sharing decision making. If agencies are anxious about the risk to the adult then a face-to-face meeting will help to share anxiety as people plan together. Planning via the telephone can be a pragmatic solution when only one other agency is involved with the local authority acting as coordinator in a straightforward enquiry. It is important that the busy nature of agencies is not allowed to get in the way of face-to-face planning when it is needed. Face-to-face meetings may no longer be part of the business culture of organisations, but adult safeguarding should challenge these cultures, remembering to use the principles of proportionality and partnership at all times. While simple plans may mean a short conversation, plans that involve several strands of enquiry, or that may create risks for the adult or others, must be fully discussed and explored. More time and resources will be needed if badly made plans do not prevent further harm: adults will be referred back for more intervention, or left in a more traumatic situation. Planning an enquiry can involve a range of considerations, which we now set out.

What facts do we need to ascertain? What is the focus of the enquiry?

The focus of the enquiry is often exactly what the adult wishes the enquiry to focus on. As we have argued in Chapter 6, adults are experts in their own lives and about their needs for protection, redress and recovery. We also need to remember the balance between protection, prevention and proportionality: we should not be gathering facts that have no relevance to the concern. However, there are situations where the focus may be on facts which the adult finds hard to understand. For many adults, their supporters and, sometimes, practitioners, the facts that need to be understood in order to prevent harm or protect the adult and others are outside our life experience. Examples may include: coercive control in domestic abuse; high-risk violent behaviour; coercive control which is used to enact exploitative disability hate crime or sexual exploitation of individuals or groups; the psychological mechanisms with which internet and other scammers keep people 'hooked' into being scammed; the plausible reasons given by practised confidence tricksters to gain money and resources; exploitation via cuckooing or other drug-related activity; and human trafficking. These complex areas require careful exploration with the adult together with partnership planning and working together from a range of agencies.

How the adult is and will be involved

What are the adult's views, wishes and outcomes, and how these will be updated and continue to be understood? How will the adult's wishes inform the enquiry? Are there agencies or people the adult thinks should be involved? Are there agencies or people the adult does not want to be approached? How will this affect the enquiry? Are there evidenced reasons to override this wish? Does the adult have significant difficulty in being involved? Is there someone appropriate they want to represent them? If not, has advocacy been commissioned? If the adult has been assessed as not having the mental capacity to make decisions about outcomes, who is representing them and how will they be involved? How will we observe the adult's best interests at all times? How will we monitor the adult's well-being as the enquiry progresses?

Known risks

Is there a need for an interim safeguarding plan to promote the well-being of the adult or adults involved while enquiries are undertaken? How will risk be assessed with the adult or their representative, and how will any risks caused to the adult concerned by the enquiry be addressed?

Assessments needed

Is an assessment of the adult's care and support needs under section 9 of the Care Act 2014 needed? Or an assessment of their mental capacity regarding specific decisions about the concerns expressed, their safety or involvement in the process?

If there are a range of enquiries, for example a police investigation of a potential criminal act, or a medical assessment, or care and support needs assessment, how will these be coordinated in a way that is least disruptive to the adult, make best use of the enquiry officer's expertise, and maximise the best outcome negotiated with the adult? How will the information be shared and coordinated? How will the enquiry officers be supported? As new facts emerge or circumstances change, the enquiry plan will need to be changed. Good attention from the local authority that is coordinating the enquiry plan will ensure that the plan continues to respond to emerging needs, risks, the adult's wishes and changing circumstances.

REFLECTIVE ACTIVITY

Case study: Mrs Swift's enquiry plan

After planning with you and their manager, **Mrs Swift**'s two regular home carers spoke with her while they were supporting her to shower two days after the ambulance referral. She is bruised from being pushed but otherwise physically OK. Mrs Swift says she has had enough; she loves Nigel but is afraid of him: he is shouting at her more and drinking alcohol heavily. Now the shock of his behaviour towards her has worn off she has decided that she wants him to leave, and for him to get some help. Mrs Swift is aware that she is in breach of her tenancy. She wanted to help him but matters seem to be getting worse. Mrs Swift does not want the police to prosecute Nigel but wants some peace from him for now. She wants someone to help her to tell him to go. After getting this report, you convene an enquiry planning meeting with the housing association landlord, the police, the home care agency and a social worker.

Reflective questions

–   What is your assessment of the risk of further harm to Mrs Swift?

> – How urgently should a response be made?
> – What avenues are open to support Mrs Swift, taking account of her currently expressed wishes and the risk of creating further risk or damaging her quality of life?
>
> *Our thoughts* are that the risk of Mrs Swift being harmed are high and imminent given Nigel's previous and current behaviour and the escalation of his drinking alcohol. Mrs Swift wants to have a break from him, and for him to "get help". A joint visit from the landlord – to explain breach of tenancy and the need to leave that same day to Nigel – and a social worker – to support Mrs Swift and explain options to her – may help, but the police will need to be on stand-by should this fail.

Involving adults in enquiries and using advocacy

Adult safeguarding enquiries are intended to empower those whose human rights they seek to uphold, but the experience of adult safeguarding risks being disempowering, and can lead to adults feeling singled out and considered separately from their relationships and networks, being judged and intruded on, and fearful that the adult safeguarding process takes then to a point of no return, which they have little control over (Sherwood-Johnson et al, 2013). The safeguarding process can reduce the resilience of the adult and the systems around them. An adult's resilience can be promoted through a sense of belonging to a network of secure relationships, a sense of self-esteem and of self-efficacy, the feeling of control and competence to influence their situation (Bloom, 1996; Gilligan, 1997). In order to counter the risk of reducing the adult's resilience they must be supported to be involved in the adult safeguarding process.

▶ ESSENTIAL INFORMATION: PRACTICE GUIDANCE

Practical steps to take to involve people in enquiry processes

Conversations
Follow the guidance in Chapter 4 to engage, creating a relationship with the adult and their identified networks. Talk with the people the adult suggests can help. Make sure you keep the adult, or their representatives, updated as to how the enquiry plan is progressing. As discussed in Chapter 6, gather facts and assess risk together.

Information

Make sure you understand how you will communicate with the adult. Do have accessible information to leave with them, including how they can contact you and anyone else who will be a contact during the enquiry. Discuss timescales, what is realistic and acceptable to the adult, what can be done quickly, what will take more time.

Meetings

Make sure meetings are accessible to the adult and their supporters. Start by talking with the adult about what arrangements will be best for them. It may be preferable to hold meetings at the adult's house or in a place they feel comfortable and most able to participate in. The adult can bring supporters or a representative or may have an advocate. They may not wish to attend the meeting but have their views represented by another either verbally or in writing. A shorter meeting may be more manageable for everyone, including the adult. You may need to build in breaks and hold the meeting at a time when the adult is most able to participate and/or their representative is available. The meeting must be conducted at the adult's pace. The adult could work with you to set the agenda for the meeting. Consider how the meeting will conduct itself to ensure maximum participation, listening and responding to the adult's contribution.

Advocates instructed by the local authority

It is important to understand what type of advocate may be able to support and represent the adult. There are several roles with 'advocate' in their job title, but it should not be presumed that all specialist advocates are able to advocate on behalf of adults regarding adult safeguarding. Care Act advocates commissioned by the local authority will be able to meet the requirements of advocacy within adult safeguarding. This is 'instructed advocacy', as the adult has the mental capacity to make decisions relevant to the concern.

If the adult has substantial difficulty because they do not have the mental capacity to make the relevant decisions then an IMCA is the appropriate advocate. Many advocacy organisations who provide Care Act advocates also provide IMCAs and it is helpful and reasonable that the adult is represented by the same advocate for different aspects of their needs. IMCAs are specialist advocates trained to support decision making and act as 'non-instructed' advocates. They can act as the voice of the adult, making sure that their wishes, views and beliefs are represented and their rights are secured. IMCAs use a range of approaches to inform their understanding of the adult's perspective. These include a rights-based model that focuses on the adult's human rights, a witness observer model where the advocate spends time with the person observing how they interact with others and the environment around them, and a person-centred model, which focuses on getting to know the person and what is important in their life.

Advocates that cannot be instructed by the local authority

The adult may have access to an Independent Mental Health Advocate (IMHA). An IMHA is also a specialist advocate and can act as an instructed or non-instructed advocate depending on the adult's capacity to instruct. The right to an IMHA was introduced in 2007 under amendments to the Mental Health Act 1983. The IMHA's role is to help people to understand their legal rights under the Mental Health Act 1983 (SCIE, 2014b). Advocating in an adult safeguarding situation is not part of the IMHA's role, unless that situation is related to the care and treatment the adult is receiving whilst detained under the Mental Health Act 1983, for example neglect or ill treatment in a mental health hospital. IMHAs may offer to advocate and, especially if they have a relationship with the adult, are helpful, but they are under no legal obligation to do so.

Independent Domestic Abuse Advisors (IDVAs) have a distinct role in domestic abuse situations. Their purpose is to address the safety of victims at high risk of harm from intimate partners, ex-partners or family members in order to secure their safety and the safety of any children in the situation. IDVAs work with adults from the point of crisis to assess their level of risk, discuss the range of suitable options and develop safety plans. These plans will include actions from the MARAC as well as sanctions and remedies available through the criminal and civil courts, housing options, and services available through other organisations. IDVAs support and work over the short to medium term to get an adult on the path to long-term safety (SafeLives, 2014). It may well be that an IDVA will accompany and support an adult through adult safeguarding relating to domestic abuse, but their role is to work with the adult to address domestic abuse concerns and create safety plans; they cannot be involved in the adult's need for advocacy regarding other aspects of well-being.

What do advocates do?

The Care and Support Statutory Guidance describes advocates as having two roles:

1. They need to *provide support* to the adult to assist them in understanding the safeguarding process.
2. *Representation*, particularly in ensuring that the individual's voice is heard and the safeguarding process takes account of their views wherever appropriate. (DHSC, 2018a, sections 7.50–7.52)

Studies of advocates in adult safeguarding in England (Lonbay and Brandon, 2017) and Scotland (Sherwood-Johnson, 2016) identify four areas of activity:

1. **Creating a supportive relationship**: Understanding the adult, their preferences, needs, strengths, circumstances and also, in non-instructed advocacy, their past wishes and views.

2. **Enabling communication**: Making sure the adult can understand the procedures and their rights within these. Taking steps to ensure that the adult is involved and that their views and wishes are central to the process.

3. **Supporting the adult to participate in meetings**: Considering options together, planning with them what they want to say and do.

4. **Acting as the adult's memory**: Keeping notes, asserting their needs and wishes, making sure the adult is not being persuaded against their interests or being rushed, going over what happened afterwards.

Advocates need time to get to know the adult and to form a relationship of trust with them. It is important to remember that the advocate is doing their best to represent the adult – they are independent of all agencies and cannot be swayed by the concerns of the agencies involved. Representing or supporting the adult's wishes is about empowering them to have as much control as possible during a time when they have lost so much control. Sometimes we might experience relationships with advocates as oppositional or uncomfortable. We need to reflect on how would we feel if the adult themselves was being assertive and challenging – the advocate is doing this on their behalf.

REFLECTIVE ACTIVITY

Case study: Mrs Swift and her advocate

The enquiry plan was only partially successful in achieving the aim of giving **Mrs Swift** a space free of Nigel and his frightening behaviour. It was Mrs Swift's decision as to whether he left the flat or not and whether she continued to breach her tenancy. Mrs Swift told Nigel that she wanted him to leave but given he had nowhere to go would allow him 'a few more days' to visit the housing point of access and get himself sorted out. This extended into a week. Fortunately, Nigel did not forbid the home carers coming in who he perceived as a 'neutral party' and so Mrs Swift's well-being could be ascertained and the multi-agency group around her could stay vigilant of her safety.

Nigel continued to drink heavily and fell into the path of a motorcyclist on his way back from the supermarket. He was taken to hospital and admitted as he had a head injury and fractured leg. The police reported this to the social worker who went straight round to see Mrs Swift. Mrs Swift was very distressed – she felt the social worker was pressuring her, she felt she couldn't think straight, that she wasn't being listened to, and wanted everyone to leave her alone. Mrs Swift was in a dilemma, she loved her son, but also did not want to lose her tenancy or spend her life in fear of him. She had no other family or friends to turn to.

Reflective question

– What can you do to support Mrs Swift during this crucial time?

Our thoughts are that, because of the deep dilemmas in her life and absence of neutral support, she is experiencing significant difficulty in being involved in the enquiry, weighing up information, and being listened to. You could talk with her about having a neutral person, a Care Act advocate, to support her to think through her wishes and to make sure that her views are listened to.

How did Mrs Swift's story end?

The initial approach to support Mrs Swift to tell Nigel to leave was not fully successful. A further meeting was being planned when events changed Mrs Swift's circumstances and brought matters to a head. In situations where there are a range of risky behaviours this sometimes happens and a good monitoring and communication plan is vital to respond to crises and opportunities.

Mrs Swift and her advocate were able to work well together. The relationship they had formed the basis for extensive conversations about Mrs Swift's feelings and wishes and Nigel's options. Nigel was discharged to a ground-floor room in a bed and breakfast. Mrs Swift visited him when she wanted to, armed with cake and details of the local Alcoholics Anonymous group. She sees her grandchildren again as Nigel's ex-partner is no longer suspicious of her. Her locks are changed as she does not want Nigel to live with her again; and as her life begins to feel good she is feeling stronger.

Who can undertake an enquiry and how to support them

A local authority has a legal duty to make an enquiry under section 42 of the Care Act, but it can ask, or 'cause', another agency to make enquiries regarding a specific and individual case: 'The local authority must make (*or cause to be made*) whatever enquiries it thinks necessary to enable it to decide whether any action should be taken in the adult's case ... and, if so, what and by whom' (Care Act 2014, S42(2)).

Remember that a local authority cannot delegate its duty under section 42, but it can cause another agency to make an enquiry on the basis that the agency is the most appropriate agency or has the expertise or the duty to do so. This means that those responsible for a section 42 enquiry can decide that another agency should undertake a section 42 enquiry and report its findings back. The statutory duty (S6(6)(c)) to cooperate does not apply if undertaking an enquiry would be incompatible with the agency's duties or would have an adverse effect on its own functions. The local authority must give the agency making the enquiry on its behalf a clear idea of what it is expected to do, it must support the agency and must assure the quality of the enquiry when returned.

▶ ESSENTIAL INFORMATION: PRACTICE GUIDANCE

When causing another agency to make an enquiry: dos and don'ts

1. **Do** set clear terms of reference – be clear about what you want the agency to enquire about. What do you understand are the important facts that need to be understood or risks considered?
2. **Do** detail how you expect the agency will involve the adult in the enquiry. Be clear and specific: 'Speak with Mrs Jones and ask her what impact this incident has had on her. How does she feel now? What would help her recover? What would improve her quality of life? What does she think is now the best way forward?' **Don't** say 'use a Making Safeguarding Personal approach' as the provider may not be clear what this is. Make sure that an advocate is instructed by the local authority if needed to support the adult.
3. **Do** be clear about who the agency should report to and give contact details. Make sure the agency knows who will support them if they have questions or make an unexpected discovery, for example that a crime has been committed.
4. **Do** negotiate the timescale for return of the enquiry report. You can follow up a few days beforehand to make sure all is well. **Don't** let matters drift, instead set new timescales and ask what barriers or challenges are being experienced. Remember it is a local authority duty to make sure the enquiry is undertaken.
5. **Do** quality assure the report. Has the enquiry been objective and thorough? Has it addressed the focus of the concern? Has the adult or their representative been involved? Has the conclusion of the enquiry been evidenced? Has any further need for protection been determined and actioned? What recommendations are made? If you cannot accept the quality of the enquiry, you can ask the agency to undertake further work with a new negotiated timescale, or you can undertake a further enquiry yourself.

While many adult safeguarding practitioners in local authorities have had training and ongoing support in using the MSP approach and have experience of involving the adult in their own safeguarding, many private, voluntary and independent sector health and social care providers have had no or little training.

Many providers will already be using person-centred, creative and preventative approaches and find that asking adults about outcomes and redress is second nature, but some are not so confident about involving adults or their representatives. Their concerns may range from worrying about upsetting people or losing the trust and confidence of those using the service, through to seeing safeguarding as a disciplinary or regulatory matter which is dealt with by managers and owners, not the adults who use the service or their representatives or indeed the frontline staff who work with them.

Lawson (2017) has written guidance on good practice and MSP for a range of organisations including housing, police, commissioners and health and care providers. Telling agencies what MSP is and how to use person-centred approaches is only a beginning. While commissioners and regulators must promote such approaches, we also need to share our knowledge and training about involving people with our provider colleagues. Our current case-auditing experience shows an emerging picture of a 'two tier' use of MSP approaches. If an adult is living in their own home, they are more likely to be involved in their own safeguarding than an adult living in a care setting. There may be several underlying reasons for this, but a clear trend is that we are more likely to ask a provided service to undertake an enquiry in a care home, that provider may not have had training and support to use an MSP approach and community organisations may be more used to using enabling approaches to care and support.

Who can be caused to make an enquiry?

Table 9.1 gives a short list of agencies that either have the role and responsibility for certain types of enquiry or may know the adult so well that they are able to use their relationship to broach sensitive areas of the adult's life with them. In complex cases there may be several activities going on, for example an assessment of the adult's care and support needs, a criminal investigation, and a health assessment. Think about when and how these activities take place. Could there be joint visits with other professionals? Check that the well-being of the adult is being supported through all enquiries; for example, while a police investigation may need to take precedence, ensuring that the adult has practical support to maintain their well-being is paramount and must be considered at all times.

Making safeguarding plans

Safeguarding planning often occurs as part of the enquiry, but if the situation is complex a plan may not be agreed until the end of the enquiry. As we have already discussed, the process of enquiry and planning can be fluid; it may be possible to make plans rapidly or it may take some time to do so. The imminence of harm, the decision-making pace the adult needs, the outcomes they seek and the need for input from a range of agencies can all influence when and how safeguarding plans are made.

Table 9.1: Agencies and organisations that may be relevant to undertake section 42 enquiries

Enquiry activities	Agency that may be able to enquire
Establishing the views, wishes and desired outcomes of the adult	The most appropriate person in the situation, the professional who knows the adult best and who the adult trusts. This could be a social worker, or could be a nurse, occupational therapist, care worker, provider manager, housing support worker, PCSO, community psychiatric nurse or GP
	Remember: If the adult has substantial difficulty in being involved in the enquiry, an appropriate person should be identified to represent them, and if there is no appropriate person, an independent advocate must be instructed
Care and support needs assessment under section 9 or 11 of the Care Act 2014	Social worker or similar social care staff
Assessment of health, including mental health needs	Appropriate health worker such as GP, district nurse or community psychiatric nurse
Allegations that a crime has been committed	Police
Anti-social behaviour – this can range from noisy neighbours, which is a civil matter, through to hate crime and threatening behaviour, criminal matters	Non-criminal: landlord, if breach of tenancy agreement, environmental health or the local authority anti-social behaviour team Criminal: police
Bogus calls, internet or post scams, rogue traders	Trading Standards and/or the police
Breach of health and safety legislation and regulations	CQC if this occurs in a regulated setting, the Health and Safety Executive (HSE) if in a non-regulated setting
Incident in an NHS setting or health funded care	An incident of harm may well meet the criteria for Serious Incident investigation by health colleagues
Breach of terms of employment and/or disciplinary procedures	The person's employer
Misuse of enduring or lasting power of attorney or misconduct of a court-appointed deputy	Office of the Public Guardian (OPG), Court of Protection or the police
Person making decisions about the care and well-being of an adult who does not have mental capacity to make decisions about their safety, are made without authority or are not in the best interests of the adult	OPG or the Court of Protection
Misuse of appointeeship	Department for Work and Pensions (DWP)

Essential components of a safeguarding plan

The statutory guidance tells us that 'Once enquiries are completed, the outcome should be notified to the local authority which should then determine with the adult what, if any, further action is necessary and acceptable. It is for the local authority to determine the appropriateness of the outcome of the enquiry' (14.110). And also: 'The local authority must determine what further action is necessary. Where the local authority determines that it should itself take further action (for example, a protection plan), then the authority would be under a duty to do so' (14.107).

The local authority's section 42 duty continues as plans are made and monitored. The local authority is the lead agency in decision making about whether a safeguarding plan is needed and what actions should be part of the plan. Once it decides that a plan is needed, the local authority has a duty to put a protection plan in place.

The statutory guidance notes that:

> If the adult has the capacity to make decisions in this area of their life and declines assistance, this can limit the intervention that organisations can make. The focus should therefore be on harm reduction. It should not however limit the action that may be required to protect others who are at risk of harm. The potential for 'undue influence' will need to be considered if relevant. If the adult is thought to be refusing intervention on the grounds of duress then action must be taken. (14.108)

What kinds of action can be taken if we believe that another person is preventing the adult making their own decisions? It is important not to collude with this type of control by closing the case and ending contact with the adult. We need to find opportunities to continue to work with the adult, and to understand how coercive control is manifested in this situation, and how we can support the adult to escape, using the law, including inherent jurisdiction, as necessary.

When an adult does not have the mental capacity to make decisions about their own safety the principles of best-interests decision making must be observed. As discussed in Chapter 4, we must look for and use the least restrictive option that will keep the adult safe while restricting their rights and freedoms as little as is possible. We must consider the adult's human rights (as considered in Chapter 2), in particular the ECHR Article 2 right to life, Article 3 freedom from inhuman or degrading treatment, Article 5 right to liberty and Article 8 right to private and family life, and how these will be supported within a safeguarding plan.

The statutory guidance summarises what should be noted within a plan:

- what steps are to be taken to assure their safety in future;
- the provision of any support, treatment or therapy including on-going advocacy;

- any modifications needed in the way services are provided (for example, same gender care or placement; appointment of an OPG deputy);
- how best to support the adult through any action they take to seek justice or redress;
- any on-going risk management strategy as appropriate;
- any action to be taken in relation to the person or organisation that has caused the concern. (14.111)

Plans will be as unique as the adult they are used to protect, taking account of the adult's views, wishes and outcomes and containing creative solutions to ensure that the adult has the best quality of life along with the most reliable resources to support them. Some safeguarding plans are simple, for example the plan (earlier in this chapter) made with Ron Wise that involved Ron, his social worker and his support worker. Some plans involve several agencies or are complicated or have a number of actions that need to be taken jointly or in a specific order, as with Mrs Swift. Other plans may involve more than one agency and have a degree of risk attached, for the adult and/or for the agencies involved. Safeguarding plans that are not simple are best formulated at a face-to-face meeting where the adult, their supporters and agencies can share ideas and anxieties, and plan creatively together.

The principles of empowerment and proportionality must guide the decisions made. Adults have autonomy and having their expertise valued and wishes respected and acted on can promote the adult's self-esteem and reduce the possibility of harm and exploitation in the future. Options that increase the adult's capability to protect themselves must be considered. As well as practical steps, this may include therapeutic work which helps the adult recover from past and present abuse.

A plan agreed by the adult and those closest to them will be more effective in preventing further harm; if the adult and their informal supporters are involved in problem solving, they are likely to be able to continue to problem solve together in the future (Taylor and Tapper, 2017). We can work with the adult and their supporters through best-interests meetings, family meetings or by engaging individuals in a family separately.

Statutory children's services in England are using family group conferences (FCGs), as an empowering and effective approach to enabling problem solving within the 'system' around the child. Three quarters of local authorities in England and Wales currently run or commission FGCs for children in their area (Family Rights Group, 2019) but Taylor and Tapper (2017) were only able to identify four local authorities in England and one in Scotland using the approach for adults. Awareness of the usefulness of the approach is developing, but resource limitations appear to be preventing the development of FGCs in adult safeguarding. In New Zealand, where the approach was initiated by Māori families, and in a number of other countries, including Northern Ireland and the Netherlands, the approach can be requested as a citizen's right rather than something that is offered or restricted by professionals (Hobbs and Alonzi, 2013). In the meantime, FCG practitioners continue to gather data on the success of the approach, both in terms of successful outcomes and resources reduced.

▶ **ESSENTIAL INFORMATION: PRACTICE GUIDANCE**

Family group conferences

Family group conferences are not to be confused with family meetings and are a specific approach to family decision making. They have distinct features:

- The process begins with preparation. An FGC facilitator visits and prepares all participants, identifying and addressing the concerns of the participants, any long-standing relationship difficulties and any potential risk factors. The adult decides who they want to be at the meeting, where and when it will take place. This process can take weeks but completing this first stage is essential, as each participant must fully understand why the FGC is being called, what will happen there and what their role is. The adult decides how they want to be supported through the meeting: this can be by an advocate or maybe someone they have a close and trusting relationship with. The facilitator is neutral – they are independent of all agencies and professionals involved. They are skilled and experienced in facilitating and coordinating FGCs.

- The meeting has three stages. The first is information sharing: the adult, their family and friends and the professionals involved are facilitated to share information about the concern. The emphasis is on problem solving, not blame, and on the strengths in the room. The second part of the meeting is 'private family time'. The adult, their family and friends and, if applicable, the adult's advocate meet without the professionals and neutral facilitator present and make a Family Action Plan. This is presented to the referrer of the concern in the third part of the meeting for discussion facilitated by the coordinator. Once finalised, arrangements for monitoring and review of the plan are agreed. FGCs can be used as consultation and information gathering to inform a best-interests decision and are useful when there is disagreement between family members or between family members and professionals.

Reflective questions
- Which situations would you find an FGC useful?
- Are there elements within the approach that you may be able to use in practice now?
- Can you share your awareness of the FGC approach to inspire colleagues to request that your local authority invests in an FGC project?

Safeguarding planning with individuals and families

White (2017, pp 111–21) notes some key questions to consider when creating a safeguarding plan:

- How can safety be promoted without damaging the adult's human rights, or the benefits they gain from the situation?
- Are there ways of supporting the adult to change the situation to reduce risk while still respecting their choice and promoting the quality of life they want?
- What could go wrong – what contingencies are needed?
- Does everyone involved have a joined-up understanding of the adult's situation, what is important to them and what the risks are?

It is important to think through the adult's desired outcomes from the adult safeguarding process alongside their views on how their overall well-being can be maintained or improved. The adult's thoughts on recovery and resolution should also be discussed, and options presented to them to achieve this if they are unsure of what may be available. We will explore recovery and resolution further in Chapter 10. This process should not be rushed. Many adults complain that they feel rushed by the safeguarding timescales and efficiency of the enquiry officer. Adults need time to think through what they wish to happen, and for this reason it is recommended that the adult's desired outcomes are reviewed at the beginning, middle and end of the adult safeguarding process. This will also give you time to talk through with the adult what outcomes are and are not possible.

While there are occasions when the adult's outcomes are not possible, for example to close a care home or arrest someone who has not committed a crime, there will be others when to meet the adult's outcomes would cause an unacceptable risk of harm to the adult or other adults or children. The duty of care to safeguard the adult will always need to be balanced with their right to self-determination. These situations need careful negotiation with the adult and others involved, and all decisions should be discussed and explained to the adult in a way they can understand.

Remember that an adult may have had years of experience of living with an abusive partner or adult child and developed strategies in the past for dealing with the abuse that are no longer working, as frailty or illness changes relationships and abilities. An adult may value a relationship with the person who is now harming them and may decide that some elements of abuse are preferable to losing the valued relationship. Others may be very afraid of the person harming them and fear taking any action that may increase the person's abusive behaviour towards them. They may be experiencing coercion and/or control from an intimate. Other adults may be clear that they want action to be taken on their behalf and want the police or regulator to be involved. The adult's previous experiences may affect how they view the harm and what they feel will support them to either self-protect or be protected.

The policies and procedures produced by the West Midlands Adult Safeguarding Editorial Group (2016) describe a range of potential actions that serve as a useful prompt in considering creating a safeguarding plan. We have extended and described these in the Essential Information boxes.

▶ **ESSENTIAL INFORMATION: PRACTICE GUIDANCE**

Actions to promote the safety and well-being of an adult

- Meeting the individual expressed outcomes of the adult.
- Provision of care and support services to promote safety and well-being (for example, home care, telecare).
- Security measures such as door locks and entry devices, personal alarms, telephone or pager, CCTV. Telephone call blocking, mail preference services, changing telephone numbers or email addresses.
- Installing smoke alarms or other anti-fire equipment.
- Formalised arrangements for monitoring safety and well-being (for example, 'Keeping in Touch' plans – usually used where an adult with capacity will not accept any other form of support).
- Putting a flag on agency systems with documented and agreed actions to be taken when the agency is alerted.
- Activities including personal development and awareness raising that increase a person's capacity to protect themselves, support or activities that increase self-esteem and confidence.
- Ongoing advocacy services to make sure the adult is in control of their life or a particular aspect of it. Reducing isolation using befriending services, creating 'circles of support'. Linking the adult up with local crime prevention organisations via the PCSO or Neighbourhood Watch.
- Support through the criminal justice system; IDVA or Independent Sexual Violence Advocate, Intermediary Service.
- Prevention orders: domestic abuse, forced marriage. Civil injunctions.
- Guardianship order under the Mental Health Act.
- Application to the High Court under inherent jurisdiction if the adult is prevented from exercising their free will by another.

Useful organisations that can inform and contribute to the plan
- health services
- housing providers
- domestic abuse support services
- Trading Standards

- fire and rescue
- police
- access to support for people who are victims of modern slavery/human trafficking via the National Referral Mechanism

Adapted from West Midlands Adult Safeguarding Editorial Group, 2016

In addition to actions that promote the safety and well–being of the adult there may be actions we can take to prevent further harm by an individual or organisation.

▶ **ESSENTIAL INFORMATION: PRACTICE GUIDANCE**

Actions to prevent further abuse or neglect by a person or an organisation

- Meeting with an individual who poses a risk of harm and negotiating changes to their behaviour.
- Family group conferencing to agree changes to harmful behaviour.
- Carrying out a carer's assessment and providing services to decrease risk of harm or changing the support services provided to an adult to decrease carer stress.
- Changing the support given to an adult who has care and support needs and is a source of harm to other adults.
- Criminal prosecution.
- Application for a court order, for example restraining contact or an anti-social behaviour order.
- Application to the Court of Protection to change/remove a lasting power of attorney; application to the Department of Work and Pensions to change or cancel appointeeship.
- Enforcement action by the CQC, including cancellation of registration.
- Prosecution by Trading Standards.
- Referral to the relevant registration body (for example Nursing and Midwifery Council, Health and Care Professionals Council, General Medical Council).
- Training needs assessment, supervision (of employee/volunteer) or disciplinary action following an internal investigation.
- Organisational review and action plans to address poor management or leadership, staffing levels, policies/procedures, working practices, organisational culture.

Adapted from West Midlands Adult Safeguarding Editorial Group, 2016

Safeguarding plans can be ineffective, and even increase the risk to the adult, if they are not carefully monitored and reviewed. Agencies may believe that an adult is living in a safe situation 'because there is a plan in place' without stopping to review the impact of changes in the adult's life with the adult and those close to them. How this will be done, when and who by, needs to be set out in the safeguarding plan. Some useful questions to consider when setting out how the plan will be reviewed are:

- Does the adult feel safer? If they are concerned, who will they contact and how?
- When will you both agree that the need for the plan has ended?
- If the adult cannot tell you themselves, how will you assess the success of any plan? Who will tell you, how often?

The impact of existing risk on the adult's well-being must be considered with the adult at every review of the safeguarding plan, if one needs to be in place. New concerns should result in a new assessment of risk and review of any plan, together with a consideration of whether another enquiry is needed.

The s42 duty ceases at the time when the adult safeguarding plan is no longer required, such as when the adult is no longer at risk of abuse or neglect, or risks have reduced to the level that the adult wishes to live with and that present no risk to their 'vital interests' (ECHR Article 2 rights) or risk to others (public interest). The adult must inform the decision to end a safeguarding plan and a review of the plan will be the best way of achieving this. When the safeguarding plan is no longer needed it is important to let other agencies still working with the adult, and the referrer if appropriate, know that the plan has ended so that they do not assume that the adult has supports in place, and also know they must refer to adult safeguarding should they have new concerns in the future, something that should be done even if a plan is in place but may not reliably occur.

The importance of escalation

It is important to understand what to do if partnerships with other agencies or within your own agency go wrong. Common scenarios include disputes about decision making, poor practice, agencies not completing the actions they have committed to do as part of an enquiry or safeguarding plan, or agencies who have agreed to progress a 'caused' enquiry failing to do so. Your local SAB will have developed an escalation policy that has been agreed by all SAB partners. It is worth having a copy of this and discussing the principles with your colleagues.

Gloucestershire SAB have used restorative practice principles to inform their escalation procedure. The procedure is intended to promote a quick and straightforward means of resolving professional disagreements while ensuring that the safety of the adult remains the most important consideration and that disagreements do not detract from this. Gloucestershire have been using restorative approaches to improve the effectiveness of meetings, communications and problem solving, and to promote shared responsibility and accountability. In common with other escalation pathways, escalation begins with practitioner-to-practitioner challenge; if not resolved then manager-to-manager challenge; and ultimately, in Gloucestershire, to a SAB Resolution Panel which will make a decision binding on all parties.

▶ ESSENTIAL INFORMATION: PRACTICE GUIDANCE

Principles to use in professional disagreements

- Respond positively to feedback – it is not personal, it's about an adult; issues have been raised because there are concerns about the level of risk/lived experiences for an adult(s). Being able to positively accept challenge is equally as important as being able to rise to a challenge.
- Seek to resolve any professional disagreements at the lowest possible level as part of everyday working practice and within the timescales laid out in guidance.
- Encourage others to challenge or question your own practice to ensure healthy challenge becomes part of all of our professional and learning cultures.
- Wherever possible, discussions should take place face-to-face or by telephone. Try to avoid the use of email alone to raise a challenge. However, it is good practice to follow up your conversation by email to document the discussions that took place.
- The tone of challenge should be one of respectful enquiry, not criticism – be curious and remain curious until you understand and accept the reasons behind the decision that has been made or an alternative decision has been reached.
- Challenge should always be evidence based and solution focused.
- Be persistent and keep asking questions.
- Discuss your concerns with the named/designated safeguarding lead within your organisation or through supervision arrangements.
- Always keep a written record of actions and decisions taken in line with your own organisation's information governance and record keeping policies.

REMEMBER, you are acting in the best interests of the adult and they must always remain central to your discussions and decision making.

Gloucestershire Safeguarding Adults Board, 2018

(▶) KEY MESSAGES

- Enquiries are fluid, rather than a defined set of linear activities, that meet a set of objectives as specified in statutory guidance in a proportionate, person-centred way.

- There are many reasons why you might be prevented from meeting with an adult. You will need to understand these in order to plan your approach to the person obstructing or hindering.

- Enquiries, no matter how short, need to be planned. Enquiries that involve several agencies are best planned in a face-to-face meeting.

- Care Act advocates and IMCAs can be instructed (commissioned) to represent the adult and can make sure the adult is involved in their own safeguarding through creating relationships, enabling communication, supporting the adult in meetings and acting as their 'memory'.

- A range of agencies can be 'caused' to make an enquiry, but this must be compatible with the agencies' existing duties and must cause no adverse effect to the agencies' exercise of their existing functions.

KNOWLEDGE REVIEW

- WHAT factors would cause you to consider moving from an enquiry focused on a conversation with the adult into a more extended enquiry into the abuse or neglect?

- WHAT approaches can you use to gain access to an adult if a third party appears to be preventing this? If these approaches fail, in what circumstance would you consider the use of legal powers?

- WHAT should you expect from different types of advocate?

- WHAT are your duties, and your role and responsibility, in relation to 'caused' enquiries?

- WHAT are the crucial elements in ensuring the success of a safeguarding plan?

- WHEN might you need to use an escalation pathway? What will your first step be?

📖 FURTHER READING

- We recommend Emily White again, for her reflections on Making Safeguarding Personal through the enquiry process: White, E. (2017) 'Assessing and Responding to Risk', in A. Cooper and E. White (eds) *Safeguarding Adults Under the Care Act 2014: Understanding Good Practice*, London: Jessica Kingsley, pp 110–27.

- You can find out more about family group conferences from: Taylor, M. and Tapper, L. (2017) 'Participative Practice and Family Group Conferencing', in A. Cooper and E. White (eds) *Safeguarding Adults Under the Care Act 2014: Understanding Good Practice*, London: Jessica Kingsley, pp 57–73.

- Guidance on gaining access to an adult at risk is available from SCIE. See SCIE (Social Care Institute for Excellence) (2018) 'Gaining Access to an Adult Suspected to Be at Risk of Neglect or Abuse'. Available from: www.scie.org.uk/safeguarding/adults/practice/gaining-access.

10

Recovery and resolution

Chapter aim

In this chapter we will explore the resources and methods needed by adults at risk and by practitioners to move on from adult safeguarding work. We illustrate a range of approaches to recovery and resolution for adults at risk, including mediation and restorative justice, together with access to counselling and supportive interventions or victim support organisations.

In this chapter we will explore:

- What do recovery, resolution and restoration mean to adults and those working with them?

- The impact of harm on adults;

- counselling and therapeutic approaches;

- mediation;

- restorative justice;

- criminal justice;

- compensation.

The statutory guidance stipulates that a section 42 enquiry should consider how the adult will recover from the harm and/or achieve a resolution of the experience, and that plans for recovery and resolution should be part of ongoing discussion and planning after the enquiry is completed (statutory guidance 14.95 and 14.106). This element of adult safeguarding is often neglected. There may be many reasons for this omission – stretched resources may mean that practitioners do not look beyond initial protection work, or perhaps practitioners are unsure how to support an adult's recovery or resolution between people. The long-term impact of harm on the well-being of adults at risk may not be adequately considered, and agencies that might assist adults to recover are unknown.

REFLECTIVE ACTIVITY

Throughout the chapter reflect on what you would expect to happen after you were assaulted or harmed in any way.

Reflective questions

- What support would you expect?
- How are your expectations about your own well-being mirrored in how you support adults to recover from and resolve the impact of harm on their lives?
- What challenges or barriers can you identify in your own thinking about recovery and resolution for adults? What assumptions or biases are there in your thinking?

Our thoughts are that we do not tend to think about ourselves as practitioners as needing recovery, resolution or restoration and this can also apply to adult safeguarding as we are not often encouraged to consider this in the adult social care model. Prioritising these can act as preventative measures for future abuse as well as improving well-being and outcomes for the adult overall.

What do recovery, resolution and restoration mean to adults and those working with them?

The term 'recovery' can denote a return to one's previous condition of well-being before harm occurred. 'Resolution' is a more ambiguous term, implying that a difficulty or dispute is finished or agreed: a problem solved. For adults who continue to live in potentially harmful circumstances this may not always be possible but it is always worth asking the question "How would you like matters to be resolved or when would you feel that the problem has ended?" Although not mentioned in the statutory guidance, the term 'restoration' is also worth thinking about: the act of being restored, gaining something back that was lost. All these terms have assumed more than their actual meanings within adult safeguarding, largely because of the potentially empowering effect on adults of support to recover, and the impact on the adult's self-esteem and confidence in being actively involved in restorative approaches. Craig (1998) describes the potential impact of engagement in mediation for older people:

> Mediation promotes self-esteem through the experience of having one's point of view heard and valued, and in the ability to resolve matters oneself. Mediation can be seen as valorising for anxious older people who experience achievement through the mediation process of helping them construct improvements in their relationships. It also

encourages self-protection as they become assertive and confident in communication. (p 178)

The immediate actions we take after harm is disclosed will support recovery, but for many, recovery is a long-term endeavour. Recovery from the immediate impact of abuse can be focused on practical measures as well as giving advice or listening and reassuring, whereas long-term recovery work focuses on addressing the trauma of abuse in order to enable the adult towards recovery and restoration in its fullest sense. Pritchard (2013) distinguishes between recovery and healing in her work: 'recovery is immediately after something; healing is long-term' (p 19). Pritchard derives much of her practice wisdom from listening to adults; participants in her 'Beyond Existing' therapeutic support groups describe 'recovery' as attending to their physical needs and immediate emotional reactions to abuse, but 'healing' as the promotion of long-term change that will address their psychological state and ultimately result in the restoration or development of self-esteem, confidence, being at peace with oneself, and being free of the emotions relating to the harm.

What immediate actions are needed to promote recovery in the short term?

Adults may be left without food, heating or accommodation, or be unsafe or physically injured. Activities to restore the adult's basic needs will include:

- organising food, heating, money;
- getting medical attention for injuries;
- finding suitable clothing;
- moving accommodation;
- changing locks, making premises secure;
- changes to care and support plans or changes in the provider or staff supporting them;
- meeting immediate emotional needs, shock and distress, the need for reassurance;
- making sure the adult can talk with someone who will listen and if needed can give advice on recovery activities.

The impact of harm on adults

All adults will have emotional needs caused by being abused, and for some these are made more complex by the stirring up of emotions and memories of previous harm. Feelings of loss, shame and anger, and the trauma of being abused, will not only cause the adult's enjoyment of life to diminish but may affect their relationships with others and their physical health. Support to recover is not a case of one size fits all. We must ask the adult what they think will help them in the short and longer term. The facts you have ascertained during the enquiry may have revealed historical abuse and long-term harm. You may need to include these experiences in talking with the adult about recovery. Each adult will have a different reaction to being abused. For some there will be weeks or even months of distress, which might manifest in physical decline or illness or in behavioural changes. For a few there may be long-term consequences. These may include symptoms that can be described as post-traumatic stress disorder (PTSD) or other long-term mental health issues.

It is important to explore with the adult the impact that abuse has had, and put their reactions into context. Adults and those close to them may feel very distressed for weeks or months after being harmed. Do make sure that there are opportunities for the adult to talk if they wish and be listened to, encourage them to experience whatever feelings arise and take steps to reduce social isolation if the adult wishes you to do so.

There are few research studies on the long-term impact of harm on adults at risk, but research on the impact of abuse on the general adult population applies just as much to adults at risk as it does to people with no care and support needs. Some researchers identify that the circumstances of adults with care and support needs will increase the risk of long-term damage to emotional and physical well-being. Rowsell et al (2013) claims that trauma resulting from the violation of a carer's duty to provide protection and attachment security to a more vulnerable person is associated with a higher risk of developing PTSD.

Psychological harm may be more pronounced for individuals who have had long-term frequent experiences of harm or witnessing abuse, for example adults who spent their childhood or young adulthood in settings where their human rights were not respected, who were bullied or assaulted, or who are living in domestic or institutional settings where they are frequently harmed. Disabled people are more likely to report that domestic abuse led to them experiencing anxiety, depression or panic attacks than adults without a disability, and domestic abuse can negatively impact a women's ability to manage her primary physical disabilities, leading to the onset of debilitating secondary conditions (Public Health England, 2015).

Bows (2018) describes the physical and emotional effects on older people of sexual violence. Physical effects included genital and other injuries including broken bones related to frailer skin and bodies, which create long-term health conditions, and exacerbated existing health conditions. Older survivors of sexual violence experienced a decline in health which included heart attacks, PTSD, urinary incontinence and other life-damaging effects. The practitioners within Bows' research felt these symptoms were worse for older people because they had fewer opportunities to develop or use supportive networks through employment or social relationships.

Both the physical and emotional effects of sexual violence are thought to result in a number of lifestyle changes for older survivors leading to social isolation (Lachs and Pillemer, 2004); older survivors are more likely to develop agoraphobia, altered relationships with family or friends, and disengagement from support organisations. Bows (2018) notes that the type and nature of sexual violence to older women is similar to that of younger women; however, 'there is still a poverty of research examining the effects of sexual violence on older people, their support needs and coping strategies, and experiences of accessing support services' (p 1072).

Rowsell et al (2013) have researched how symptoms of PTSD manifest in adults who have profound learning disabilities and simple communication skills: 'Marked increases were reported in the frequency and severity of a range of emotional, physiological and behavioural symptoms of psychological distress in men and women with severe intellectual disabilities following alleged abuse. Over time, there was some alleviation in the victims' difficulties, but their psychological functioning remained severely compromised' (p 263).

The responses of the 18 people in the research were similar to those in the general population. However, unlike members of the general population, the research subjects had no access to services specialising in the treatment of PTSD. The very limited recovery made by the group two years after being abused is attributed to the lack of recognition of their distress and lack of specialist services to address their PTSD.

In common with the rest of the population, some adults may continue to experience distress long after the harm has ceased. Some may experience distress some years afterwards. An understanding of PTSD is useful in understanding what the impact of harm might be, and the reasons for changes in how the adult feels and behaves after being harmed. There are steps we can take to make sure that we are considering the impact of abuse on adults and, as discussed in the next section, can explore options with them to support recovery. The first step is developing an awareness of the symptoms of damage caused by abuse.

▶ ESSENTIAL INFORMATION: PRACTICE GUIDANCE

Post-traumatic stress disorder (PTSD) symptoms to be aware of

PTSD may be 'acute' (the symptoms are experienced for less than three months), 'chronic' (symptoms are experienced for more than three months) or have a 'delayed onset' (occurring at least six months after the traumatic event).

Impacts can be:

- **Physical**, including heart symptoms, exhaustion, exacerbation of aches and pains, digestive disorders, acute sensitivity to noise and light, sudden sounds; some research indicates risk of development of serious illness in frail or older adults.

- **Emotional**, including hypervigilance (looking out for danger all the time), anxiety including panic attacks, depression, being angry or fearful, easily moved to tears, insomnia. Avoidance reactions which include inability to remember some aspects of the trauma, avoidance of certain people or places, feeling numb or empty, feeling life is no longer interesting, there are no exciting possibilities to look forward to, there is no 'future'. The adult may numb their feelings; for example, they are unable to be as affectionate or loving as previously, or to experience deep feelings of sadness or happiness.
- Some experience the traumatic event in terms of **flashbacks**, nightmares or re-experiencing acute emotions associated with the event or constant rumination about the harm.
- In order to cope with the these issues, some adults may develop **drug or alcohol issues**, self-harm or have/act on suicidal feelings. The adult may fear being alone, but also fear crowds, lose trust in others or be suspicious of their intentions.

Adapted from NICE, 2018b

We need to be aware of our own and others' assumptions and prejudices about the impact of abuse on adults. For example, these assumptions may be informed by stereotypes (Bows, 2018) caused by ageist attitudes that think of older people as asexual and outside the accepted boundaries of concern as survivors of sexual violence (Bows and Westmarland, 2017) or think that people who are cognitively impaired do not experience the impact of trauma, such as adults with dementia-related memory impairment who are sometimes described as having no memory of the abuse and therefore being unharmed. The subsequent changes in behaviour, as described in the Vera Jones story in Chapter 5, may go unnoticed. Recognition of the need for recovery work with people who live in care homes or other communal settings can be lost when agencies focus on remedying the situation through changes in staff and management and do not consider the impact on individuals.

The absence of recognition of PTSD or other post-abuse physical and mental health conditions has implications for the long-term recovery of adults and may also limit any thoughts of attempting to gain compensation for the significant and life-changing effects of abuse. Attempts to support the adult to regain well-being will be unsuccessful unless the distress they have experienced is addressed. There is growing evidence that given good support an individual's quality of life can actually improve post-abuse. Weiss (2014) argues that successful growth after trauma for older people rests on avoiding a sense of rejection, receipt of social support (particularly for emotional comfort) and having a sense of participation in society.

A full awareness of the impact of abuse on adults means that safeguarding plans must always consider a longer term plan about how the adult will be supported to fully recover in accordance with their wishes of a best-interests decision.

Counselling and therapeutic approaches

A significant amount of work is needed to recognise the impact of harm on adults, to identify existing specialist services that can help and to promote the creation of services that can address the full range of recovery needs of adults at risk of harm. You need to be aware of the options for recovery open to adults and to actively support the adult to access these as wished.

What actions can we take now?

- Explore with adults the options to help them recover from harm. If your service is closing down the case, make sure you work with the adult to identify who they will talk with to discuss their emotional and physical well-being at monthly intervals for the first six months to a year. Discuss what the adult's thoughts are on getting help and support and the options open to them to pursue. If the adult is part of a group living setting where harm has occurred, consider how recovery support be arranged for all individuals within the group as necessary.
- Identify agencies in your area that offer counselling or therapeutic responses to address the needs of all adults, or who could do so if support to enable access was offered. Keep this information handy to use when discussing options with adults. Options may include NHS services that can be accessed through the adult's GP (specialist counselling, PTSD support including cognitive behavioural therapy, other mental health supports), or via a Community Learning Disabilities Team (CLDT).
- There may be support available via local services set up to support adults who have been sexually abused or have experienced domestic abuse. Domestic abuse services in your area may offer a version of The Freedom Programme suitable for women who have a learning disability. It is designed for women experiencing domestic abuse; group sessions help participants make sense of and understand what has happened to them. The Freedom Programme (2018) has developed training with Bristol CLDT for existing facilitators to enable them to run sessions for women who have learning disabilities. The Freedom Programme can be offered on a one-to-one basis or in very small group sessions to women with a learning disability who are currently in an abusive relationship. There may be a programme in your area. You can also identify national agencies who may be able to help. Respond, a national charity, offer survivor support services and psychotherapy for people with learning disabilities traumatised by abuse. Victim Support (2019) may be able to put you in touch with local services as well as offering support via a volunteer to the adult.

- Adults living in group settings may benefit from regular opportunities to meet and talk through their current well-being with an advocate or similar as well as using more specific services to address their individual recovery needs. Make sure that recovery is on the agenda of all planning meetings related to organisational abuse. Changing the culture of an organisation, increasing the use of person-centred and human rights-based approaches, can help to identify how individual adults are experiencing the impact of previous and current abuse, and give opportunities to address specific needs.
- It is worth highlighting any gaps in provision for recovery to commissioners in both the local authority and the clinical commissioning group. Keep raising your own and your colleagues' awareness of the impact of harm and of useful responses; reflect on and challenge any discriminatory assumptions you and others make about the impact of abuse on adults and how their recovery needs should be addressed.

Mediation

Recovery can involve not only personal recovery but the recovery of relationships or of a valued previous way of life, or the recovery of confidence and self-esteem from being actively involved in making decisions about how future relationships will progress. Mediation approaches promote the resolution of problems between people. Mediation skills are used in a range of processes useful to plan protection and recovery including FGCs and restorative justice. Mediation is a process in which an impartial third party (the 'mediator') meets with those in conflict to help them to reach agreement on the issues that divide them and is most effective when the issues being addressed are open to resolution through the modification of perceptions, attitudes or behaviour. Mediators avoid taking sides, making judgements or giving guidance and should have had recognised training in mediation, and be able to demonstrate active listening skills. Mediation in adult safeguarding is under-researched in the UK although some researchers (Craig, 1998; Bagshaw et al, 2015) have explored the potential impact of mediation schemes on outcomes for older people.

Civil or non-restorative justice mediation can be used in a variety of settings, from family disputes to disputes between neighbours or people who live in the same care home or supported accommodation. Practitioners who want to use mediation skills in everyday practice will need mediation training. Do also consider that if you have been involved in an enquiry about harm, you may well not be seen as a neutral party by the source of harm or others in the situation, and you may have your own feelings about the rights and wrongs of the situation.

Potential strengths of mediation

Mediation is concerned to equalise power relations between people and should be an empowering experience for the adult, enabling their voice to be heard and understood by others in the situation and promoting their self-determination as decisions are agreed by the adult and others directly involved. Resolution may be supported via the mediation principle of solving problems and reaching understanding or agreement rather than blame.

Further harm may be prevented if problems between people can be resolved and relationships promoted. Mediation may support an adult's desired outcome regarding retaining or improving relationships with those who have harmed them. Mediation helps people communicate: sometimes harm occurs because people do not understand the other's perspective or there has been miscommunication.

The approach should not be considered if:

- the adult or others do not have the mental capacity to participate;
- there is violence or risk of violence in the relationship;
- the process of mediation is likely to increase harm;
- there are imbalances of power that cannot be balanced by the intervention of a neutral mediator. The relationship between an adult and a professional who has a duty of care towards them cannot be open to mediation because of that duty of care owed to the adult and the inherent power imbalance in the situation. In these cases, other approaches may help, for example a genuine apology and an assisted discussion on future plans.

REFLECTIVE ACTIVITY

Case study: mediation between Agnes Milton and her grandson

Agnes Milton cared for her grandson, Kevin, after his mother emigrated to Australia with her new partner. Kevin was 15 at the time and is now 19 years old. He had not wanted to emigrate and leave his friends and school, and was very close to his grandmother. Agnes was referred to adult safeguarding via her church. Agnes asked the priest to contact adult safeguarding as Kevin was disturbing her sleep with rowdy friends, taking odd sums of money from her purse and was 'disrespectful' in his attitude.

Agnes has Parkinson's disease and has just started having carers to support her with her personal care as she is struggling to do this independently. Her health is suffering from lack of sleep and she is worried that the small instances of theft may indicate that Kevin has a problem with drugs or drink. At his age Agnes thought her grandson should be 'grateful' she had given him a roof over his head but he had shouted at her that he wanted to go to Australia and make his own life. Agnes wanted help to 'clear the air, and sort things out' with this much loved but upsetting young man.

Reflective question

- Would mediation be an appropriate approach to support Agnes and Kevin to resolve their differences?

Our thoughts are that there appears to be no risk of violence in the relationship or risk of increasing harm by taking an approach to enable both grandmother and grandson to discuss their different perspectives, hopes and wishes and make plans for their future relationship.

Face-to-face mediation meetings are most productive, but if the adult is not ready to face a person they are afraid of or very angry with then 'shuttle mediation', when the neutral mediator relays the thoughts, feelings and wishes between parties, may be useful. A Care Act advocate can be commissioned to support an adult who may have substantial difficulties in participating in the mediation process, but who has the mental capacity to make the decision to do so.

REFLECTIVE ACTIVITY

Case study: shuttle mediation in Whitegulls supported living

Pete Grainger and Jason Dodge once lived in the same care home and disliked each other. Pete moved to a supported living flat in a complex for people with learning disabilities three years ago. He was an active member of the complex and organised the film night and enjoyed regular pub visits with others who lived at Whitegulls. Jason moved in a month ago and was pleased to see Pete.

Pete was shocked to see Jason and has either avoided meeting him, so missing out on social activities, or been rude when they inadvertently meet in the communal areas. Jason has started to tell others that he will 'get Pete back' for this. It is hard to know how to move things forward as neither man will discuss their previous relationship, but it has caused a bad feeling throughout the complex and there is a risk that matters will deteriorate and one will harm the other in some way. Neither Jason nor Pete are happy about the situation.

Reflective questions

- Could mediation help?
- What approach would you use?

> *Our thoughts* are that a mediator needs to meet with Pete and Jason separately. If one or the other is not ready to meet together then a 'shuttle mediation' approach would be a good starting point in trying to get the other to see the predicament from the other's point of view and start to move forward.

Restorative justice

Restorative justice is a form of mediation used when a crime has been committed. It is also sometimes referred to as 'restorative practices', and has much in common with all mediation approaches although there is an additional emphasis on the identified offender understanding the impact of the harm they have caused. Victims of crime are entitled to be actively informed about restorative justice services in their area and what restorative justice can offer:

> Restorative Justice offers you an opportunity to be heard and sometimes to have a say in the resolution of offences. This can include agreeing activities for the offender to do as part of taking responsibility for their actions and to repair the harm that they have done. Restorative Justice can provide a means of closure and enable you to move on, while providing an opportunity for offenders to face the consequences of their actions and to understand the impact that it has had upon other people. (Code of Practice for Victims, S7.2, MoJ, 2015, p 34)

Restorative justice (RJ) is voluntary. Both the victim of crime and the offender must agree to engage with the process, which is managed by a trained RJ facilitator. Any risk to the victim's physical or psychological well-being is carefully considered and, if there are any doubts about the safety of a meeting, 'shuttle mediation' is used. The offender must have already admitted the offence, although an RJ process can take place before a trial and after sentencing, potentially when the offender is in prison. Practitioners need to work with RJ facilitators to make sure that the adult is able to engage as fully as they wish and that their specific needs are considered. The practitioner may give information to inform the RJ risk assessment with the adult's consent. Advocacy may need to be commissioned to support the adult, and as RJ can be seen as recovery and resolution from adult abuse this will be a Care Act advocate commissioned by the local authority as part of the section 68 duties.

REFLECTIVE ACTIVITY

Case study: restorative justice after a hate crime

Wendy Young has been the target of harassment by young people in her local area for the past year. She has learning disabilities and uses hearing aids. A group of young people regularly shouted at her in the street, three of them really 'targeted' her, continually knocking at her door and shouting in her face when she opened it, pushing notes through her door threatening her, and following her in the local Co-op making loud comments about her. The police arrested and cautioned the three youths, which appeared to have deterred two of them. However, one young woman, Rosalyn, continued a campaign against Wendy and has now been arrested again and charged with criminal damage after breaking a window and using 'threatening or abusive words or behaviour likely to cause harassment, alarm or distress'. Wendy was approached by the police about the possibility of a restorative justice meeting with Rosalyn, and after talking it through with her mother and social worker decided to agree to this.

Reflective questions

- What support might Wendy need?
- Are there any risks to Wendy from using this approach?
- What might be the benefits?

Our thoughts are that we need to find out from Wendy how she feels about meeting Rosalyn and the way the RJ facilitator will work with her.

- Does she have confidence in the RJ facilitator?
- Are there any access issues the facilitator and police need to consider?

It is Wendy's choice whether she wishes to do this or not, and she stands to gain a great deal in terms of self-esteem and confidence should the RJ meeting go well.

What happened?

Rosalyn began the meeting in the local community centre by giving an account of the incidents when she abused Wendy. After each incident account Wendy told Rosalyn how frightened she had been. Wendy's mother supported her and with her permission told Rosalyn how long it had taken Wendy to feel safe in her own home and what damage she felt she had done to Wendy's confidence; she had ruined her quality of life.

Rosalyn gave a long and sincere apology to Wendy and handed over an agreed amount to compensate for the breakage of the window. Wendy thanked her for this and Rosalyn told her that she had nothing further to fear, she would never frighten Wendy again and would stop her friends from doing so.

Criminal justice

Some adults will feel a sense of resolution through the prosecution and sentencing of the person who harmed them. This route to resolution can be uncertain. When supporting the adult to engage with criminal justice agencies it will be important for all those involved to keep a sense of realism about what might happen. Some cases do not pass the evidential test for prosecution and will not go forward for prosecution in a court. Others may result in a prosecution but not the type of sentence that the adult hoped for. Make sure that police colleagues explain the stages of criminal justice decision making as outlined in Chapter 8. Do keep other options, RJ or civil action, on the table. For some adults, the 'day in court' is the only pathway that will demonstrate to them that the harm caused to them has been taken seriously, but do continue to be honest and realistic about the steps that must be taken before this happens, and what alternatives there may be.

Experiences of the criminal justice system can help or hinder an adult's recovery from harm. Where there is a potential for criminal prosecution it is important to ensure that counselling or therapeutic support provided to the adult will not interfere with criminal processes and evidence. This should be discussed as part of the safeguarding planning processes and where needed guidance can be obtained from the CPS about an individual's case. Court proceedings will involve discussions of the harm and can reactivate traumatic memories and feelings; you may need to arrange extra support.

Special measures

There are a range of formal measures that can be taken to support the adult through the criminal justice system. Remember that these measures are intended to increase the adult's ability to give their 'best evidence', not to provide emotional support. Introduced under the Youth Justice and Criminal Evidence Act 1999, these special measures apply to witnesses in criminal proceedings who may be intimidated or vulnerable and include any witness whose quality of evidence is likely to be diminished because they:

- are suffering from a mental disorder (as defined by the MHA);
- have a significant impairment of intelligence and social functioning; or
- have a physical disability or are suffering from a physical disorder. (CPS, 2019)

The CPS (2019) 'eligibility for special measures' guidance notes that 'some disabilities are obvious, some are hidden. Witnesses may have a combination of disabilities. They may not wish to disclose the fact that they have a disability during initial and subsequent needs assessments … different witnesses on the autistic spectrum may have very different needs from each other.' People who have been allegedly trafficked or subject to sexual assault are considered 'intimidated witnesses'.

It is vital that the need for special measures is identified early so that arrangements can be planned. The practitioner may need to make sure that an assessment of the adult's needs has been initiated by the police or prosecuting solicitors to establish whether special measures are needed. The court may not grant the application, however. It will only do so if it is satisfied that the special measures will enable the witness to give their best evidence.

Special measures can include changes to the environment in which the adult gives evidence:

- use of screens to shield the witness;
- a live link to enable the witness to give evidence during the trial from outside the court through a televised link to the courtroom;
- evidence given in private–exclusion from the court of members of the public and the press (except for one named person to represent the press);
- video recorded interviews and removal of wigs and gowns by judges and barristers.

Special measures can also provide supports to communication before and during court hearings; an intermediary may be appointed by the court to assist the witness to give their evidence at court. They can also provide communication assistance in the investigation stage – approval for admission of evidence so taken is then sought retrospectively. The intermediary is allowed to explain questions or answers so far as is necessary to enable them to be understood by the witness or the questioner but without changing the substance of the evidence. Other aids to communication may be permitted to enable a witness to give their best evidence whether through a communicator or interpreter, or through a communication aid or technique, provided that the communication can be independently verified and understood by the court. This can include computers, voice synthesisers, symbol boards and books.

Adults may also be distressed when details revealed in court are reported in the local or national press. Courts can impose restrictions on reporting the details of adult witnesses using section 46 of the Youth Justice and Criminal Evidence Act 1999. The court must be satisfied that the quality of the witness's evidence or cooperation with the preparation of the case is likely to be diminished because of fear or distress in connection with being identified by the public as a witness. The court must balance the 'interests of justice' against the public interest and must not impose unreasonable restrictions on reporting the proceedings. Our experience is that such orders are rarely made; adults at risk are not protected from press interest with sometimes distressing consequences. The MCA did not include any legislation regarding the protection from media interest of people who lack mental capacity and full details of their harm can be published in the media.

Compensation

Some of the adults who lived at Winterbourne View hospital were awarded compensation by the Department of Health who also commissioned Respond to offer therapeutic services to 19 people who were harmed there (BBC News, 2013). We are not aware of other compensation awards to adults who have experienced harm through organisational abuse, and consideration of whether and how an adult can claim compensation is not part of usual considerations during safeguarding enquiry or planning.

The failure to appreciate the symptoms of trauma can impede compensation claims (Rowsell et al, 2013) as lasting harm to the person's well-being must be evidenced. Compensation could be used to pay for specialist recovery support or to fund measures to improve the adult's damaged quality of life and well-being. There are two options for an adult or their representative to consider regarding compensation. First, a civil claim through a solicitor. The purpose of civil claims is to recognise a wrong by awarding 'damages', or compensation for injury. The adult can claim compensation for damages against the person who abused them, or their employer, or the organisation for which they were working at the time. The abuse should be reported as a crime to the police before any civil action is taken. Compensation claims relating to abuse are sometimes settled out of court so avoiding court action and the risk of adverse publicity and hardship to all involved. A compensation claim should be registered at court within three years of abuse occurring, although this can sometimes be extended by the court in certain circumstances, for example historical child abuse.

The second route to compensation is through the Criminal Injuries Compensation Authority (CICA). CICA is a body set up by the government to compensate victims of any crime of violence. It makes financial awards to those who have suffered physical and psychological injury caused by a criminal offence committed against them. The adult must claim within two years of the abuse and must be able to demonstrate that they reported the matter to the police and cooperated with police investigations. The injury must be diagnosed and evidenced by the relevant medical professional (MoJ, 2012). Victim Support services will help adults and their representatives to access CICA and provide emotional support if discussing the crime in order to make a compensation claim is distressing.

▶ KEY MESSAGES

- Being abused and harmed can be traumatic for any person, no matter what their circumstances or degree of cognitive impairment. There is little research on this matter, but the studies that have been carried out suggest that the risk of long-term damage to physical or emotional health is increased for many adults at risk.

- It is important to be aware of the impact of harm and to reflect on any bias or prejudice you may have that prevents you from understanding the short- and long-term effects of trauma.

- You must research the options for recovery for adults in your area and highlight gaps in provision to commissioners.

- There are special measures available for people to give evidence in court, and adults who have experienced abuse by an organisation or who have suffered physical and psychological injury caused by a criminal offence committed against them may be entitled to compensation.

KNOWLEDGE REVIEW

- WHAT current and historical circumstances might affect an adult's ability to recover from harm?

- WHAT are the indicators of PTSD? What other effects can being abused have on those who have been harmed?

- WHAT approaches to recovery and resolution are informed by mediation practices?

- WHAT are the two main sources of compensation for adults harmed by abuse?

FURTHER READING

- If you want to know more about restorative justice, a good handbook to start with is: Liebmann, M. (2007) *Restorative Justice: How It Works*, London: Jessica Kingsley.

References

Acquired Brain Injury and Mental Capacity Act Interest Group (2014) 'Recommendations for action following the House of Lords Select Committee Post-Legislative Scrutiny Report into the Mental Capacity Act: Making the Abstract Real'. Available from: www.researchgate.net/publication/279535601_Making_the_Abstract_Real_Acquired_Brain_Injury_and_Mental_Capacity_A_report_making_recommendations_following_the_House_of_Lords_Select_Committee_review_of_the_Mental_Capacity_Act [Accessed 9 January 2017].

ADASS (Association of Directors of Adult Social Services) (2017) 'Making Safeguarding Personal'. Available from: www.adass.org.uk/making-safeguarding-personal-publications [Accessed 6 January 2019].

ADASS (Association of Directors of Adult Social Services) (2019) 'A Framework for Making Decisions on the Duty to Carry Out Safeguarding Adults Enquiries'. Available from: www.adass.org.uk/media/7326/adass-advice-note.pdf [Accessed 9 September 2019].

Age UK (2011) 'Safeguarding the Convoy'. Available from: www.campaigntoendloneliness.org/wp-content/uploads/Safeguarding-the-Convoy.-A-call-to-action-from-the-Campaign-to-End-Loneliness.pdf [Accessed 12 May 2019].

Association for Real Change (2013) 'Safety Net'. Available from: https://arcuk.org.uk/safetynet/ [Accessed 14 November 2018].

Association for the Prevention of Torture (2017) 'What Is Torture?' Available from: www.apt.ch/en/what-is-torture/ [Accessed 5 January 2019].

Bachman, C. and Gooch, B. (2018a) 'LGBT in Britain: Health Report'. Available from: www.stonewall.org.uk/lgbt-britain-health [Accessed 7 January 2019].

Bachman, C. and Gooch, B. (2018b) 'LGBT in Britain: Trans Report'. Available from: www.stonewall.org.uk/lgbt-britain-trans-report [Accessed 7 January 2019].

Bagshaw, D., Adams, V., Zannettino, L. and Wendt, S. (2015) 'Elder Mediation and the Financial Abuse of Older People by a Family Member', *Conflict Resolution Quarterly*, 32(4): 443–80.

Baker, D. (2017) 'Mental Capacity Act and Adult Safeguarding', in A. Cooper and E. White (eds) *Safeguarding Adults Under the Care Act 2014: Understanding Good Practice*, London: Jessica Kingsley, pp 128–46.

Bartley, S. (2015) 'Domestic Abuse of Older People: A Hidden Problem'. Available from: www.safelives.org.uk/sites/default/files/resources/Domestic%20abuse%20of%20older%20people%20a%20hidden%20problem.pdf [Accessed 28 January 2019].

BASW (British Association of Social Workers) (2014) 'Code of Ethics for Social Workers: Statement of Principles', October. Available from: www.basw.co.uk/about-basw/code-ethics [Accessed 11 August 2018].

BBC News (2013) 'Winterbourne View Victims to Receive Compensation', 27 November. Available from: www.bbc.co.uk/news/uk-england-bristol-25127564 [Accessed 10 May 2019].

BBC News (2018) 'Why Disabled Women Can't Access All Refuges', 28 November. Available from: www.bbc.co.uk/news/uk-46371441 [Accessed 3 January 2019].

Beckett, C., Maynard, A. and Jordan, P. (2017) *Values and Ethics in Social Work* (3rd edn), London: Sage.

BIHR (British Institute of Human Rights) (2008) 'The Human Rights Act: Changing Lives' (2nd edn). Available from: www.bihr.org.uk/Handlers/Download.ashx?IDMF=3c184cd7-847f-41b0-b1d1-aac57d1eacc4 [Accessed 5 January 2019].

BIHR (British Institute of Human Rights) (2013) 'Mental Health Advocacy and Human Rights: Your Guide'. Available from: www.bihr.org.uk/mental-health-advocacy-and-human-rights-your-guide [Accessed 19 November 2018].

BILD (British Institute of Learning Disabilities) (2019) 'Keeping Safe'. Available from: www.bild.org.uk/resources/easy-read-information/keeping-safe-easy-read-information/ [Accessed 12 May 2019].

Bishop, E. (2012) 'Where Social Workers Are Going Wrong on the Mental Capacity Act', *Community Care*, 30 October. Available from: www.communitycare.co.uk/2012/10/30/where-social-workers-are-going-wrong-on-the-mental-capacity-act/ [Accessed 11 August 2018].

Bloom, M. (1996) *Primary Prevention Practices*, Thousand Oaks, CA: Sage.

Bows, H. (2018) 'Practitioner Views on the Impacts, Challenges, and Barriers in Supporting Older Survivors of Sexual Violence', *Violence Against Women*, 24(9): 1070–90.

Bows, H. and Westmarland, N. (2017) 'Rape of Older People in the United Kingdom: Challenging the "Real Rape" Stereotype', *British Journal of Criminology*, 57(1): 1–17.

Braye, S. and Preston-Shoot, M. (2017) 'Learning from SARs: A Report for the London Safeguarding Adults Board'. Available from: http://londonadass.org.uk/wp-content/uploads/2014/12/London-SARs-Report-Final-Version.pdf [Accessed 30 August 2018].

Braye, S., Orr, D. and Preston-Shoot, M. (2011) 'Conceptualising and Responding to Self-Neglect: The Challenges for Adult Safeguarding', *The Journal of Adult Protection*, 13(4): 182–93.

Braye, S., Orr, D. and Preston-Shoot, M. (2015) 'Self-Neglect Policy and Practice: Research Messages for Practitioners'. Available from: www.scie.org.uk/files/self-neglect/policy-practice/self-neglect_practitioners_briefing.pdf [Accessed 10 December 2018].

Brown, K. and Lee, S. (2017) 'Financial Scamming and Fraud'. Available from: https://ncpp.co.uk/publications/financial-scamming-and-fraud/ [Accessed 3 January 2019].

Burke, B. and Harrison, P. (2016) 'Exploring the Political and Ethical Dimensions of Social Work Practice with the "Other"', in C. Williams and M.J. Graham (eds) *Social Work in a Diverse Society: Transformative Practice with Black and Minority Ethnic Individuals and Communities*, Bristol: Policy Press, pp 39–56.

Burke, C. (2006) *Building Community Through Circles of Friends*, Foundation for People with Learning Disabilities, London: Mental Health Foundation. Available from: www.mentalhealth.org.uk/publications/building-community-through-circles-friends [Accessed 5 April 2019].

Centre of Excellence for Information Sharing (2017) 'Multi-agency Safeguarding Hubs'. Available from: http://informationsharing.org.uk/download/502/ [Accessed 6 February 2019].

Clawson, R. (2017) 'My Marriage My Choice: Toolkit', Nottingham University. Available from: www.nottingham.ac.uk/research/groups/mymarriagemychoice/documents/toolkit.pdf [Accessed 2 January 2019].

College of Policing (2014) 'Code of Ethics: A Code of Practice for the Principles and Standards of Professional Behaviour for the Policing Profession of England and Wales', July. Available from: www.college.police.uk/What-we-do/Ethics/Documents/Code_of_Ethics.pdf [Accessed 15 September 2018].

College of Policing (2019) 'Investigation Process'. Available from: www.app.college.police.uk/app-content/investigations/investigation-process/ [Accessed 20 December 2019].

Collingbourne T. (2014) 'The Care Act 2014: A Missed Opportunity?' *European Journal of Current Legal Issues*, 20(3). Available from: http://webjcli.org/article/view/365/464 [Accessed 4 January 2019].

Commissioner for Older People in Northern Ireland (2014) 'Protecting Our Older People in Northern Ireland: A Call for Adult Safeguarding Legislation', June. Available from: www.copni.org/media/1299/final-protecting-our-older-people-_-a-call-for-adult-safeguarding-legislation.pdf [Accessed 3 January 2019].

Conservative Party (2010) 'Invitation to Join the Government of Britain: Conservative Party Manifesto 2010'. Available from: https://conservativehome.blogs.com/files/conservative-manifesto-2010.pdf [Accessed 5 January 2019].

CPS (Crown Prosecution Service) (2016) 'Victims Right to Review Service', July. Available from: www.cps.gov.uk/legal-guidance/victims-right-review-scheme [Accessed 7 February 2018].

CPS (Crown Prosecution Service) (2017) 'Honour Based Violence and Forced Marriage'. Available from: www.cps.gov.uk/publication/honour-based-violence-and-forced-marriage [Accessed 10 November 2018].

CPS (Crown Prosecution Service) (2018a) 'Disability Hate Crime and Other Crimes Against Disabled People: Prosecution Guidance', August. Available from: www.cps.gov.uk/legal-guidance/disability-hate-crime-and-other-crimes-against-disabled-people-prosecution-guidance [Accessed 14 January 2018].

CPS (Crown Prosecution Service) (2018b) 'Fraud and Economic Crime'. Available from: www.cps.gov.uk/fraud-and-economic-crime [Accessed 6 December 2018].

CPS (Crown Prosecution Service) (2018c) 'Domestic Abuse Guidelines for Prosecutors'. Available from: www.cps.gov.uk/legal-guidance/domestic-abuse-guidelines-prosecutors [Accessed 18 December 2019].

CPS (Crown Prosecution Service) (2019) 'Reporting a Crime; Decision to charge'. Available from: www.cps.gov.uk/reporting-crime [Accessed 20 December 2019].

CQC (Care Quality Commission) (2017) 'Enforcement Decision Tree', January. Available from: www.cqc.org.uk/sites/default/files/20170217_enforcement_decision_tree.pdf [Accessed 7 February 2019].

Craig, G. and Clay, S. (2017) 'Who Is Vulnerable? Adult Social Care and Modern Slavery', *The Journal of Adult Protection*, 19(1): 21–32.

Craig, Y. (1998) 'Intergenerational Mediation: Its Potential for Contributing to the Prevention of Elder Abuse', *Journal of Social Work Practice*, 12(2): 175–80.

Crenshaw, K. (1991) 'Mapping the Margins: Intersectionality, Identity Politics, and Violence Against Women of Color', *Stanford Law Review*, 43(6): 1241–99.

Davison, S., Rossall, P. and Hart, S. (2015) *Financial Abuse Evidence Review, Age UK*, November. Available from: www.ageuk.org.uk/globalassets/age-uk/documents/reports-and-publications/reports-and-briefings/money-matters/financial_abuse_evidence_review-nov_2015.pdf [Accessed 6 December 2018].

Department for Constitutional Affairs (2007) *Mental Capacity Act 2005 Code of Practice*. Available from: www.gov.uk/government/publications/mental-capacity-act-code-of-practice [Accessed 30 August 2018].

DH (Department of Health) (2011) 'Adult Safeguarding: Statement of Government Policy', May. Available from: www.gov.uk/government/publications/adult-safeguarding-statement-of-government-policy [Accessed 5 January 2019].

DH (Department of Health) (2012) 'Consultation on New Safeguarding Power'. Available from: www.gov.uk/government/consultations/consultation-on-a-new-adult-safeguarding-power#history [Accessed 3 January 2019].

DH (Department of Health) (2013) 'Government response to the Safeguarding Power of Entry consultation'. Available from: https://assets.publishing.service.gov.uk/government/uploads/system/uploads/attachment_data/file/197739/Gov_Response_to_PoE.pdf [Accessed 18 February 2020].

DH (Department of Health) (2015) 'Care and Support: What's Changing?', September. Available from: www.gov.uk/government/publications/care-and-support-whats-changing/care-and-support-whats-changing [Accessed 4 October 2018].

DHSC (Department of Health and Social Care) (2018a) 'Care and Support Statutory Guidance'. Available from: www.gov.uk/government/publications/care-act-statutory-guidance/care-and-support-statutory-guidance [Accessed 21 August 2018].

DHSC (Department of Health and Social Care) (2018b) 'Modernising the Mental Health Act: Increasing Choice, Reducing Compulsion – Final report of the Independent Review of the Mental Health Act 1983', December. Available from: https://assets.publishing.service.gov.uk/government/uploads/system/uploads/attachment_data/file/762206/MHA_reviewFINAL.pdf [Accessed 5 January 2019].

Dixon, J. (2018) 'Screening Adult Safeguarding Risks: A Qualitative Study into How Adult Safeguarding Teams Assess and Prioritise Safeguarding Referrals' (unpublished abstract). Available from: https://researchportal.bath.ac.uk/en/publications/screening-adult-safeguarding-risks-a-qualitative-study-into-how-a [Accessed 6 February 2019].

Dong, X. and Gorbien, M. (2006) 'Decision-Making Capacity: The Core of Self-Neglect', *Journal of Elder Abuse & Neglect*, 17(3): 19–36.

Dybicz, P. (2004) 'An Inquiry into Practice Wisdom', *Families in Society*, 85(2): 197–203.

Edge Training (2019) 'Liberty Protection Safeguards (LPS): Overview', August. Available from: www.edgetraining.org.uk/wp-content/uploads/2019/07/LPS_one_page_overview_chart_August_2019.pdf [Accessed 8 September 2019].

European Parliament (2016) 'Regulation (EU) 2016/679 of the European Parliament and of the Council of 27 April 2016 on the Protection of Natural Persons with Regard to the Processing of Personal Data and on the Free Movement of Such Data, and Repealing Directive 95/46/EC (General Data Protection Regulation)', *Official Journal of the European Union*. Available from: http://eur-lex.europa.eu/legal-content/EN/TXT/PDF/?uri=CELEX:32016R0679&from=EN [Accessed 12 December 2019].

Family Rights Group (2019) 'Family Group Conferences and Lifelong Links'. Available from: https://frg.org.uk/involving-families/family-group-conferences [Accessed 5 March 2019].

Fitzpatrick, S., Pawson, H., Bramley, G., Wood, J., Watts, B., Stephens, M. and Blenkinsopp, J. (2019) 'The homelessness monitor: England 2019'. Institute for Social Policy, Housing and Equalities Research (I-SPHERE), and The Urban Institute, Heriot-Watt University; City Futures Research Centre, University of New South Wales. Available at: www.crisis.org.uk/media/240419/the_homelessness_monitor_england_2019.pdf [Accessed 20 December 2019].

Francis, R. (2013) 'Report of the Mid Staffordshire NHS Foundation Trust Public Inquiry', 3 vols. Available from: www.gov.uk/government/publications/report-of-the-mid-staffordshire-nhs-foundation-trust-public-inquiry [Accessed 2 January 2019].

Frost, L. (2016) 'Exploring the Concepts of Recognition and Shame for Social Work', *Journal of Social Work Practice*, 30(4): 431–46.

Furedi, F. (2011) 'Changing Societal Attitudes and Regulatory Responses to Risk-Taking in Adult Care'. Joseph Rowntree Foundation, September. Available from: www.jrf.org.uk/report/changing-societal-attitudes-and-regulatory-responses-risk-taking-adult-care [Accessed 12 December 2018].

Ghaye, T. (2008) *Building the Reflective Healthcare Organisation*, Oxford: Blackwell.

Gilligan, R. (1997) 'Beyond Permanence? The Importance of Resilience in Child Placement Practice and Planning', *Adoption and Fostering*, 21(1): 12-20.

Gloucestershire Safeguarding Adults Board (2018) 'Escalation of Professional Differences Guidance', May. Available from: www.gloucestershire.gov.uk/media/2081534/gsab-escalation-protocol-may-2018.pdf [Accessed 24 April 2019].

Graham, M. and Cowley, J. (2015) *A Practical Guide to the Mental Capacity Act 2005: Putting the Principles of the Act into Practice*, London: Jessica Kingsley.

HCPC (Health and Care Professions Council) (2016) 'Standards of Conduct, Performance and Ethics'. Available from: www.hcpc-uk.org/standards/standards-of-conduct-performance-and-ethics/ [Accessed 1 September 2018].

Heath, H. and Phair, L. (2009) 'The Concept of Frailty and Its Significance in the Consequences of Care or Neglect for Older People: An Analysis', *International Journal of Older People Nursing*, 4(2): 120–31.

Heath, H. and Phair, L. (2011) 'Frailty and Its Significance in Older People's Nursing', *Nursing Standard*, 26(3): 50–5.

HM Government (2018) 'Discrimination: Your Rights'. Available from: www.gov.uk/discrimination-your-rights [Accessed 6 January 2019].

Hobbs A. and Alonzi, A. (2013) 'Mediation and Family Group Conferences in Adult Safeguarding', *The Journal of Adult Protection*, 15(2): 69–84.

Homeless Link (2014) 'The Unhealthy State of Homelessness: Health Audit Results 2014'. Available from: www.homeless.org.uk/sites/default/files/site-attachments/The%20unhealthy%20state%20of%20homelessness%20FINAL.pdf [Accessed 12 October 2018].

Home Office (2011) 'Prevent Strategy', June. Available from: www.gov.uk/government/publications/prevent-strategy-2011 [Accessed 11 December 2018].

Home Office (2013) 'Information for Local Areas on the Change to the Definition of Domestic Violence and Abuse'. Available from: www.gov.uk/government/publications/definition-of-domestic-violence-and-abuse-guide-for-local-areas [Accessed 11 December 2018].

Home Office (2015a) 'Controlling or Coercive Behaviour in an Intimate or Family Relationship: Statutory Guidance Framework', December. Available from: https://assets.publishing.service.gov.uk/government/uploads/system/uploads/attachment_data/file/482528/Controlling_or_coercive_behaviour_-_statutory_guidance.pdf [Accessed 7 January 2019].

Home Office (2015b) 'Information Guide: Adolescent to Parent Violence and Abuse (APVA)'. Available from: https://assets.publishing.service.gov.uk/government/uploads/system/uploads/attachment_data/file/732573/APVA.pdf [Accessed 11 December 2018].

Home Office (2018) 'Criminal Exploitation of Children and Vulnerable Adults: County Lines Guidance', September. Available from: https://assets.publishing.service.gov.uk/government/uploads/system/uploads/attachment_data/file/741194/HOCountyLinesGuidanceSept2018.pdf [Accessed 12 July 2019].

Home Office and Department of Health (2000) 'No Secrets: Guidance on Developing and Implementing Multi-agency Policies and Procedures to Protect Vulnerable Adults from Abuse'. Available from: www.gov.uk/government/publications/no-secrets-guidance-on-protecting-vulnerable-adults-in-care [Accessed 1 October 2018].

Home Office and Foreign and Commonwealth Office (2018) 'Forced Marriage Unit Statistics 2017', March. Available from: https://assets.publishing.service.gov.uk/government/uploads/system/uploads/attachment_data/file/730155/2017_FMU_statistics_FINAL.pdf [Accessed 13 November 2018].

Hosali, S. (2015) 'Poor Practice in Care Homes: How the Human Rights Act Helps Protect Us', British Institute of Human Rights. Available from: www.bihr.org.uk/Blog/poor-practice-in-care [Accessed 6 January 2019].

House of Lords (2014) 'Select Committee on the Mental Capacity Act 2005 Report of Session 2013–14 Mental Capacity Act 2005: Post-Legislative Scrutiny'. Available from: https://publications.parliament.uk/pa/ld201314/ldselect/ldmentalcap/139/139.pdf [Accessed 30 August 2018].

Hubbard, R. and Stone, K. (2018) *The Best Interests Assessor Practice Handbook*, Bristol: Policy Press.

Ingram, R. (2013) 'Locating Emotional Intelligence at the Heart of Social Work Practice', *British Journal of Social Work*, 43(5): 987–1004.

Johns, R. (2014) *Using the Law in Social Work* (6th edn), London: Learning Matters/Sage.

Jones, K. and Spreadbury, K. (2008) 'Best Practice in Adult Protection: Safety, Choice and Inclusion', in K. Jones, B. Cooper and H. Ferguson (eds) *Best Practice in Social Work: Critical Perspectives*, Basingstoke: Palgrave, pp 181–97.

Kemshall, H., Wilkinson, B. and Baker, K. (2013) *Working with Risk: Skills for Contemporary Social Work*, Cambridge: Polity Press.

Kidd, J. and Manthorpe, J. (2017) 'Modern Slavery – The Adult Safeguarding Interface', *The Journal of Adult Protection*, 19(3): 158–66.

Lachs, M. and Pillemer, K. (2004) 'Elder Abuse', *The Lancet*, 364(9441): 1263–72.

Lammy, D. (2004) 'Mental Capacity Bill: The Parliamentary Under-Secretary of State for Constitutional Affairs Written Statement', *Hansard*, House of Commons, 18 June. Available from: https://api.parliament.uk/historic-hansard/written-statements/2004/jun/18/mental-capacity-bill [Accessed 1 October 2018].

Landman, R.A. (2014) '"A Counterfeit Friendship": Mate Crime and People with Learning Disabilities', *The Journal of Adult Protection*, 16(6): 355–66.

Lawson, J. (2017) 'The "Making Safeguarding Personal" Approach to Practice', in A. Cooper and W. White (eds) *Safeguarding Adults Under the Care Act 2014: Understanding Good Practice*, London: Jessica Kingsley, pp 20–39.

Lawson, J. (2018) 'Briefing on Working with Risk for Safeguarding Adults Boards, ADASS/LGA', Local Government Association, Ref. 25.90, November. Available from: www.local.gov.uk/our-support/our-improvement-offer/care-and-health-improvement/making-safeguarding-personal/working-risk [Accessed 12 December 2018].

Liebmann, M. (2007) *Restorative Justice: How It Works*, London: Jessica Kingsley.

Local Government Association (2018) 'Making Safeguarding Personal'. Available from: www.local.gov.uk/our-support/our-improvement-offer/care-and-health-improvement/making-safeguarding-personal [Accessed 6 January 2017].

Lonbay, S. and Brandon, T. (2017) 'Renegotiating Power in Adult Safeguarding: The Role of Advocacy', *The Journal of Adult Protection*, 19(2): 78–91.

Maclean, S. (2010) *The Social Work Pocket Guide to Reflective Practice*, Lichfield: Kirwan Maclean Associates.

Manthorpe, J., Martineau, S., Norrie, C. and Stevens, M. (2016) 'Parliamentary Arguments on Powers of Access: The Care Bill Debates', *The Journal of Adult Protection*, 18(6): 318–28.

Marsland, D. and White, C. (2012) 'Early Indicators of Concern in Residential and Nursing Homes for Older People'. Available from: https://pdfs.semanticscholar.org/ec04/cf6c3f69431c189b49946ac2daee56c1cda8.pdf [Accessed 5 December 2019].

Marsland, D., Oakes, P. and White, C. (2015) 'Abuse in Care? A Research Project to Identify Early Indicators of Concern in Residential and Nursing Homes for Older People', *The Journal of Adult Protection*, 17(2): 111–25.

McCarthy, M. (2017) '"What Kind of Abuse Is Him Spitting in My Food?": Reflections on the Similarities Between Disability Hate Crime, So-Called "Mate" Crime and Domestic Violence Against Women with Intellectual Disabilities', *Disability & Society*, 32(4): 595–600.

McNichol, A. (2016) 'DoLS Checks "Exposing Care Failings Missed by Other Assessments"', *Community Care*, 14 September. Available from: www.communitycare.co.uk/2016/09/14/dols-checks-exposing-care-failings-missed-assessments/ [Accessed 16 September 2019].

Mencap (2012) 'Death by *Indifference*: 74 Deaths and Counting – A Progress Report 5 years On', February. Available from: www.mencap.org.uk/sites/default/files/2016-08/Death%20by%20Indifference%20-%2074%20deaths%20and%20counting.pdf [Accessed 6 December 2018]

MoJ (Ministry of Justice) (2012) 'Criminal Injuries Compensation Scheme', London: TSO. Available from: https://assets.publishing.service.gov.uk/government/uploads/system/uploads/attachment_data/file/808343/criminal-injuries-compensation-scheme-2012.pdf [Accessed 5 December 2019].

MoJ (Ministry of Justice) (2015) 'Code of Practice for Victims of Crime', October. Available from: https://assets.publishing.service.gov.uk/government/uploads/system/uploads/attachment_data/file/476900/code-of-practice-for-victims-of-crime.PDF [Accessed 10 May 2019].

MoJ (Ministry of Justice) (2018) 'Multi-Agency Public Protection Arrangements: MAPPA Guidance'. Available from: https://mappa.justice.gov.uk/connect.ti/MAPPA/view?objectId=5682416 [Accessed 3 February 2019].

Mortimer, C. (2015) 'Hate Crime Against Disabled People Rises 41 per cent in One Year'. Available at: www.independent.co.uk/news/uk/hate-crime-against-disabled-people-rises-41-per-cent-in-one-year-a6713546.html [Accessed 19 December 2019].

Munro, E. (2011) 'Munro Review of Child Protection: A Child-Centred System', May. Available from: www.gov.uk/government/publications/munro-review-of-child-protection-final-report-a-child-centred-system [Accessed 6 February 2019].

National Crime Agency (2017) 'County Lines Violence, Exploitation & Drug Supply', November. Available from: https://nationalcrimeagency.gov.uk/who-we-are/publications/234-county-lines-violen-ce-exploitation-drug-supply-2017/file [Accessed 5 December 2019].

NHS Digital (2018) 'Safeguarding Adults Collection (SAC), Annual Report, England 2017–18'. Available from: https://files.digital.nhs.uk/33/EF2EBD/Safeguarding%20Adults%20Collection%202017-18%20Report%20Final.pdf [Accessed 28 November 2018].

NICE (National Institute for Health and Care Excellence) (2018a) 'NICE guideline [NG108] Decision Making and Mental Capacity'. Available from: www.nice.org.uk/guidance/ng108/chapter/Recommendations#assessment-of-mental-capacity [Accessed 10 October 2018].

NICE (National Institute for Health and Care Excellence) (2018b) 'Post-Traumatic Stress Disorder: NICE Guideline [NG116]'. Available from: www.nice.org.uk/guidance/ng116 [Accessed 9 May 2019].

Norfolk Safeguarding Adults Board (2018) 'Professional Curiosity Guidance'. Available at: www.norfolksafeguardingadultsboard.info/assets/NSAB-GUIDANCE/NSAB-Professional-Curiosity-Partnership-VersionSEPT2018FINAL02.pdf [Accessed 20 December 2019].

Norrie, C., Stevens, M., Martineau, S. and Manthorpe, J. (2018) 'Gaining Access to Possibly Abused or Neglected Adults in England: Practice Perspectives from Social Workers and Service-User Representatives', *British Journal of Social Work*, 48(4): 1071–89.

Northern Ireland Department of Health (2015) 'Adult Safeguarding: Prevention and Protection in Partnership', Available from: www.health-ni.gov.uk/sites/default/files/publications/dhssps/adult-safeguarding-policy.pdf [Accessed 11 December 2018].

Nursing and Midwifery Council (2015) 'The Code, Professional Standards of Practice and Behaviour for Nurses and Midwives'. Available from: www.nmc.org.uk/globalassets/sitedocuments/nmc-publications/nmc-code.pdf [Accessed 1 September 2018].

Osiatyński, W. (2013) 'The Historical Development of Human Rights', in S. Sheeran and N. Rodley (eds) *Routledge Handbook of International Human Rights Law*, Abingdon: Routledge, pp 9–24.

PACE (Police and Criminal Evidence Act) (1984) 'Codes of Practice Code C'. Available from: https://assets.publishing.service.gov.uk/government/uploads/system/uploads/attachment_data/file/729842/pace-code-c-2018.pdf [Accessed 5 June 2019].

Pilkington, S. (2012) 'Practice Guide 4: Sexual Activity Where a Person May Have Limited Capacity to Consent – Guidance for Workers in Area Social Work and Integrated Teams'. Available from: https://web.archive.org/web/20190303111440/www.worcestershire.gov.uk/download/downloads/id/2559/practice_guide_4_-_sexual_relationships.pdf [Accessed 5 December 2019].

Plymouth Safeguarding Adults Board (2019) 'Creative Solutions Forum: Terms of Reference', March. Available from: https://plysab.proceduresonline.com/pdfs/csf_terms_ref.pdf [Accessed 17 May 2019].

Preston-Shoot, M. (2017) 'What Difference Does Legislation Make? Adult Safeguarding Through the Lens of Serious Case Reviews and Safeguarding Adults Reviews: A Report for South West Region Safeguarding Adults Boards'. Available from: http://admin.southwest-ra.gov.uk/media/ADASS/Safeguarding_Review_2017.pdf [Accessed 30 August 2018].

Pritchard, J. (ed.) (2013) *Good Practice in Promoting Healing and Recovery for Abused Adults*, London: Jessica Kingsley.

Prochaska, J. and DiClemente, C. (1982) 'Transtheoretical Therapy: Toward a More Integrative Model of Change', *Psychotherapy*, 19(3): 276–88.

Public Health England (2015) *Disability and Domestic Abuse: Risk, Impacts and Response*. Available from: https://assets.publishing.service.gov.uk/government/uploads/system/uploads/attachment_data/file/480942/Disability_and_domestic_abuse_topic_overview_FINAL.pdf [Accessed 5 May 2019].

RiPfA (Research in Practice for Adults) (2017) 'Coercive Control'. Available from: https://coercivecontrol.ripfa.org.uk/ [Accessed 3 January 2019].

RiPfA (Research in Practice for Adults) (2019) 'Webinars'. Available from: www.ripfa.org.uk/resources/training-and-events/webinars/ [Accessed 11 June 2019].

Roch, A., Morton, J. and Ritchie, G. (2010) 'Out of sight out of mind? Transgender People's Experience of Domestic Abuse'. Available at: https://www.scottishtrans.org/wp-content/uploads/2013/03/trans_domestic_abuse.pdf [Accessed 20 December 2019].

Rogers, C.R. (1951) *Client Centred Therapy: Its Current Practice, Limitations and Theory*, London: Constable.

Rogers, J., Bright, L. and Davies, H. (2015) *Social Work with Adults*, London: Sage/Learning Matters.

Rosengren, D.B. (2017) *Building Motivational Interviewing Skills: A Practitioners Handbook* (2nd edn), London: Guilford Press.

Rowsell, A.C., Clare, I.C.H. and Murphy, G.H. (2013) 'The Psychological Impact of Abuse on Men and Women with Severe Intellectual Disabilities', *Journal of Applied Research in Intellectual Disabilities*, 26(4): 257–70.

Ruck Keene, A., Butler-Cole, V., Allen, N., Lee, A., Kohn, N., Scott, K. and Edwards, S. (2017) 'A Brief Guide to Carrying Out Capacity Assessments – November 2017'. Available from: https://web.archive.org/web/20181021021112/www.39essex.com/mental-capacity-guidance-note-brief-guide-carrying-capacity-assessments/ [Accessed 5 December 2019].

SafeLives (2014) 'National Definition of IDVA Work'. Available from: www.safelives.org.uk/sites/default/files/resources/National%20definition%20of%20IDVA%20work%20FINAL.pdf [Accessed 28 February 2019].

SafeLives (2016a) 'Older People's Care/Referral Pathway Guidance'. Available from: www.safelives.org.uk/sites/default/files/resources/Older%20peoples%20Care%20pathway%20guidance%20notes.pdf [Accessed 28 January 2019].

SafeLives (2016b) 'Spotlight #2: Disabled People and Domestic Abuse'. Available from: www.safelives.org.uk/knowledge-hub/spotlights/spotlight-2-disabled-people-and-domestic-abuse [Accessed 3 January 2019].

SafeLives (2016c) 'Spotlight #1: Older People and Domestic Abuse'. Available from: www.safelives.org.uk/node/861 [Accessed 28 January 2019].

Schön, D.A. (1983) *The Reflective Practitioner: How Professionals Think in Action*, London: Temple Smith.

SCIE (Social Care Institute for Excellence) (2013) 'Key Legislation: Articles Relevant to Dignity in Care'. Available from: www.scie.org.uk/publications/guides/guide15/legislation/humanrightsact/articles.asp [Accessed 18 November 2018].

SCIE (Social Care Institute for Excellence) (2014a) 'Gaining Access to an Adult Suspected to Be at Risk of Neglect or Abuse: A Guide for Social Workers and Their Managers in England'. Available from: www.scie.org.uk/care-act-2014/safeguarding-adults/adult-suspected-at-risk-of-neglect-abuse/files/adult-suspected-at-risk-of-neglect-abuse.pdf [Accessed 7 January 2019].

SCIE (Social Care Institute for Excellence) (2014b) 'Understanding Independent Mental Health Advocacy (IMHA) for Mental Health Staff'. Available from: www.scie.org.uk/independent-mental-health-advocacy/resources-for-staff/understanding/ [Accessed 29 March 2019].

SCIE (Social Care Institute for Excellence) (2017) 'Overview of the SARs Library Project'. Available from: www.scie.org.uk/safeguarding/adults/reviews/library/project [Accessed 11 June 2019].

SCIE (Social Care Institute for Excellence) (2018) 'Gaining Access to an Adult Suspected to Be at Risk of Neglect or Abuse'. Available from: www.scie.org.uk/safeguarding/adults/practice/gaining-access [Accessed 8 June 2019].

SCIE (Social Care Institute for Excellence) (2019) 'Latest Videos on Social Care TV'. Available from: www.scie.org.uk/socialcaretv/latest.asp [Accessed 6 June 2019].

Shemmings, D. (2000) 'Adult Attachment Theory and Its Contribution to an Understanding of Conflict and Abuse in Later-Life Relationships', *The Journal of Adult Protection*, 2(3): 40–9.

Sherwood-Johnson, F. (2016) 'Independent Advocacy in Adult Support and Protection Work', *The Journal of Adult Protection*, 18(2): 109–18.

Sherwood-Johnson, F., Cross, B. and Daniel, B. (2013) 'The Experience of Being Protected', *The Journal of Adult Protection*, 15(3): 115–26.

Sicora, A. (2017) *Reflective Practice and Learning from Mistakes in Social Work*, Bristol: Policy Press.

Sin, C.H. (2013) 'Making Disablist Hate Crime Visible: Addressing the Challenges of Improving Reporting', in A. Roulstone and H. Mason-Bish (eds) *Disability, Hate Crime and Violence*, Abingdon: Routledge, pp 147–65.

Skills for Care (2014) 'Care Act Learning and Development Materials Glossary'. Available from: www.skillsforcare.org.uk/Documents/Standards-legislation/Care-Act/Glossary.pdf [Accessed 12 November 2018].

Somerset County Council (2016) 'Leaflet A7 Keeping Safe'. Available from: www.somerset.gov.uk/EasySiteWeb/GatewayLink.aspx?alId=100207 [Accessed 15 September 2019].

South Gloucestershire Safeguarding Adults Board (2019) 'What Makes a Good Care Home'. Available from: http://sites.southglos.gov.uk/safeguarding/wp-content/uploads/sites/221/2015/07/What-Makes-a-Good-Care-Home-web.pdf [Accessed 16 September 2019].

Stacey. G., Johnston, K., Stickley, T. and Diamond, B. (2011) 'How Do Nurses Cope with Values and Practice Conflict?' *Nursing Times*, 107(5): 20–3.

Stevens, M., Martineau, S., Manthorpe, J. and Norrie, C. (2017) 'Social Workers' Power of Entry in Adult Safeguarding Concerns: Debates over Autonomy, Privacy and Protection', *The Journal of Adult Protection*, 19(6): 312–22.

Stone, K., Vicary, V. and Spencer-Lane, T. (2020) *The Approved Mental Health Professional Practice Handbook*, Bristol: Policy Press.

Swindon Local Safeguarding Adults Board (2015) 'Your Guide to Safeguarding in Swindon'. Available at: www.swindon.gov.uk/downloads/file/4539/practical_guide_for_service_users_involved_in_safeguarding [Accessed 20 December 2019].

Szerletics, A. (2011) 'Vulnerable Adults and the Inherent Jurisdiction of the High Court', Essex Autonomy Project, September. Available from: https://autonomy.essex.ac.uk/resources/vulnerable-adults-and-the-inherent-jurisdiction-of-the-high-court/ [Accessed 10 October 2018].

Taylor, M. and Tapper, L. (2017) 'Participative Practice and Family Group Conferencing', in A. Cooper and E. White (eds) *Safeguarding Adults Under the Care Act 2014: Understanding Good Practice*, London, Jessica Kingsley, pp 57–73.

The Freedom Programme (2018) 'Facilitator Training: Learning Differences Training'. Available from: www.freedomprogramme.co.uk/learning-differences-training.php [Accessed 1 May 2019].

The Journal of Adult Protection. Available from: www.emeraldgrouppublishing.com/products/journals/journals.htm?id=jap [Accessed 1 June 2019].

The Survivors Trust (2018) 'Find Support in Your Area'. Available from: www.thesurvivorstrust.org/Pages/Category/find-support-in-your-area [Accessed 5 December 2019].

Thompson, L.J. and West, D. (2013) 'Professional Development in the Contemporary Educational Context: Encouraging Practice Wisdom', *Social Work Education*, 32(1): 118–33.

United Nations Human Rights (1984) 'United Nations Convention Against Torture'. Available from: www.ohchr.org/EN/ProfessionalInterest/Pages/CAT.aspx [Accessed 29 May 2019].

University of Bristol Norah Fry Centre for Disability Studies (2018) 'The Learning Disabilities Mortality Review (LeDeR) Annual Report 2017'. Available from: www.hqip.org.uk/resource/the-learning-disabilities-mortality-review-annual-report-2017/ [Accessed 5 December 2019].

Victim Support (2019) 'How We Can Help'. Available from: www.victimsupport.org.uk/help-and-support/how-we-can-help [Accessed 10 May 2019].

Weiss, T. (2014) 'Personal Transformation: Posttraumatic Growth and Gerotranscendence', *Journal of Humanistic Psychology*, 54(2): 203–26.

West Midlands Adult Safeguarding Editorial Group (2016) 'Adult Safeguarding: Multi-agency Policy and Procedures for the Protection of Adults with Care and Support Needs in the West Midlands'. Available from: www.safeguardingwarwickshire.co.uk/wmadultdocs [Accessed 4 March 2019].

White, E. (2017) 'Assessing and Responding to Risk', in A. Cooper and E. White (eds) *Safeguarding Adults under the Care Act 2014: Understanding Good Practice*, London, Jessica Kingsley, pp 110–27.

Williams, V.J., Boyle, G., Jepson, M.J., Swift, P., Williamson, T. and Heslop, P. (2012) 'Making Best Interests Decisions: People and Processes'. Available from: https://research-information.bris.ac.uk/en/publications/making-best-interests-decisions-people-and-processes(4a89b31f-2097-4483-9a3f-73d32a243ad5).html [Accessed 5 December 2019].

Windle, K., Francis, J. and Coomber, C. (2011) 'Briefing Paper 39: Preventing Loneliness and Social Isolation: Interventions and Outcomes'. Available from: www.scie.org.uk/publications/briefings/files/briefing39.pdf [Accessed 10 May 2019].

Statute, case law, serious case reviews and Safeguarding Adults Reviews

The Houses of Parliament set out the statutory legal framework for adult safeguarding practice. In the UK law operates by the principle of precedent, which means that when judges interpret the statute created by Parliament they must consider the decisions made by other courts concerning the same situations, and where a binding decision has been made by a higher court that judgment must be used to guide decisions in lower courts.

Figure A1 shows the hierarchy of courts in which judgments relevant to adult safeguarding law practice are likely to be made.

The statutes list has been organised by date with the most recent first. The case law (or common law) has been arranged alphabetically by theme and then by date with the most recent first. It is first arranged by theme to assist readers to find cases relevant to any queries they may have. Some cases are relevant to more than one subject area so may appear under more than one heading. Within

Figure A1: Court structure relevant to adult safeguarding

European Court of Human Rights (ECHR)
European Convention on Human Rights law – based in Strasbourg

Supreme Court (UKSC)
Previously House of Lords (UKHL) – UK law

Court of Appeal (EWCA)
Criminal and civil divisions

High Court (EWHC)
Family Court (EWHC Fam), Court of Protection (EWCOP), Upper Tribunal (UKUT)

Crown Court
Criminal e.g. offences under the MCA and MHA

County Court
Court of Protection e.g. local hearings

Magistrates' Court
Criminal e.g. offences under the MCA and MHA, warrants under MHA

Tribunals
e.g. Mental Health Act

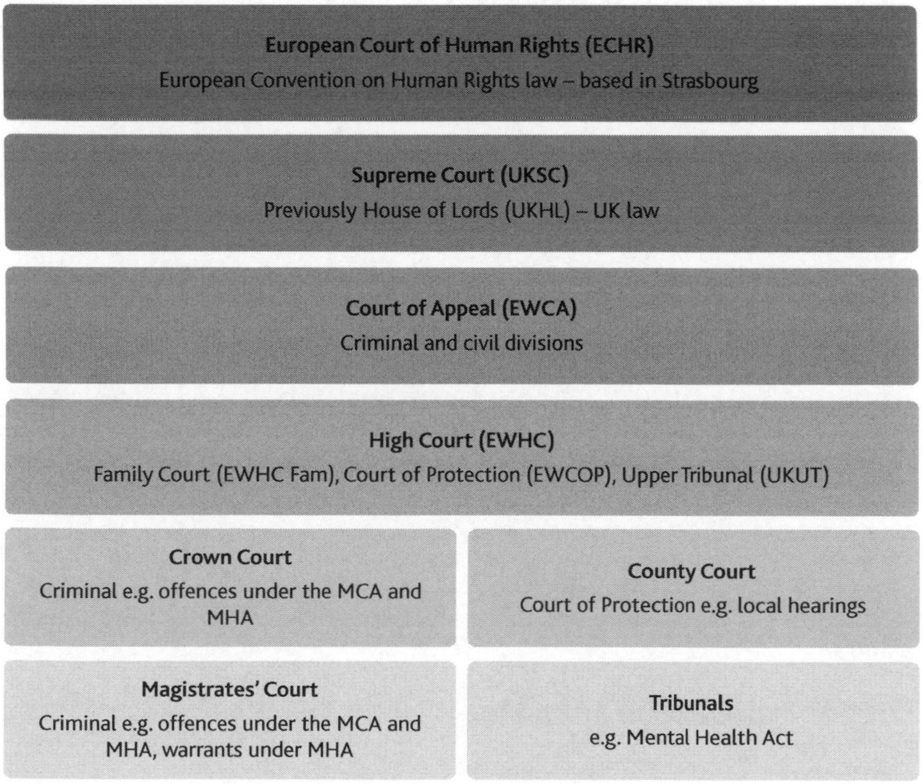

the themes, it is then organised by date, with the most recent cases appearing first. For example, the Supreme Court's decision in the *P v Cheshire West and Chester Council* and *P and Q (MIG and MEG) v Surrey County Council* cases is binding on all subsequent deprivation of liberty cases in England and Wales and has overridden all previous judgments made in these cases, for example in the Court of Protection and the Court of Appeal.

Statutes

Mental Capacity (Amendment) Act (2019). Available from: www.legislation.gov. uk/ukpga/2019/18/enacted/data.htm [Accessed 6 December 2019].

Serious Crime Act (2015). Available from: www.legislation.gov.uk/ukpga/2015/9/ contents/enacted [Accessed 21 December 2019].

Mental Health (Scotland) Act (2015). Available from: www.legislation.gov.uk/ asp/2015/9/contents/enacted [Accessed 16 January 2020].

Consumer Rights Act (2015). Available from: www.legislation.gov.uk/ ukpga/2015/15/contents/enacted [Accessed 17 November 2018].

Care Act (2014). Available from: www.legislation.gov.uk/ukpga/2014/23/ contents/enacted [Accessed 29 May 2019].

Social Services and Well-being (Wales) Act (2014). Available from: www. legislation.gov.uk/anaw/2014/4/contents [Accessed 25 June 2019].

Equality Act (2010). Available from: www.legislation.gov.uk/ukpga/2010/15/ contents [Accessed 19 December 2018].

Adult Support and Protection (Scotland) Act (2007). Available from: www. legislation.gov.uk/asp/2007/10/contents [Accessed 25 June 2019].

United Nations Convention on the Rights of Persons with Disabilities (CRPD) (2006). Available from: www.un.org/development/desa/disabilities/convention- on-the-rights-of-persons-with-disabilities.html [Accessed 11 October 2018].

Mental Capacity Act (2005). Available from: www.legislation.gov.uk/ ukpga/2005/9/contents [Accessed 1 May 2019].

Mental Health (Care and Treatment) (Scotland) (2003). Available from: www. legislation.gov.uk/asp/2003/13/contents [Accessed 16 January 2020].

Human Rights Act (1998). Available from: www.legislation.gov.uk/ ukpga/1998/42/contents [Accessed 19 December 2019].

Police and Criminal Evidence Act (1984). Available from: www.legislation.gov. uk/ukpga/1984/60/contents [Accessed 16 September 2019].

Mental Health Act (1983, as amended 2007). Available from: www.legislation. gov.uk/ukpga/1983/20/contents [Accessed 10 December 2018].

Case law

Advocacy and representation
* *Re. AJ (DOLS)* (2015) EWCOP 5. Available from: www.bailii.org/ew/cases/ EWCOP/2015/5.html [Accessed 30 December 2017].

Consent to marriage
- *XCC v AA & Anor (Rev 3)* [2012] EWCOP 2183. Available from: www.bailii. org/ew/cases/EWCOP/2012/2183.html [Accessed 5 June 2019].

Deprivation of liberty
- *P v Cheshire West and Chester Council and another* and *P and Q v Surrey County Council* [2014] UKSC 19. Available from: www.bailii.org/uk/cases/ UKSC/2014/19.html [Accessed 23 November 2018].

Imputability to the state
- *Staffordshire County Council v SRK* [2016] EWCOP 27. Available from: www. bailii.org/ew/cases/EWCOP/2016/27.html [Accessed 30 December 2018].

Inherent jurisdiction
- *Southend-on-Sea v Meyers* (2019) EWHC 399 (Fam). Available from: www. bailii.org/ew/cases/EWHC/Fam/2019/399.html [Accessed 5 June 2019].
- *Local Authority X v MM & Anor* (No. 1) [2007] EWHC 2003 (Fam). Available from: www.bailii.org/ew/cases/EWHC/Fam/2007/2003.html [Accessed 12 December 2018].

Mental capacity assessment, including salient points and causative nexus
- *PC v City of York Council* [2013] EWCA Civ 478. Available from: www.bailii. org/ew/cases/EWCA/Civ/2013/478.html [Accessed 30 March 2019].
- *CC v KK and STCC* [2012] EWCOP 2136. Available from: www.bailii.org/ ew/cases/EWCOP/2012/2136.html [Accessed 30 October 2018].
- *Re E (An alleged patient): Sheffield City Council v E* [2004] 1 FLR 965. Available from: www.bailii.org/ew/cases/EWHC/Fam/2004/2808.html [Accessed 29 May 2019].

Safeguarding and Article 8
- *Essex County Council v RF & Ors* [2015] EWCOP 1. Available from: www. bailii.org/ew/cases/EWCOP/2015/1.html [Accessed 30 December 2018].
- *MK v Somerset County Council* [2014] EWCOP B25. Available from: www. bailii.org/ew/cases/EWCOP/2014/B25.html [Accessed 30 December 2018].
- *Milton Keynes Council v RR & Ors* [2014] EWCOP B19. Available from: www. bailii.org/ew/cases/EWCOP/2014/B19.html [Accessed 30 December 2018].
- *London Borough of Hillingdon v Steven Neary & Ors* [2011] EWCOP 1377. Available from: www.bailii.org/ew/cases/EWCOP/2011/1377.html [Accessed 22 May 2019].

Risk and well-being
- *Local Authority X v MM & Anor (No. 1)* [2007] EWHC 2003 (Fam). Available from: www.bailii.org/ew/cases/EWHC/Fam/2007/2003.html [Accessed 23 January 2019].

Tort law

- *M'Alister (or Donoghue) (Pauper) appellant and Stevenson (respondent)*. Available from: www.bailii.org/uk/cases/UKHL/1932/100.html [Accessed 31 May 2019].

Serious case reviews and Safeguarding Adults Reviews

Flynn, M. (2007) 'The Murder of Steven Hoskin: A Serious Case Review'. Available from: www.cornwall.gov.uk/media/3633936/Steven-Hoskin-Serious-Case-Review-Exec-Summary.pdf [Accessed 11 December 2018].

Flynn, M. (2018) 'Mendip House'. Available from: http://ssab.safeguardingsomerset. org.uk/wp-content/uploads/20180206_Mendip-House_SAR_FOR_ PUBLICATION.pdf [Accessed 25 June 2019].

Heaton, A. (2016) 'Mr C Serious Case Review October 2016: Executive Summary'. Available from: https://bristolsafeguarding.org/adults/safeguarding-adult-reviews/bristol-sars/mr-c-serious-case-review-october-2016/ [Accessed 10 October 2018].

Spreadbury, K. (2018a) 'Safeguarding Adults Review: Adrian Munday (SAR Z) Devon Safeguarding Adults Board'. Available from: https://new.devon.gov.uk/ devonsafeguardingadultsboard/safeguarding-adult-reviews [Accessed 3 January 2019].

Spreadbury, K. (2018b) 'Nightingale Homes'. Available from: http://sites. southglos.gov.uk/safeguarding/adults/safeguarding-adults-board/serious-case-reviews-2/ [Accessed 25 June 2019].

Index

References to figures and tables are shown in *italics*.